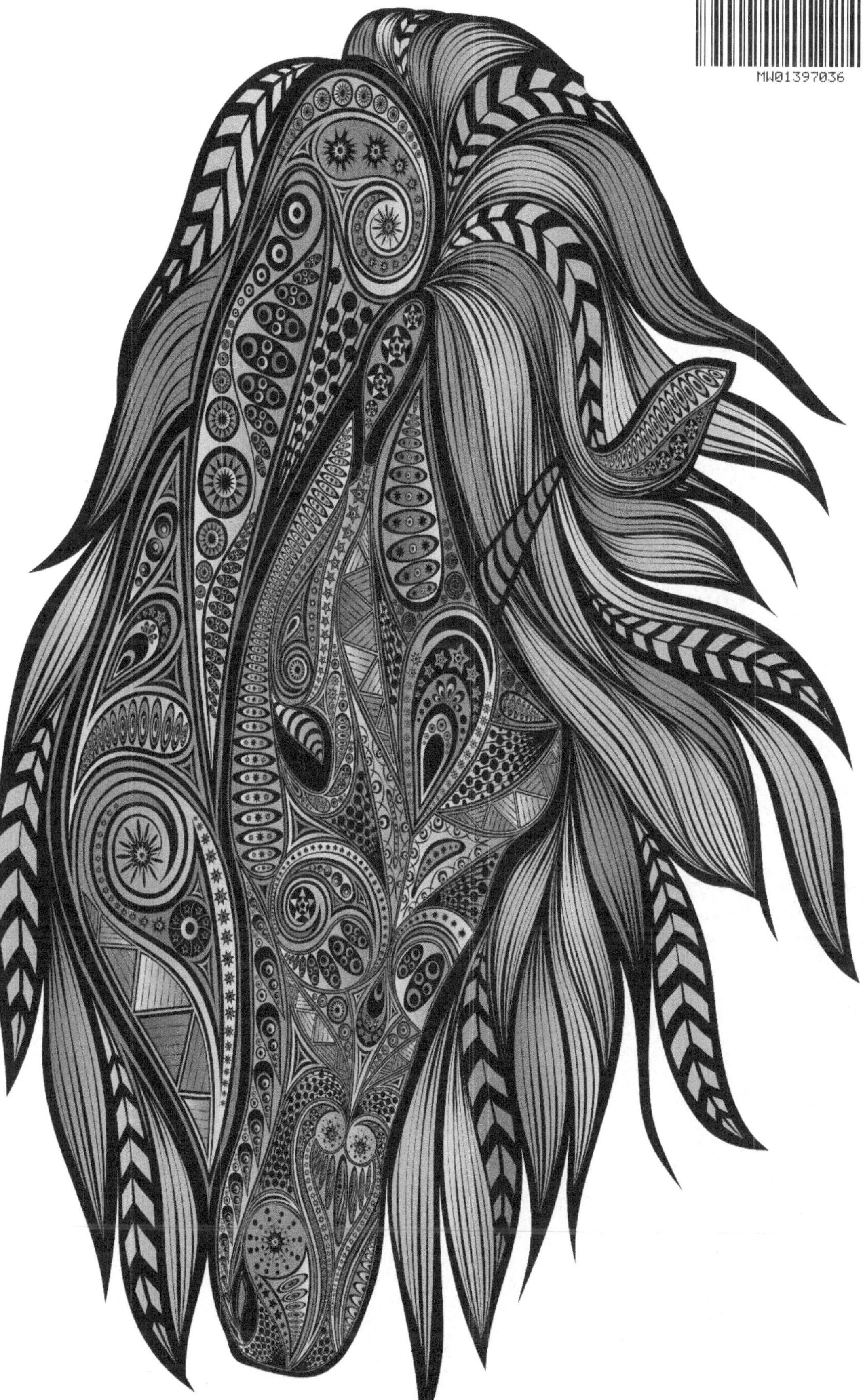

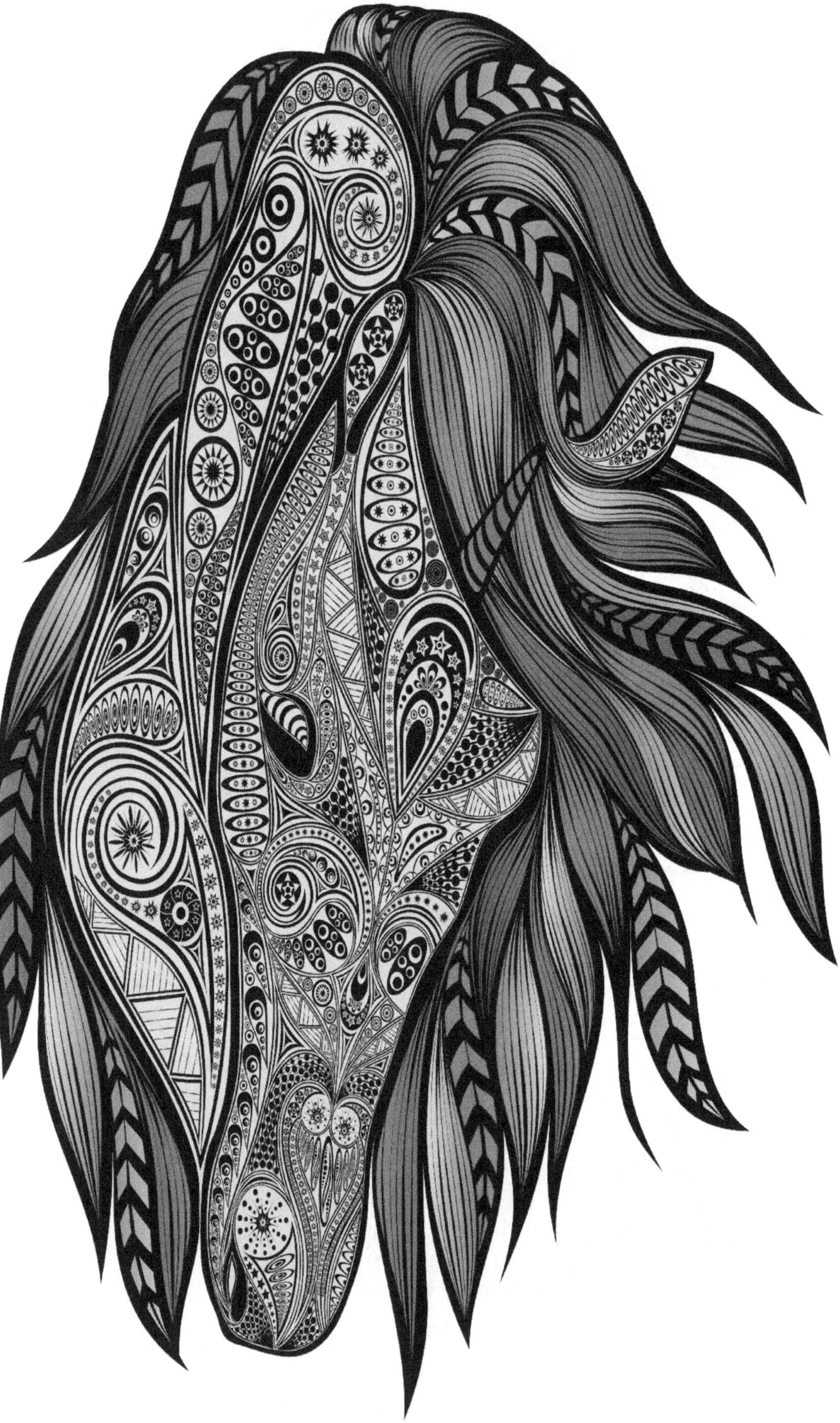

FANTASTIC UNICORNS COLORING BOOK

COPYRIGHT © 2022

DR. ROBERT K. WHEELER JR.

ALL RIGHTS RESERVED

REPRODUCTION IN ANY FORMAT IS ONLY ALLOWED WITH WRITTEN PERMISSION FROM THE AUTHOR.

ISBN 9798370553257

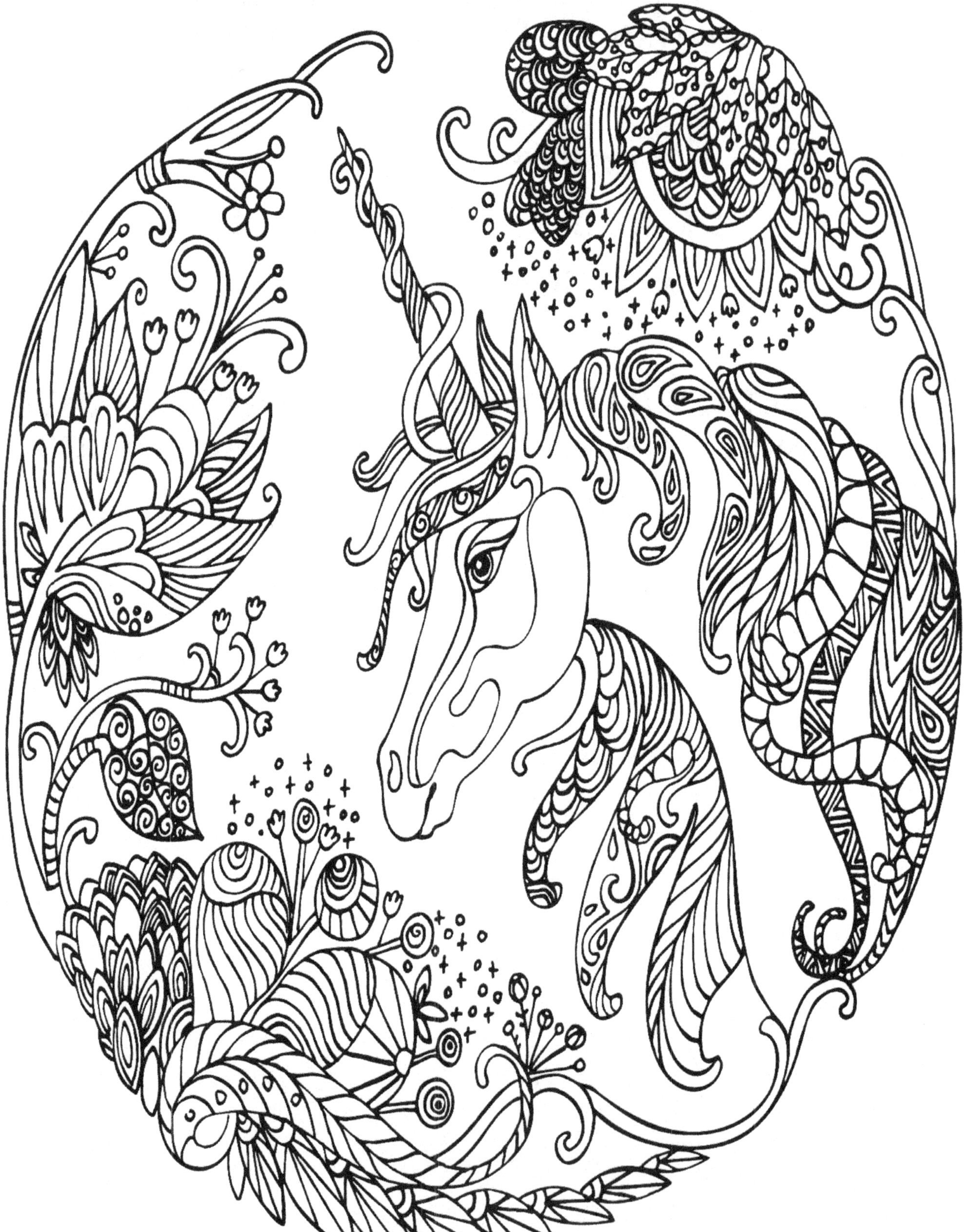

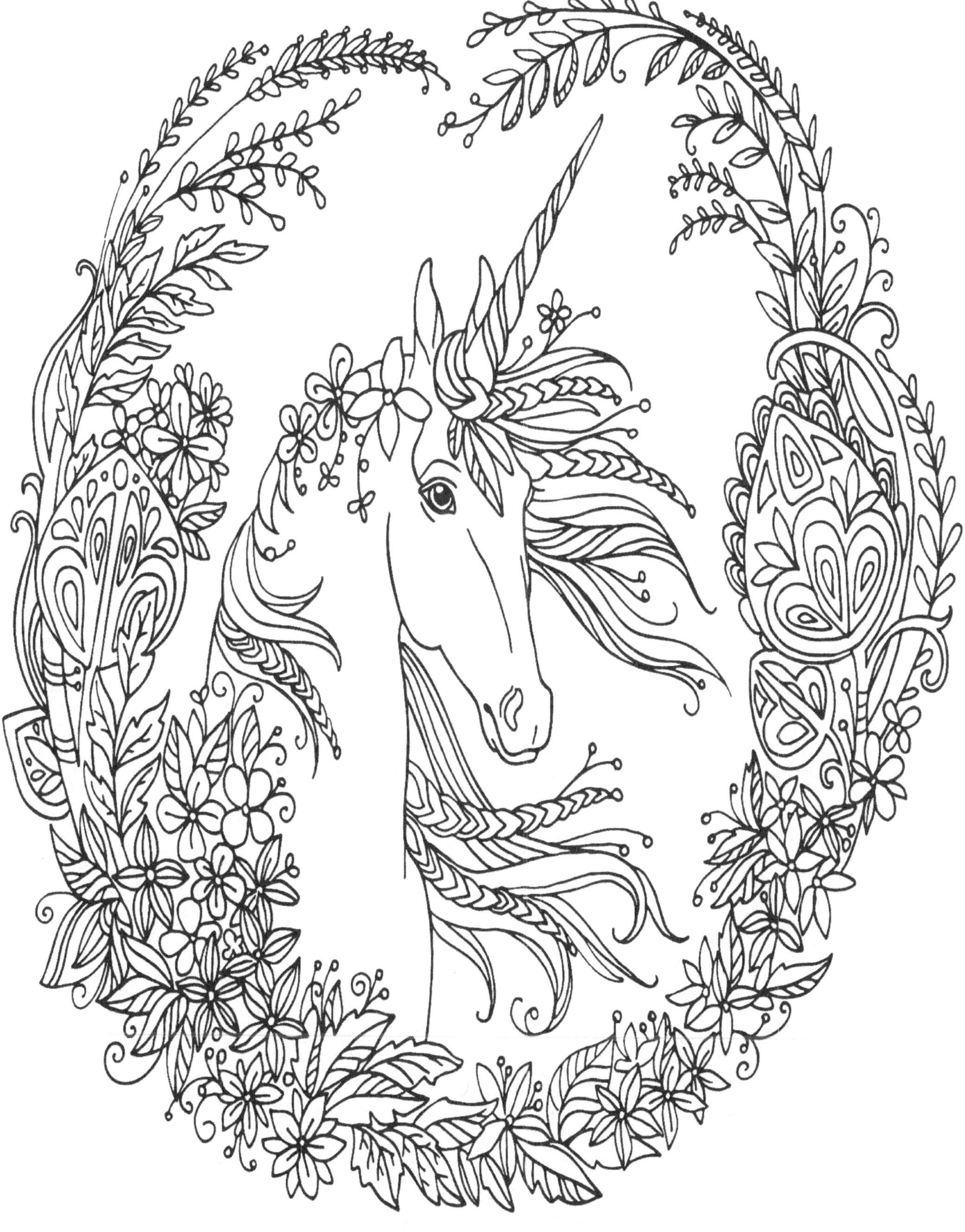

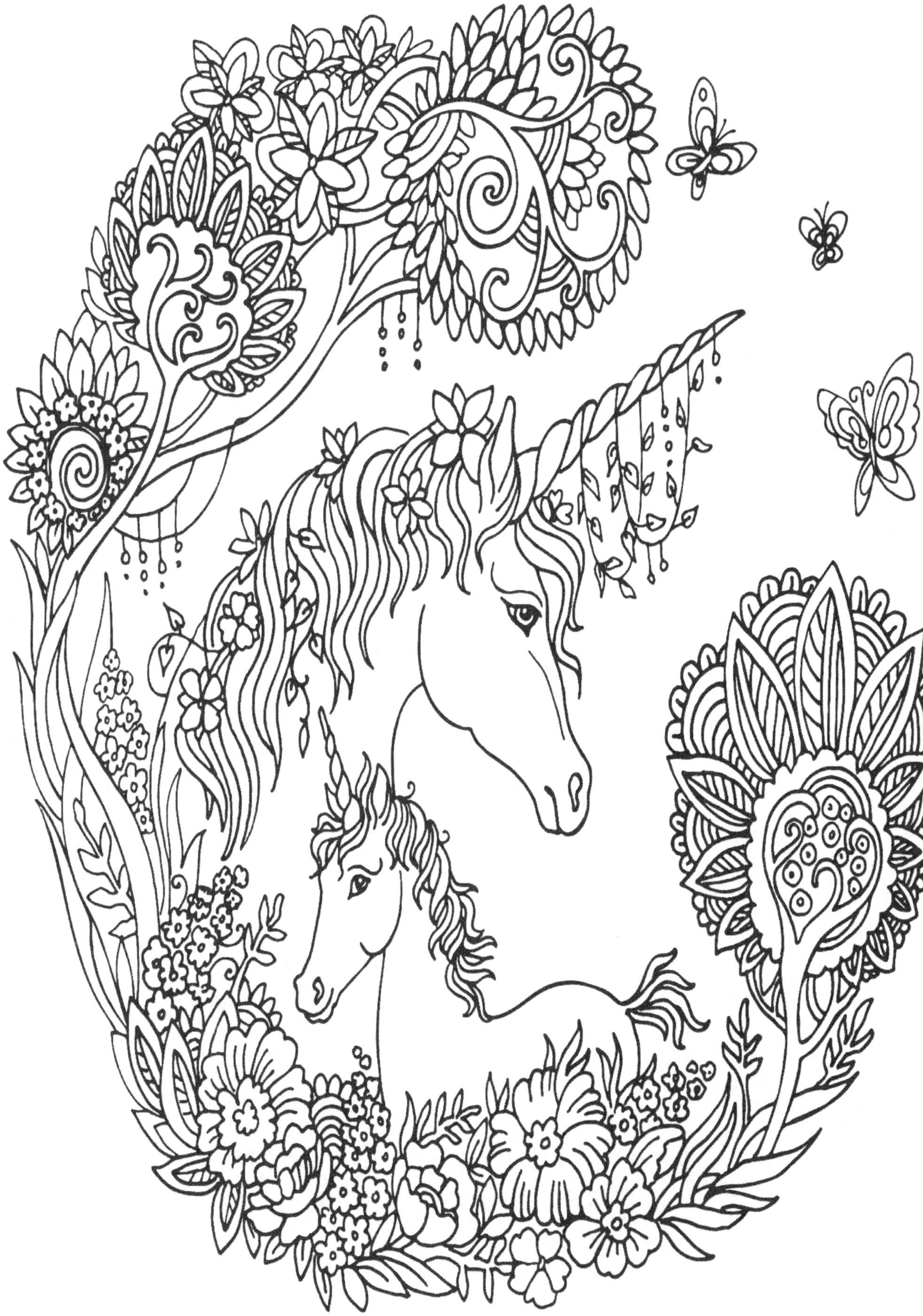

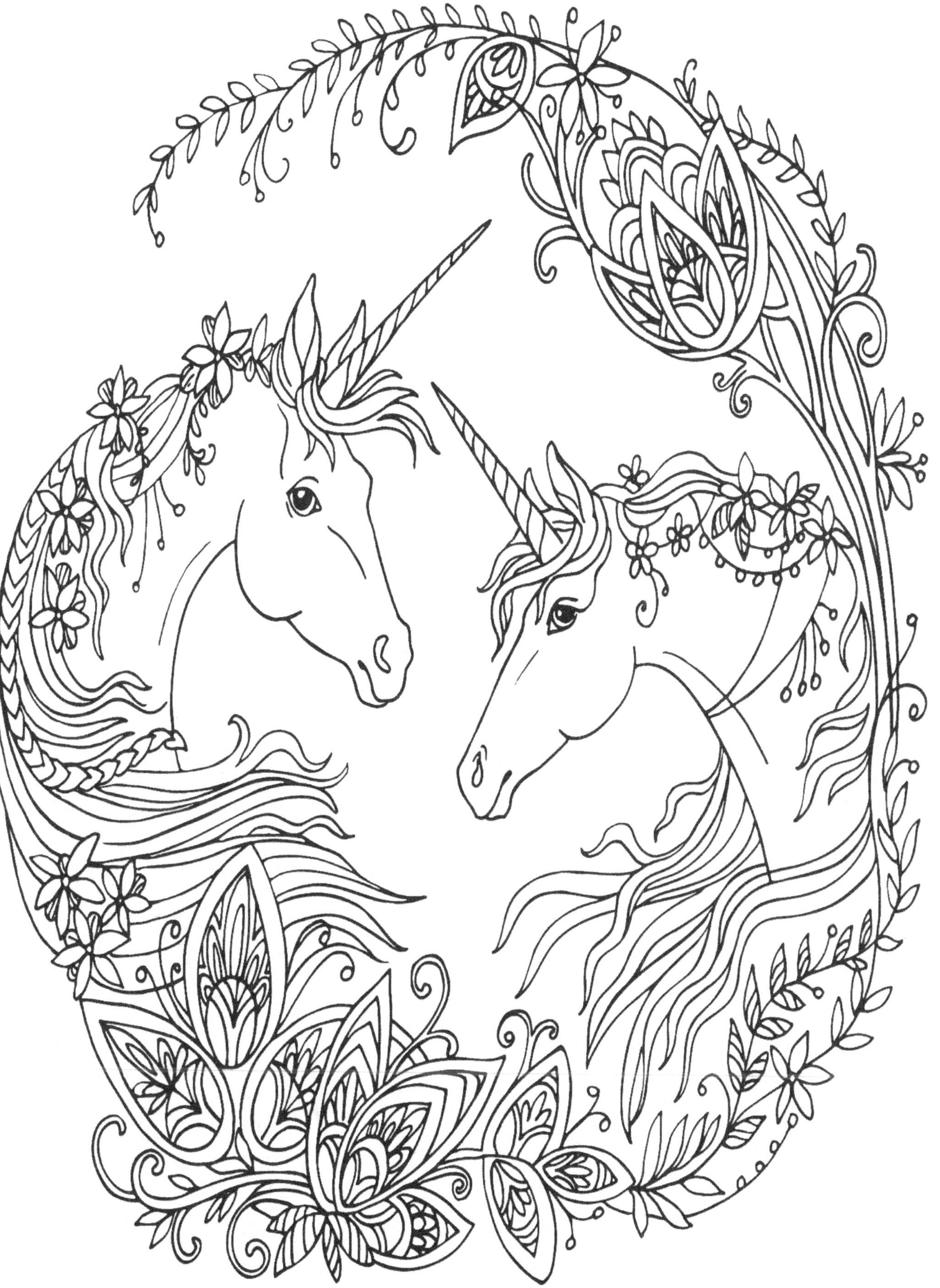

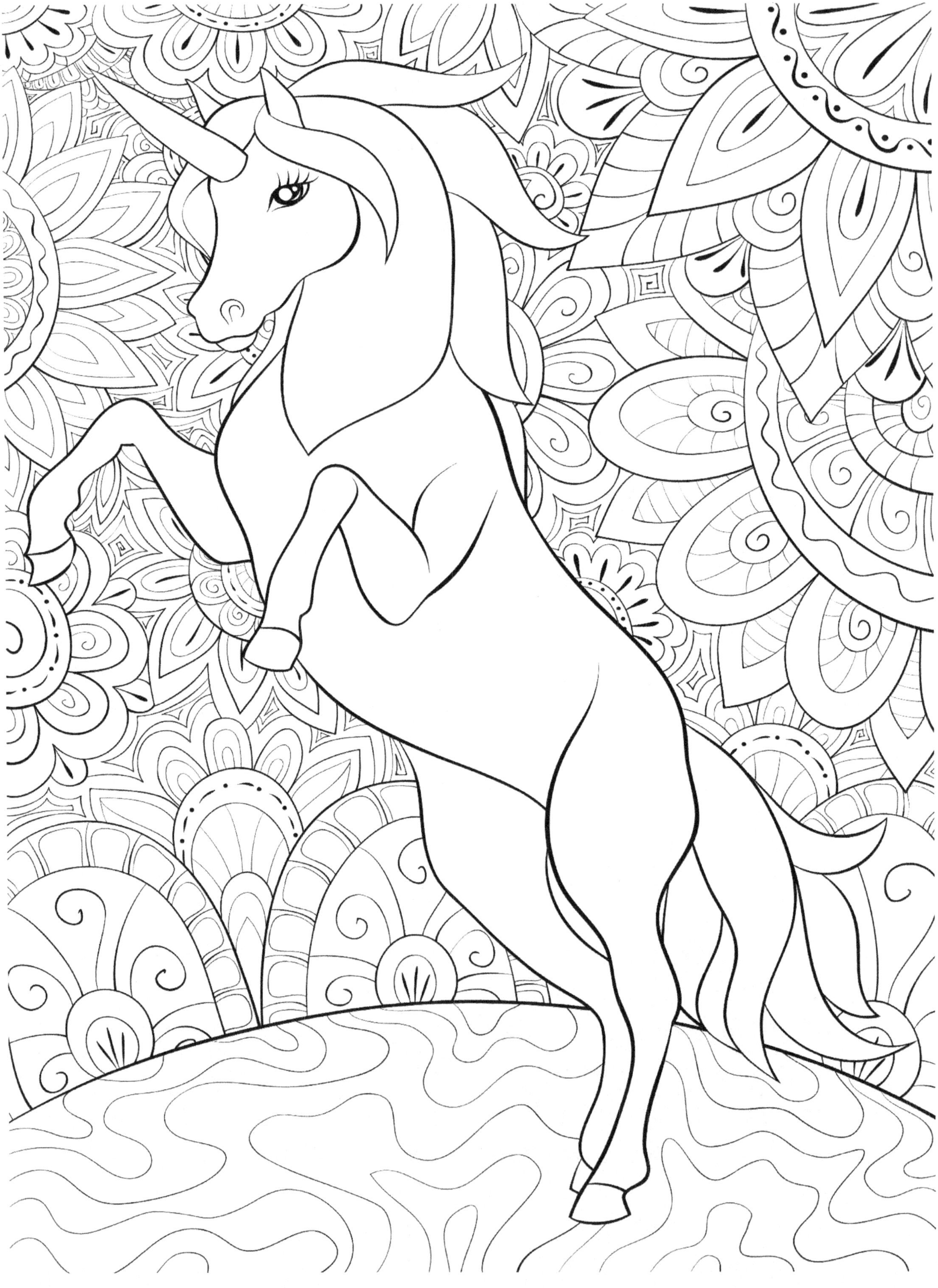

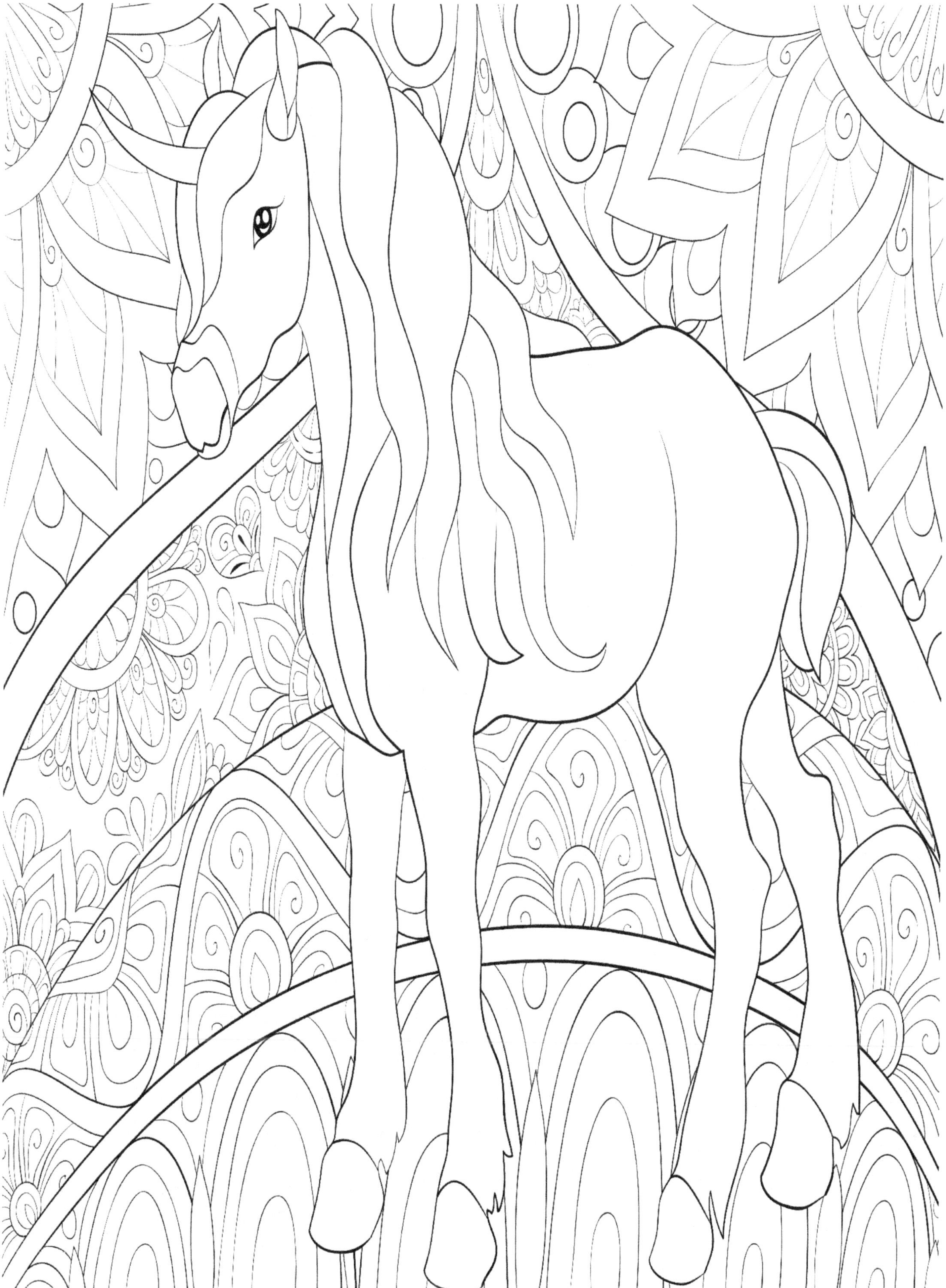

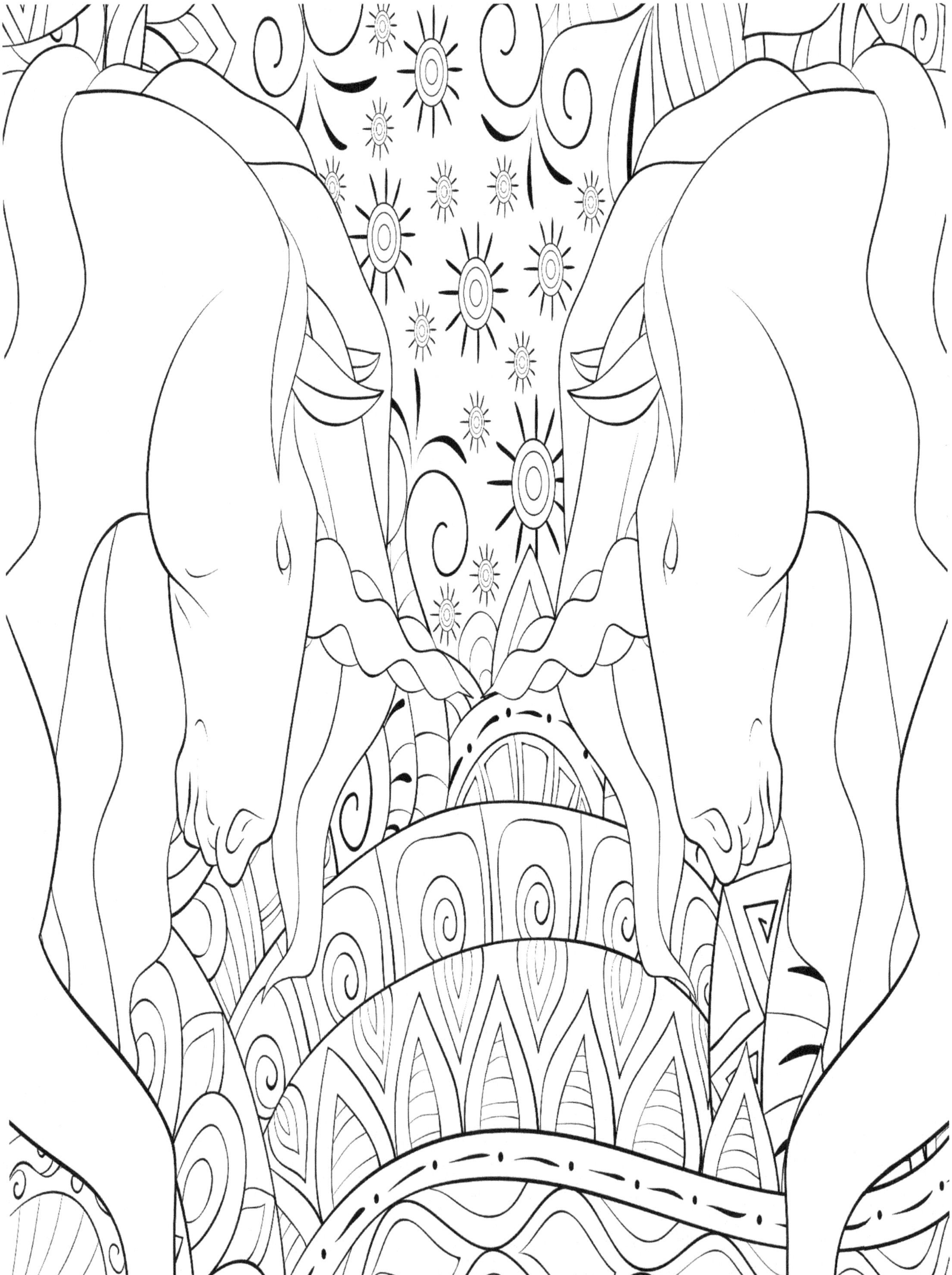

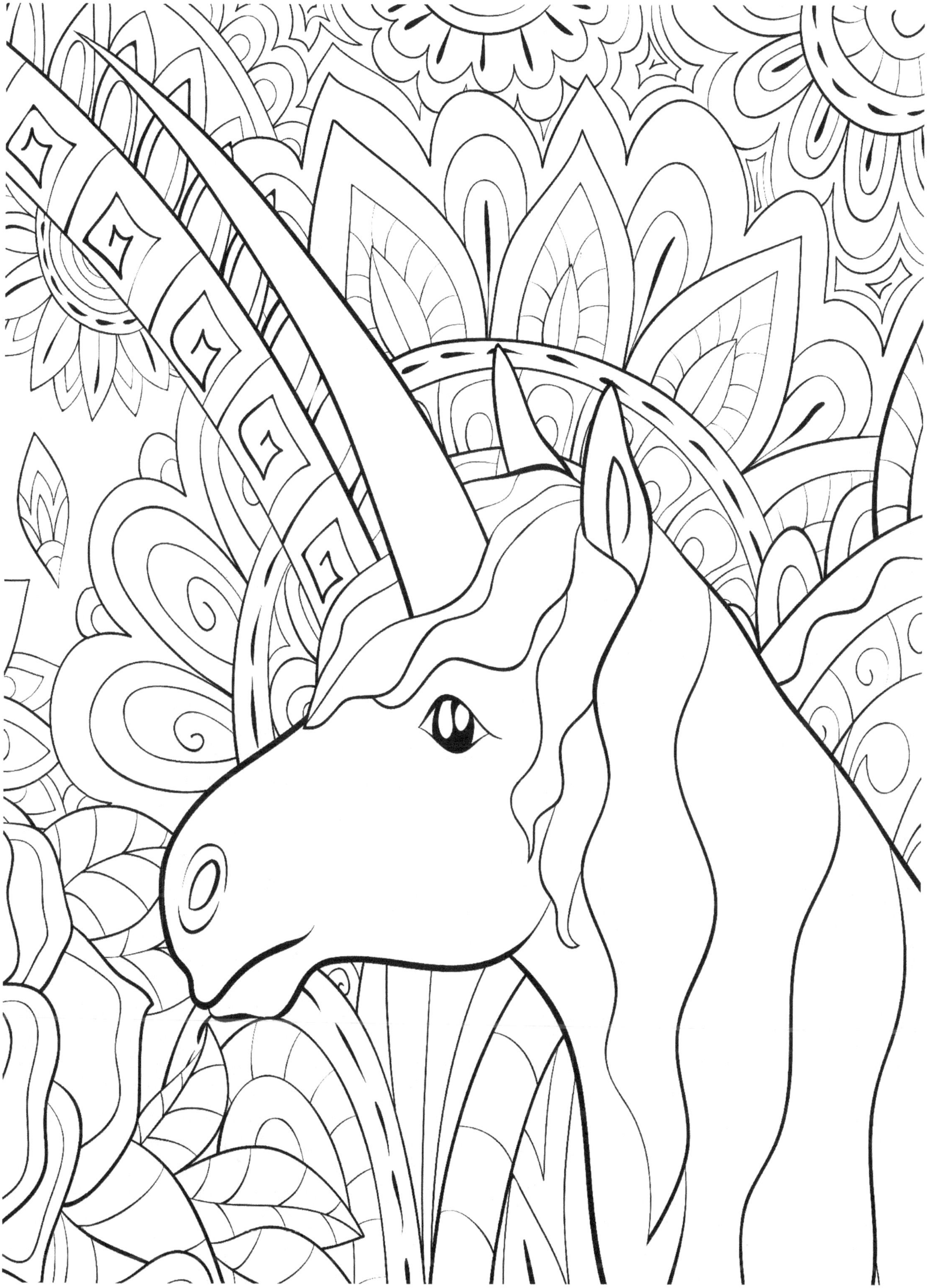

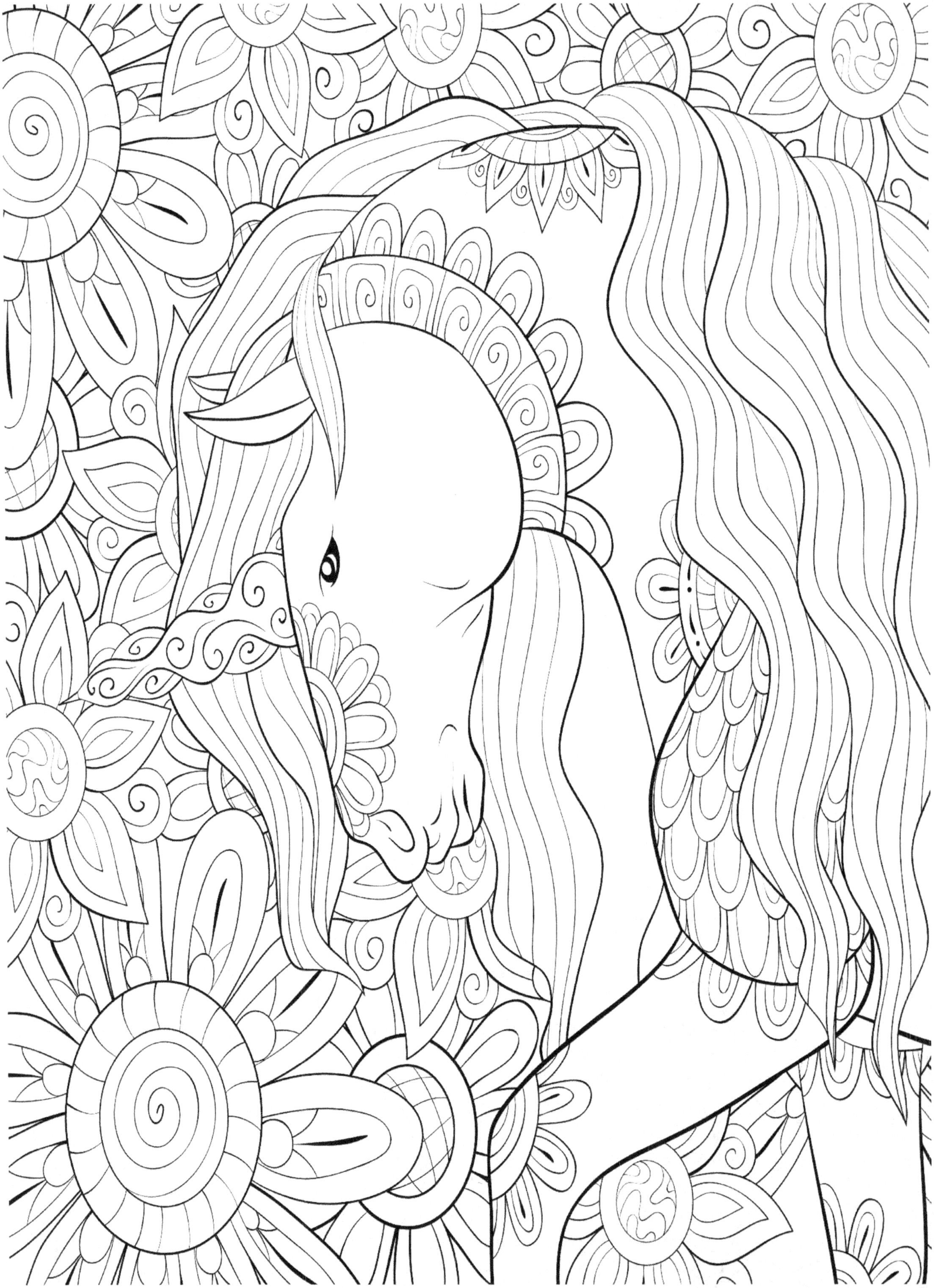

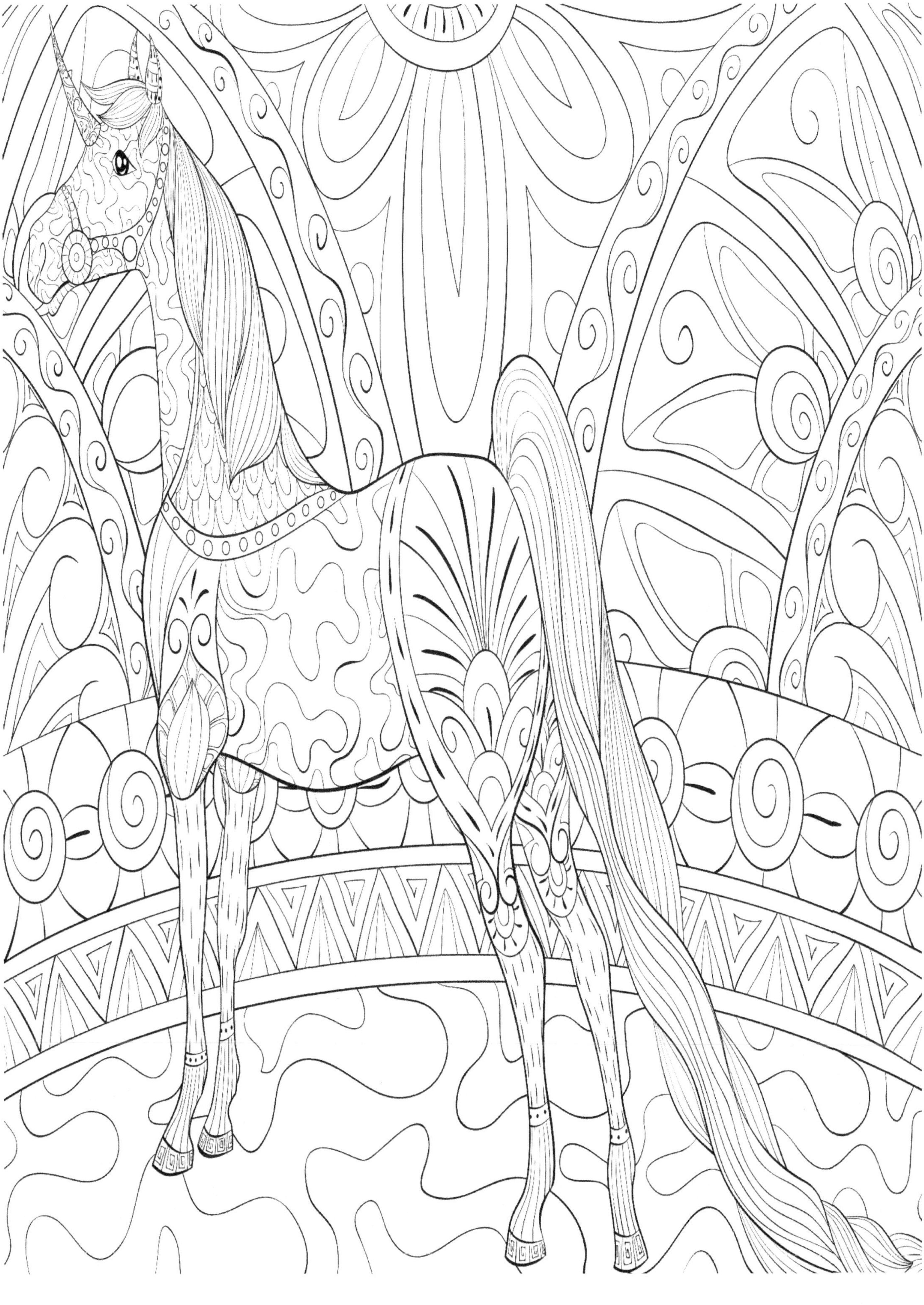

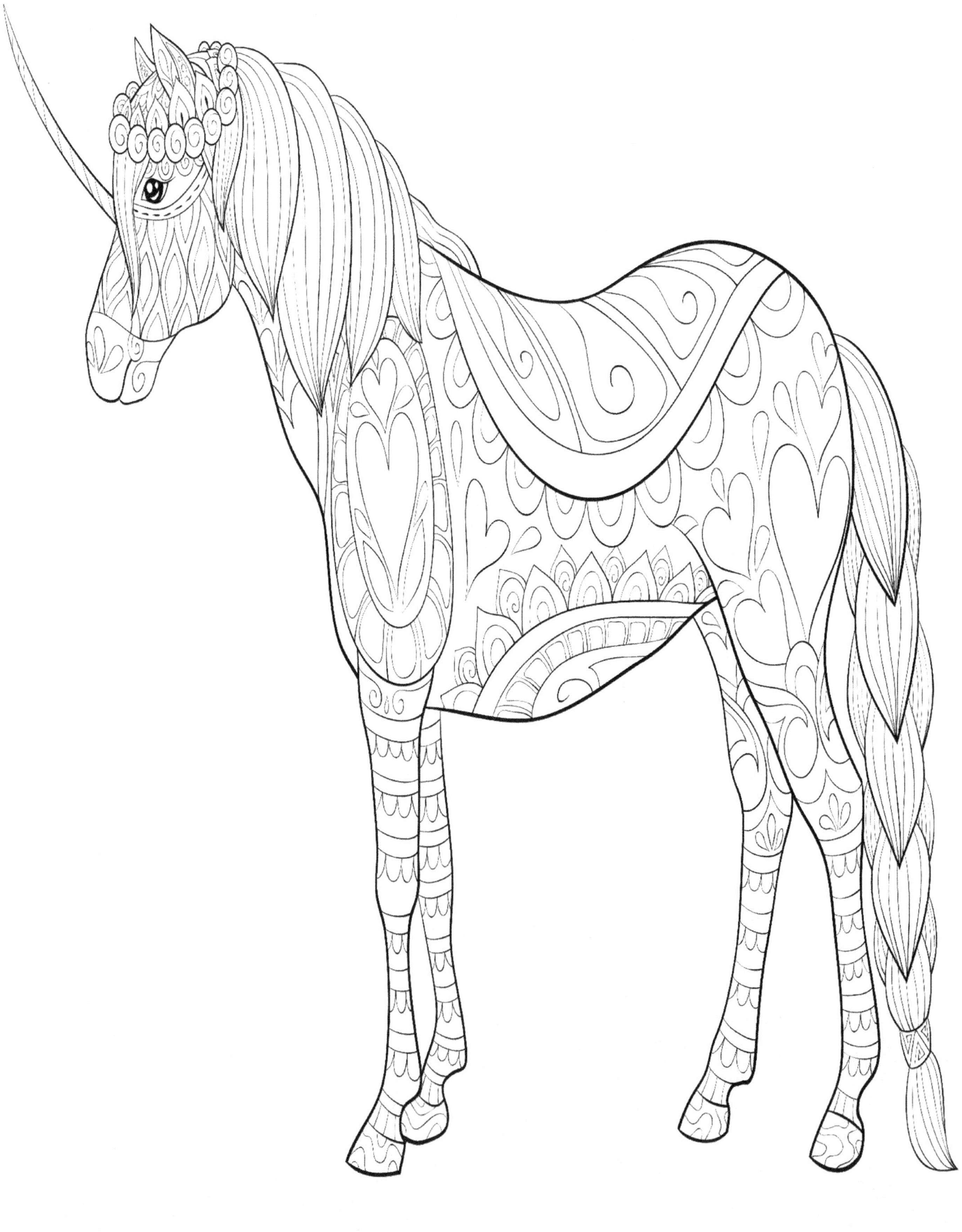

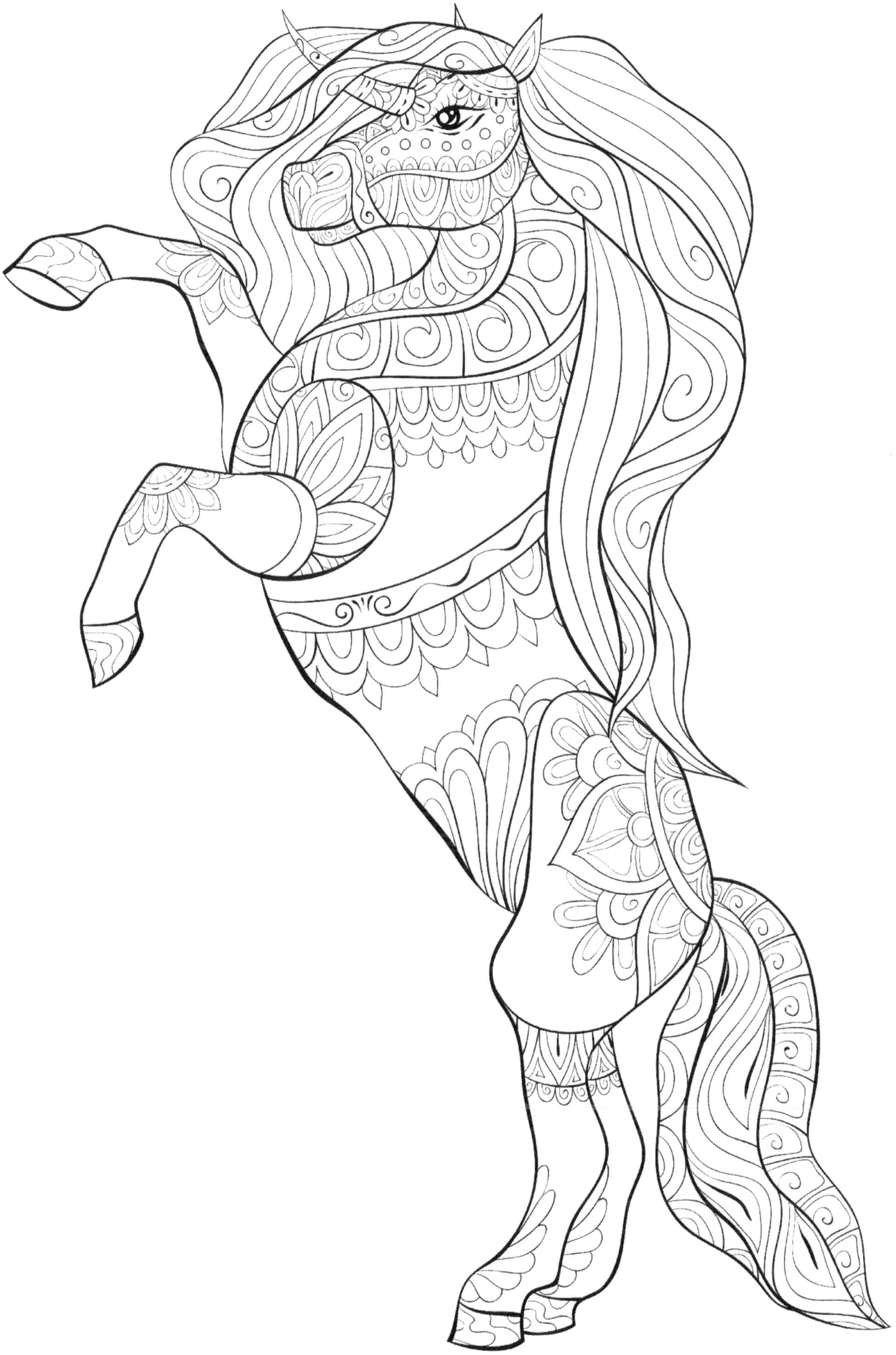

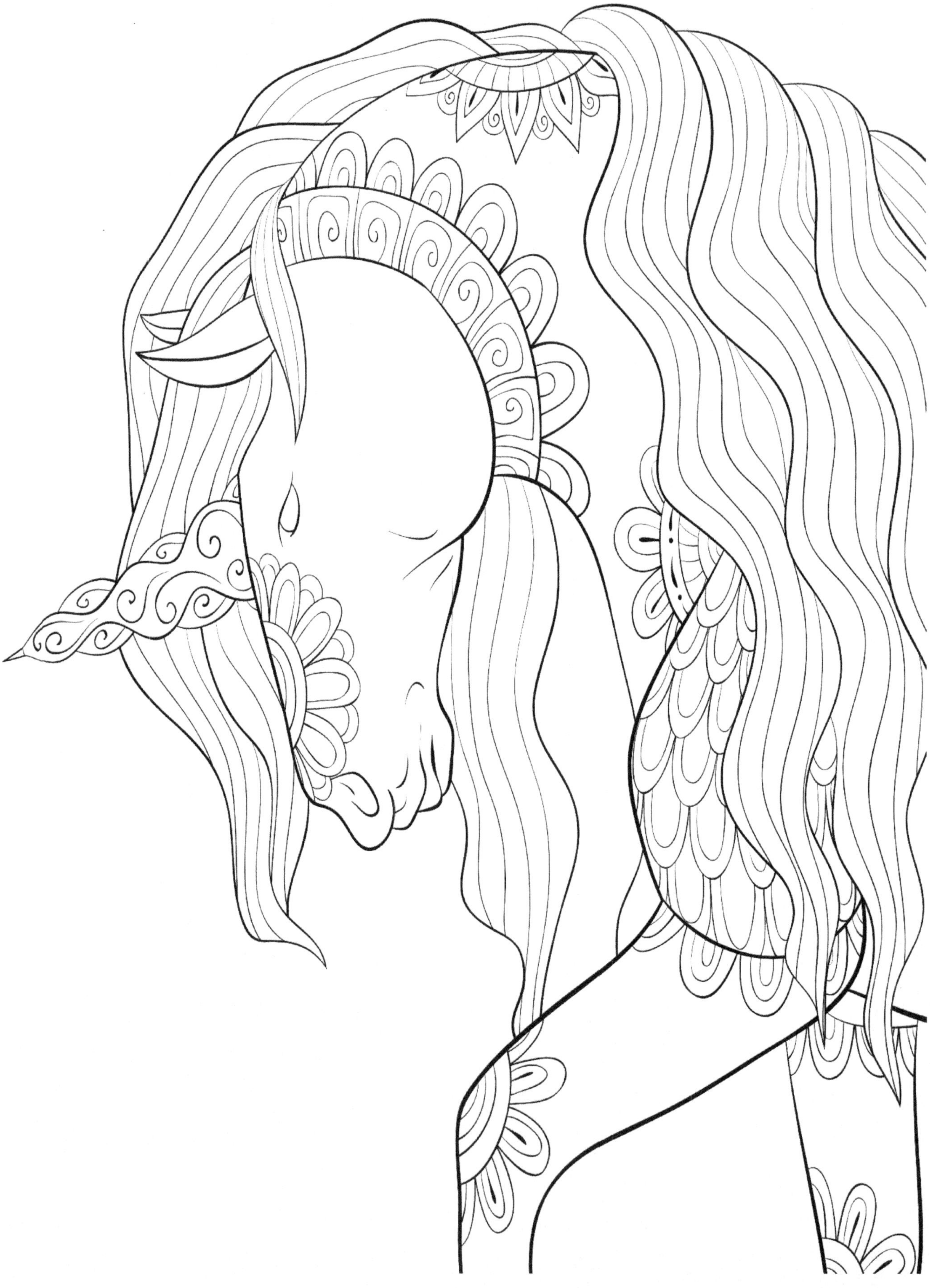

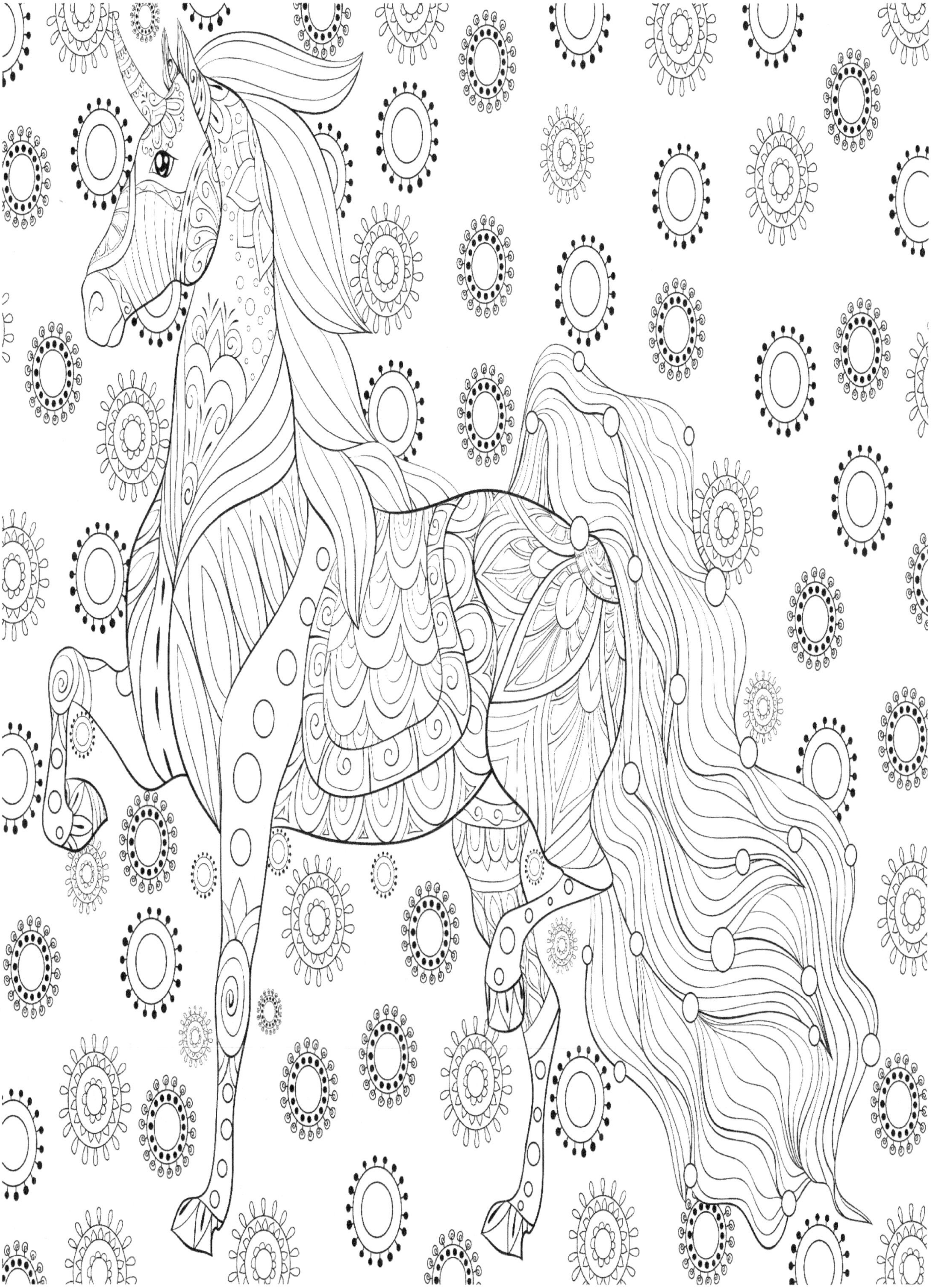

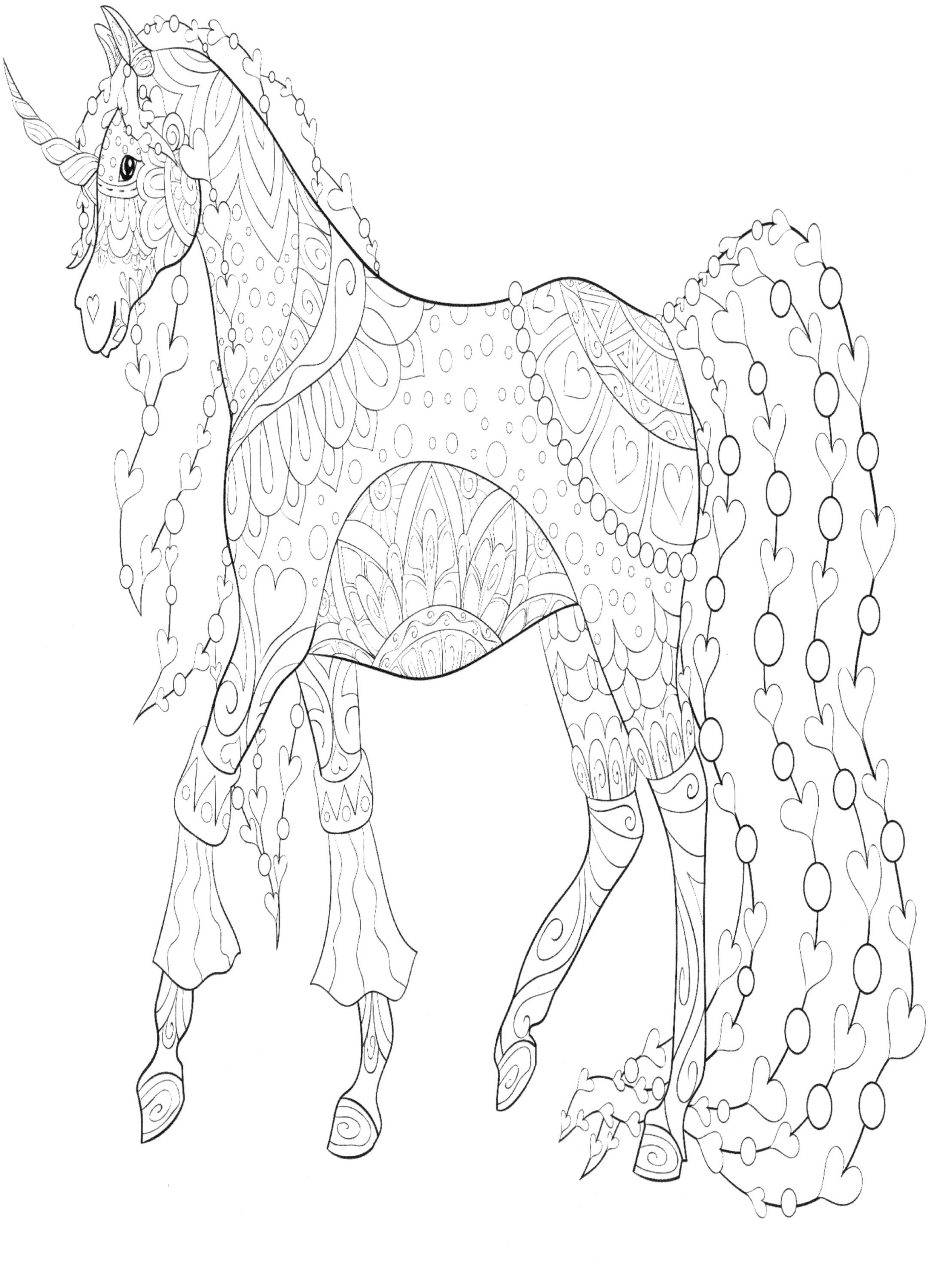

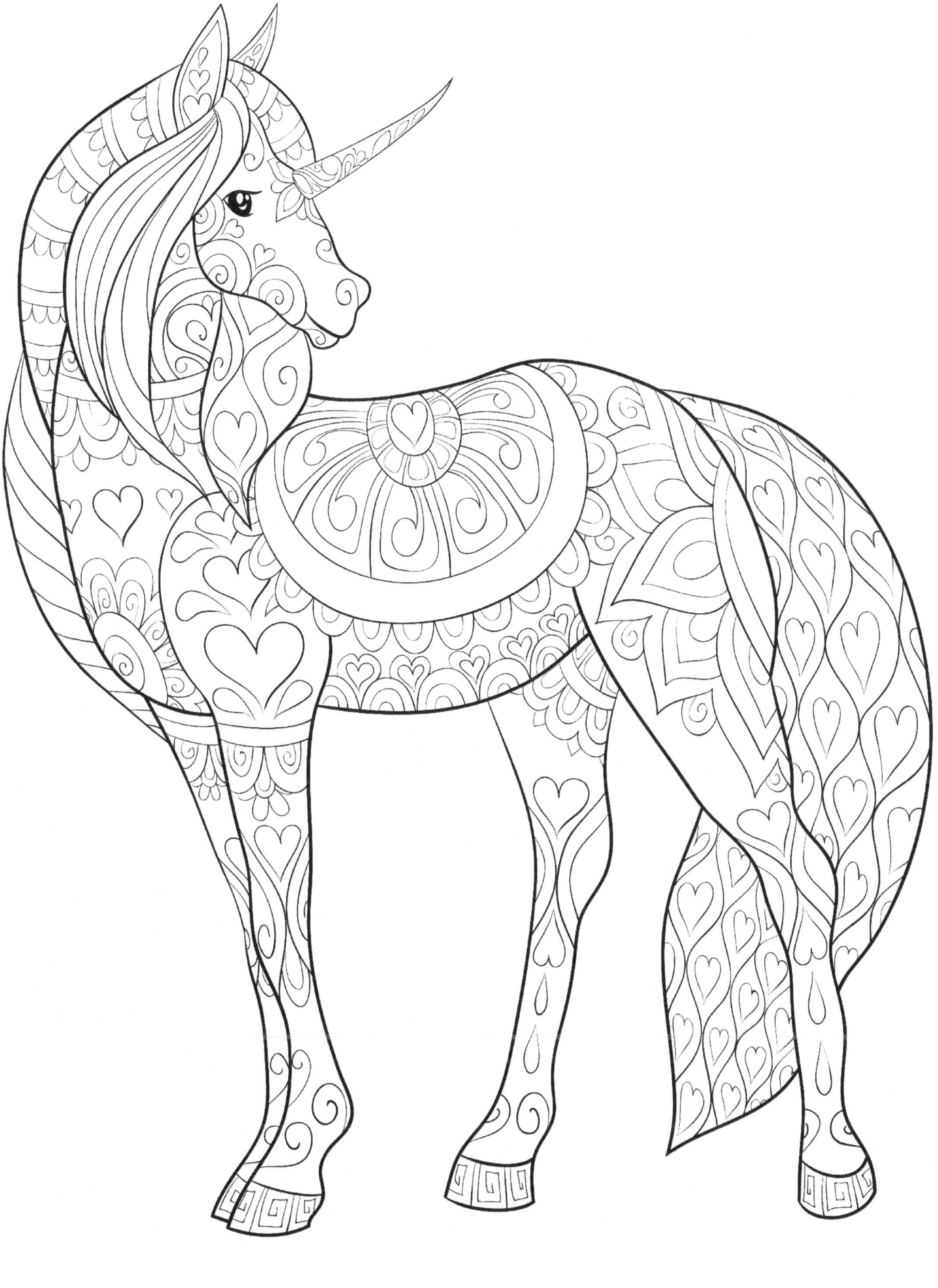

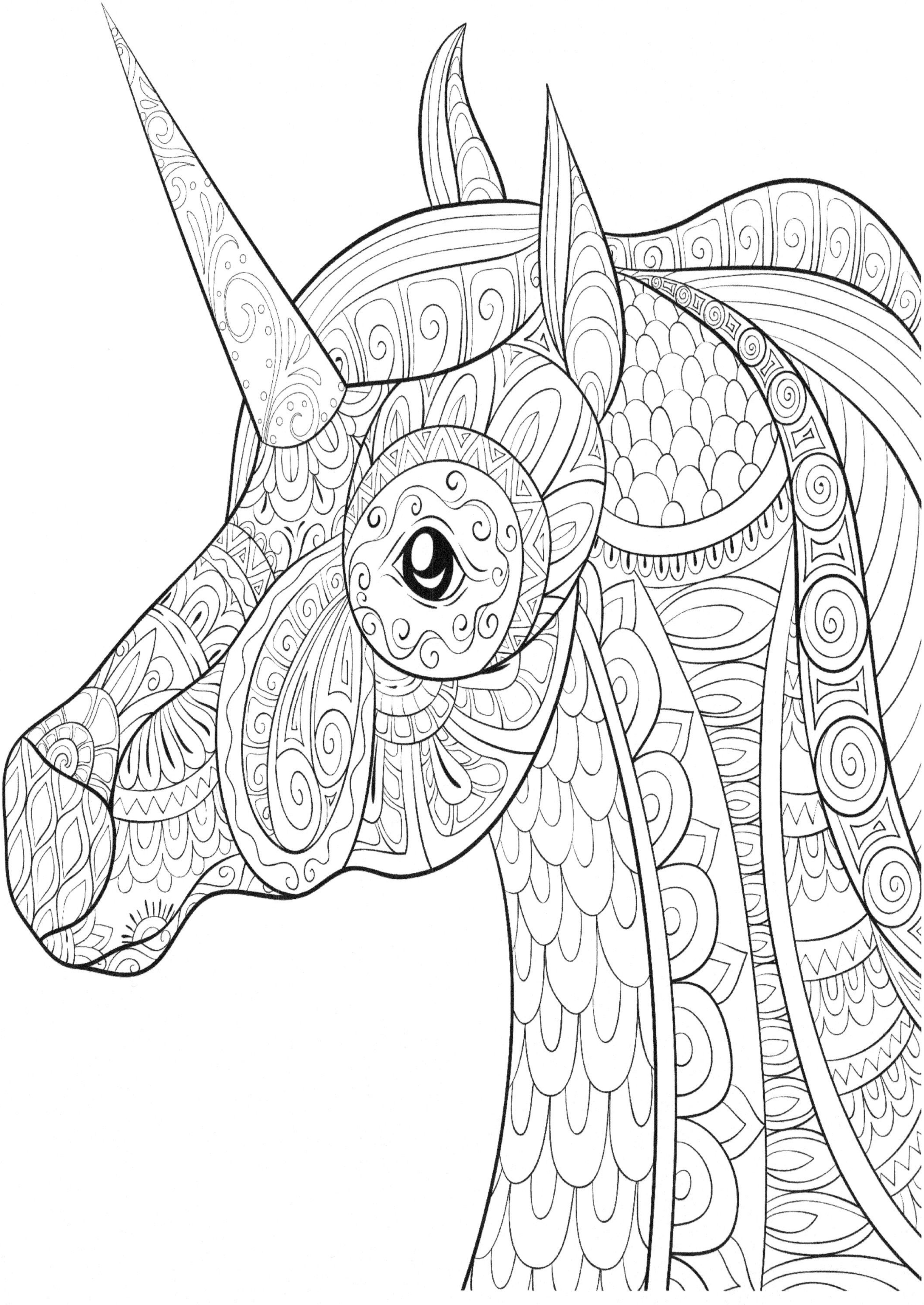

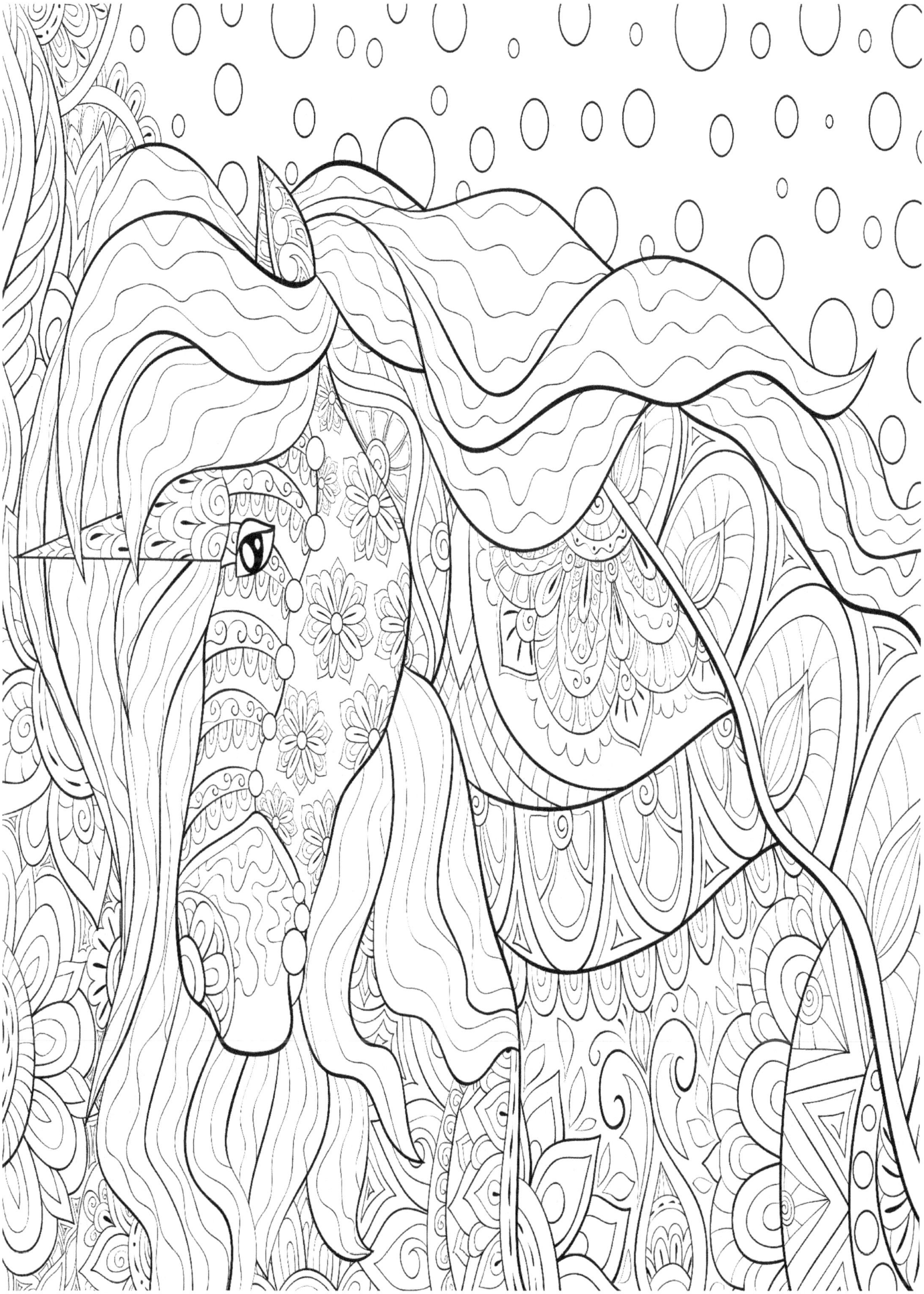

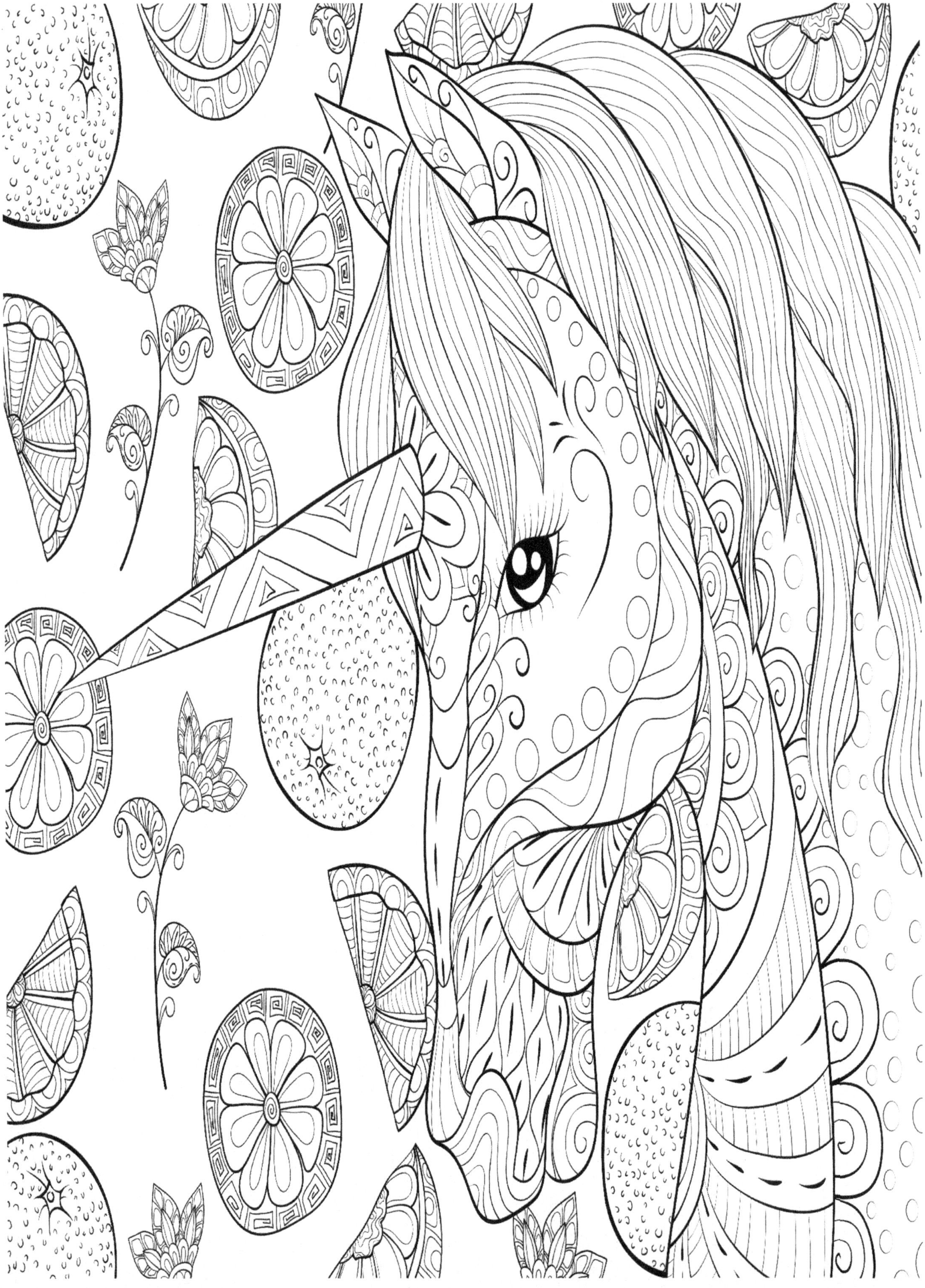

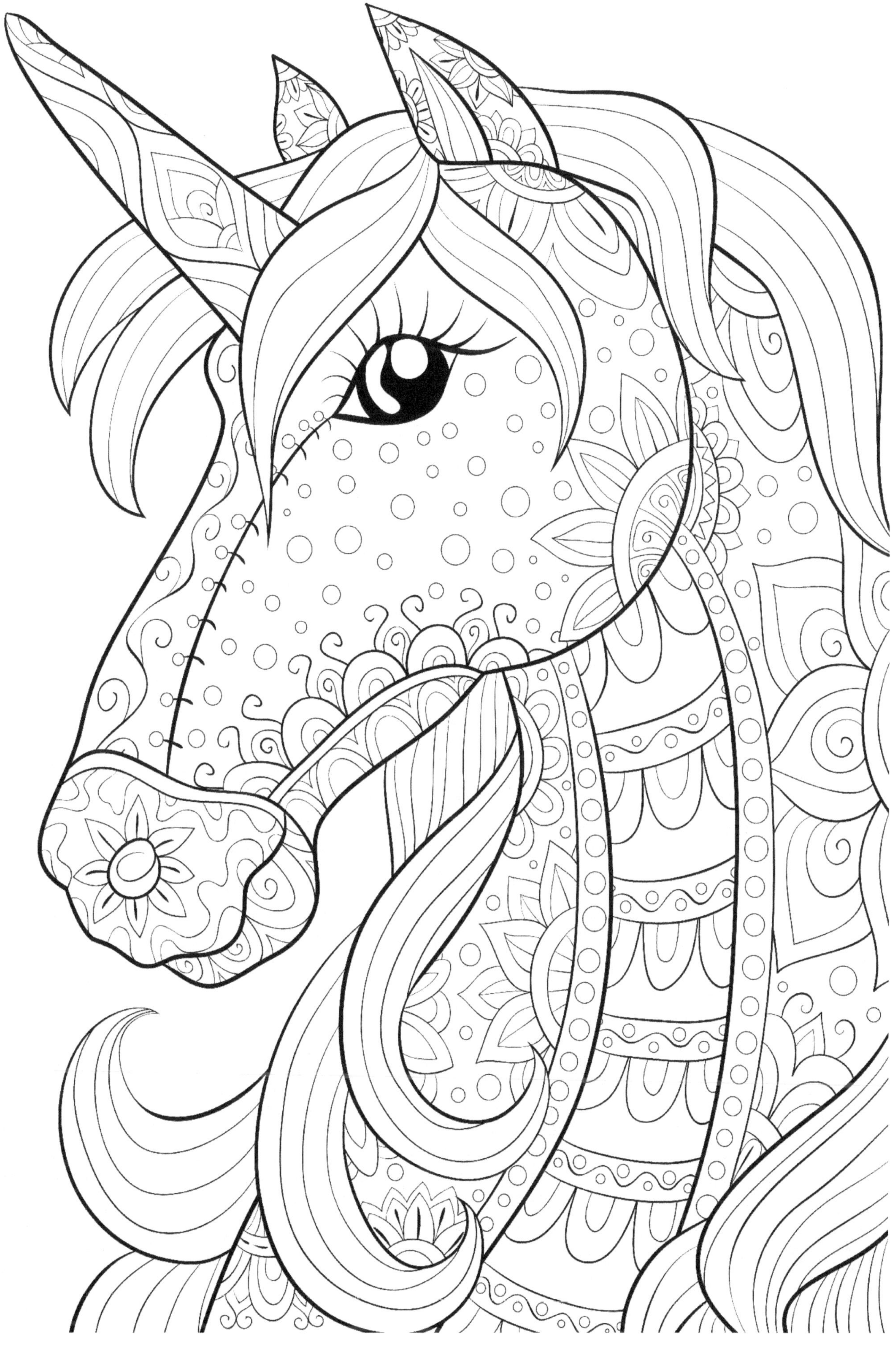

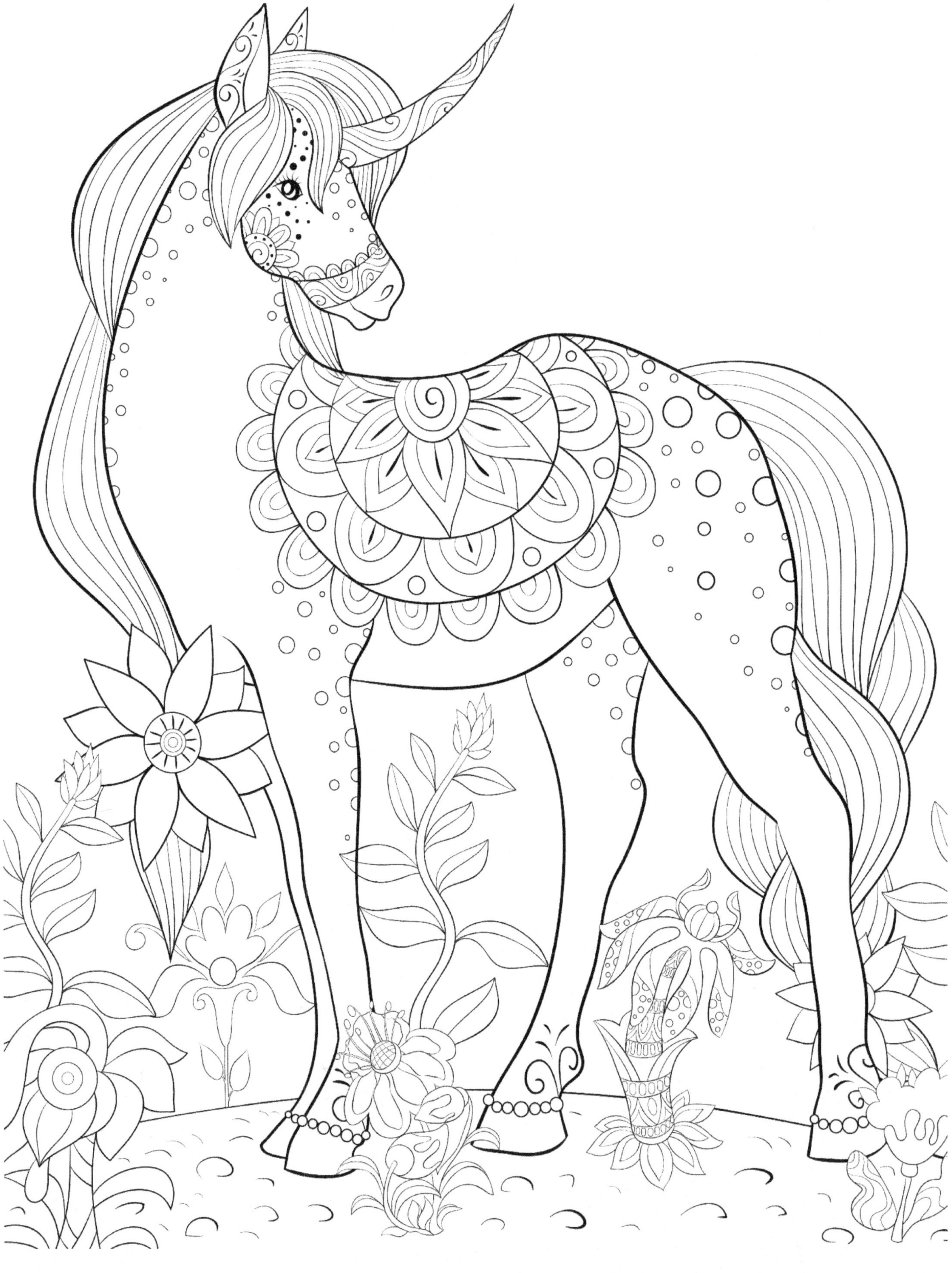

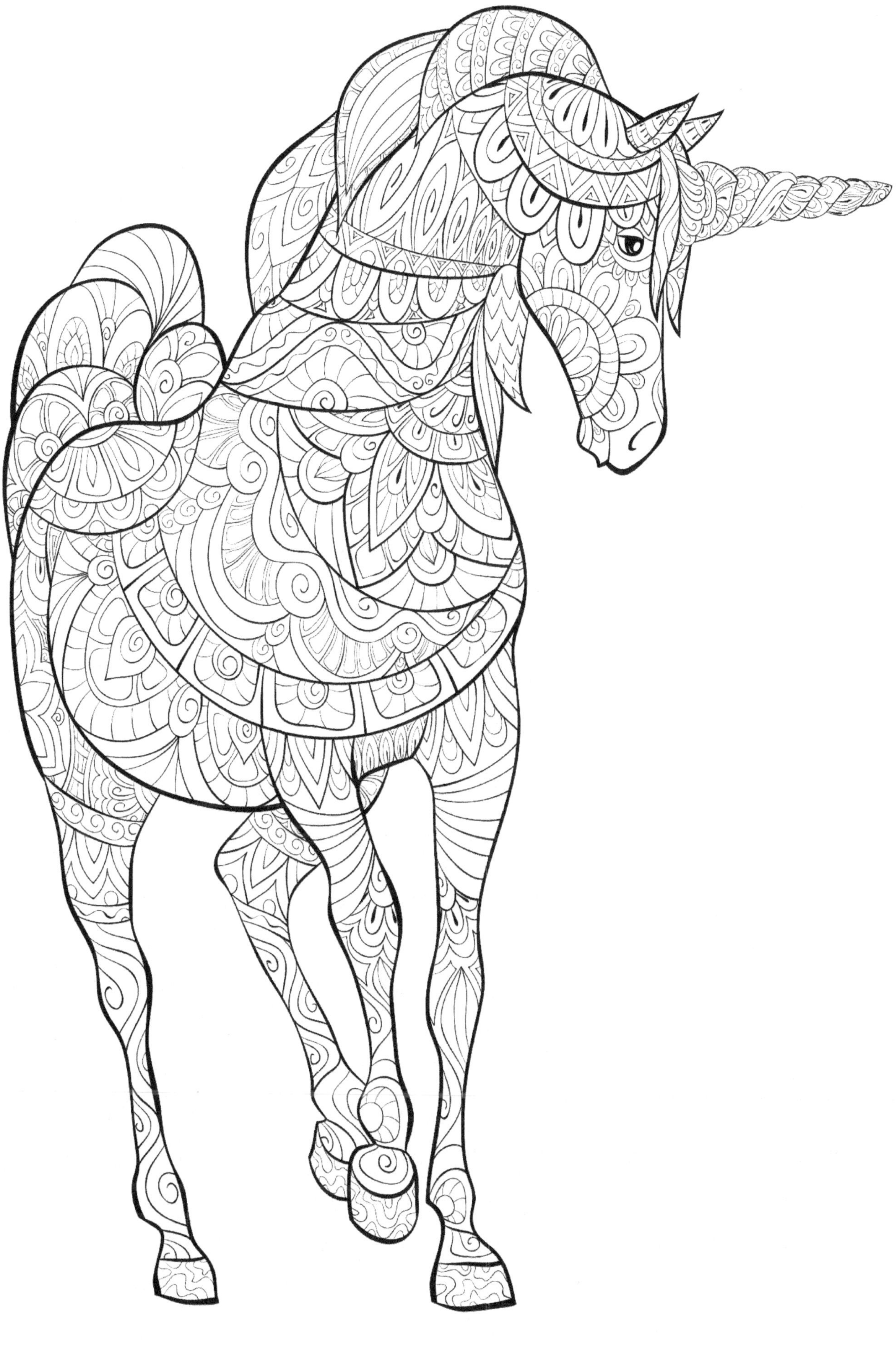

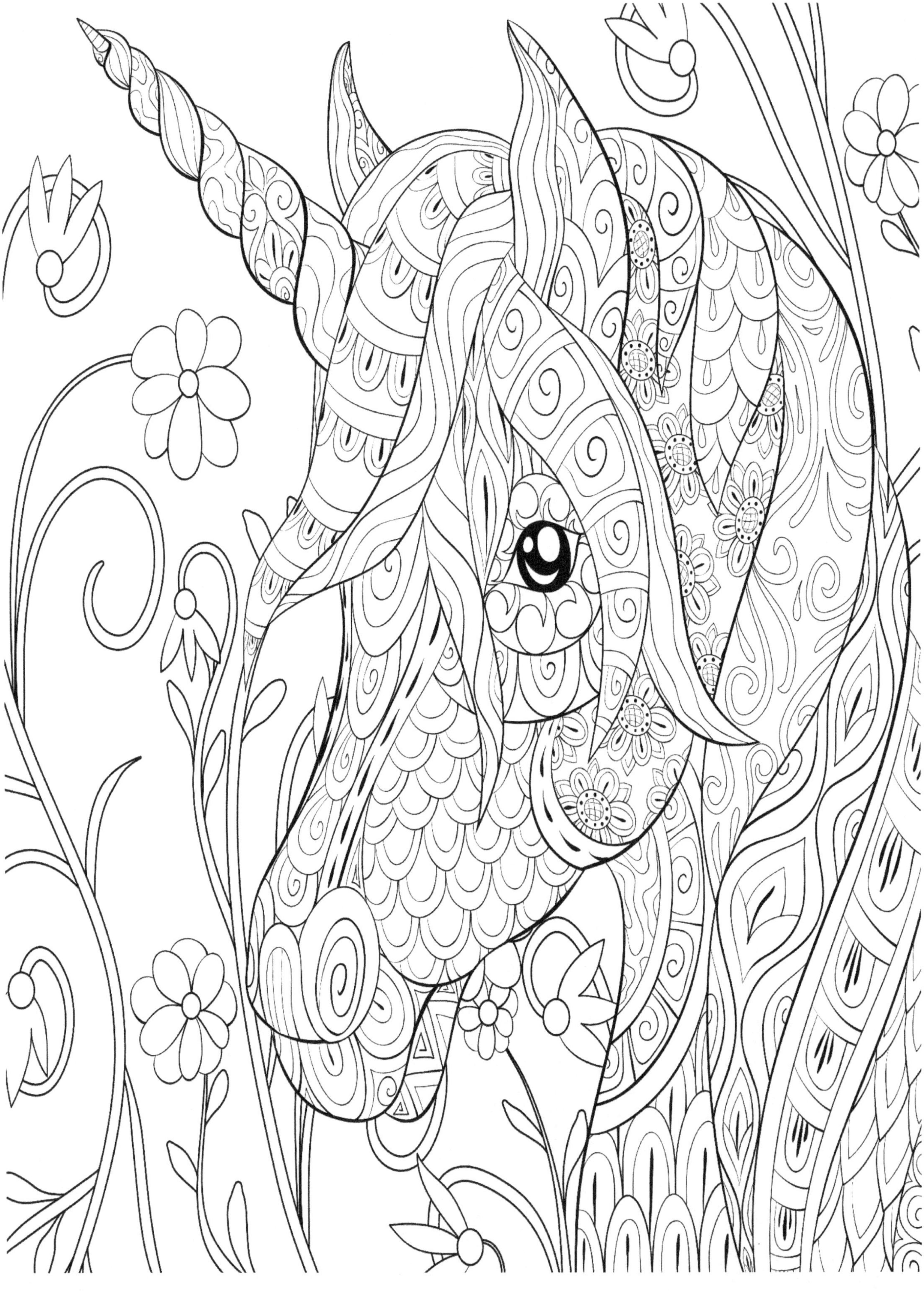

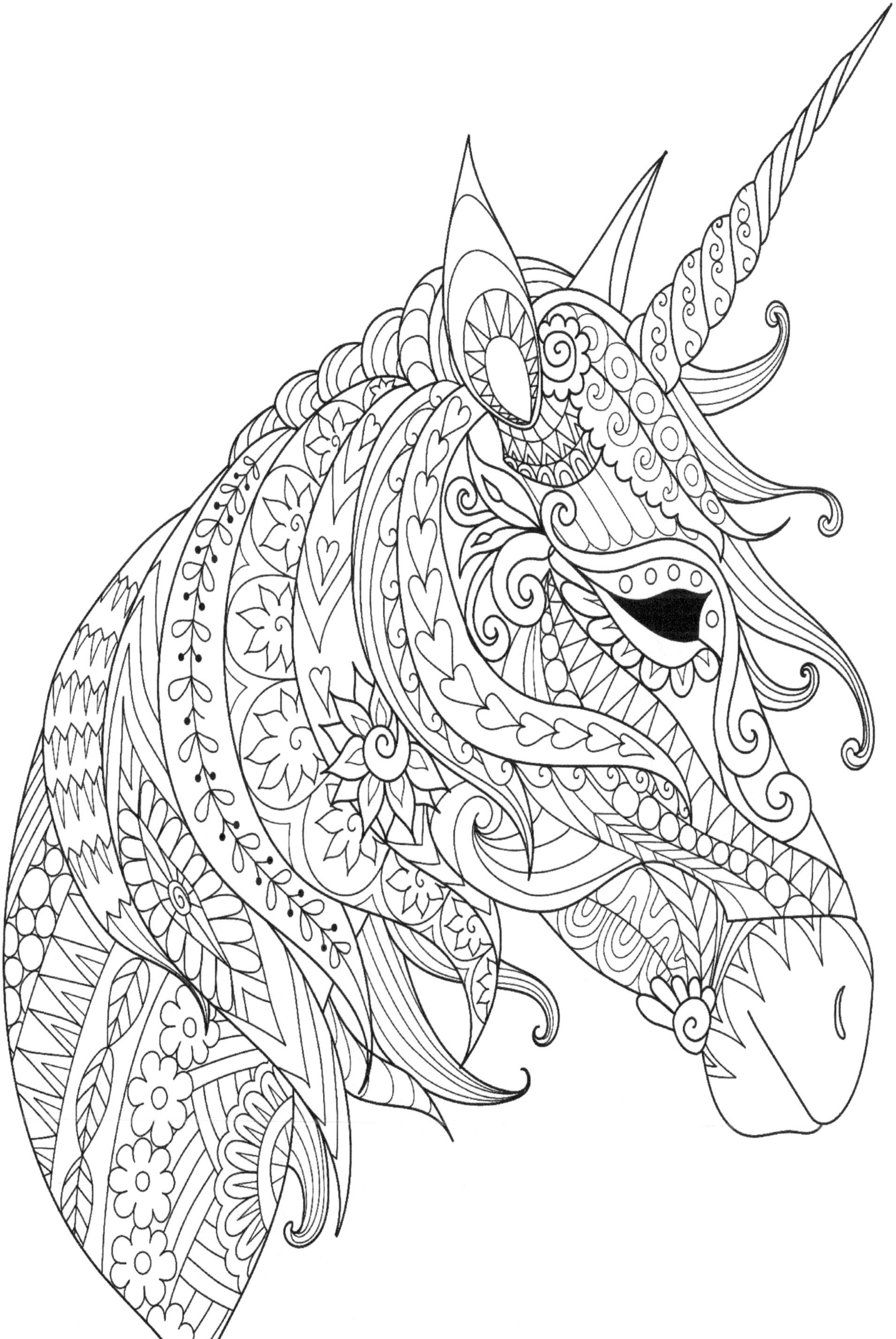

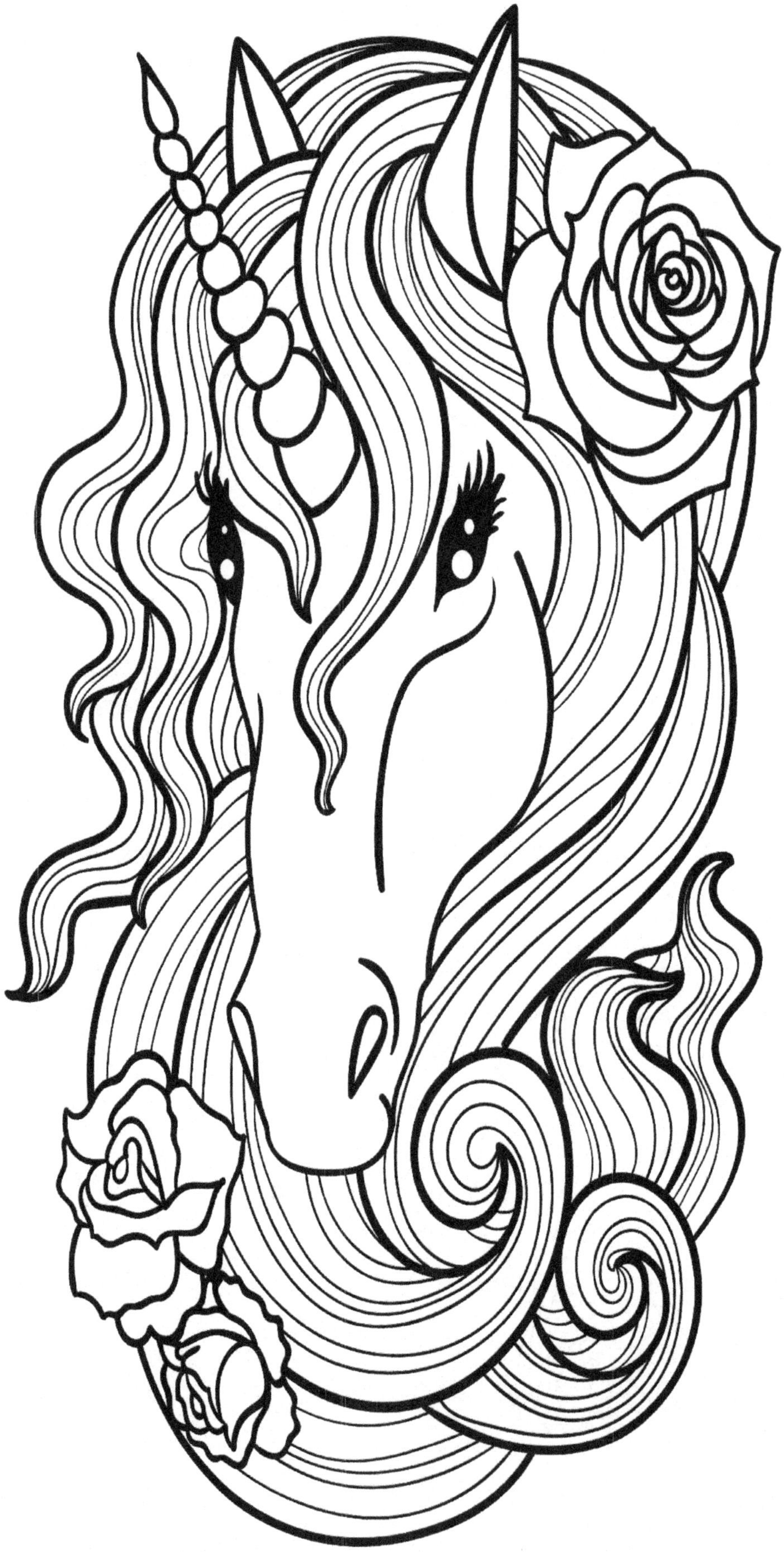

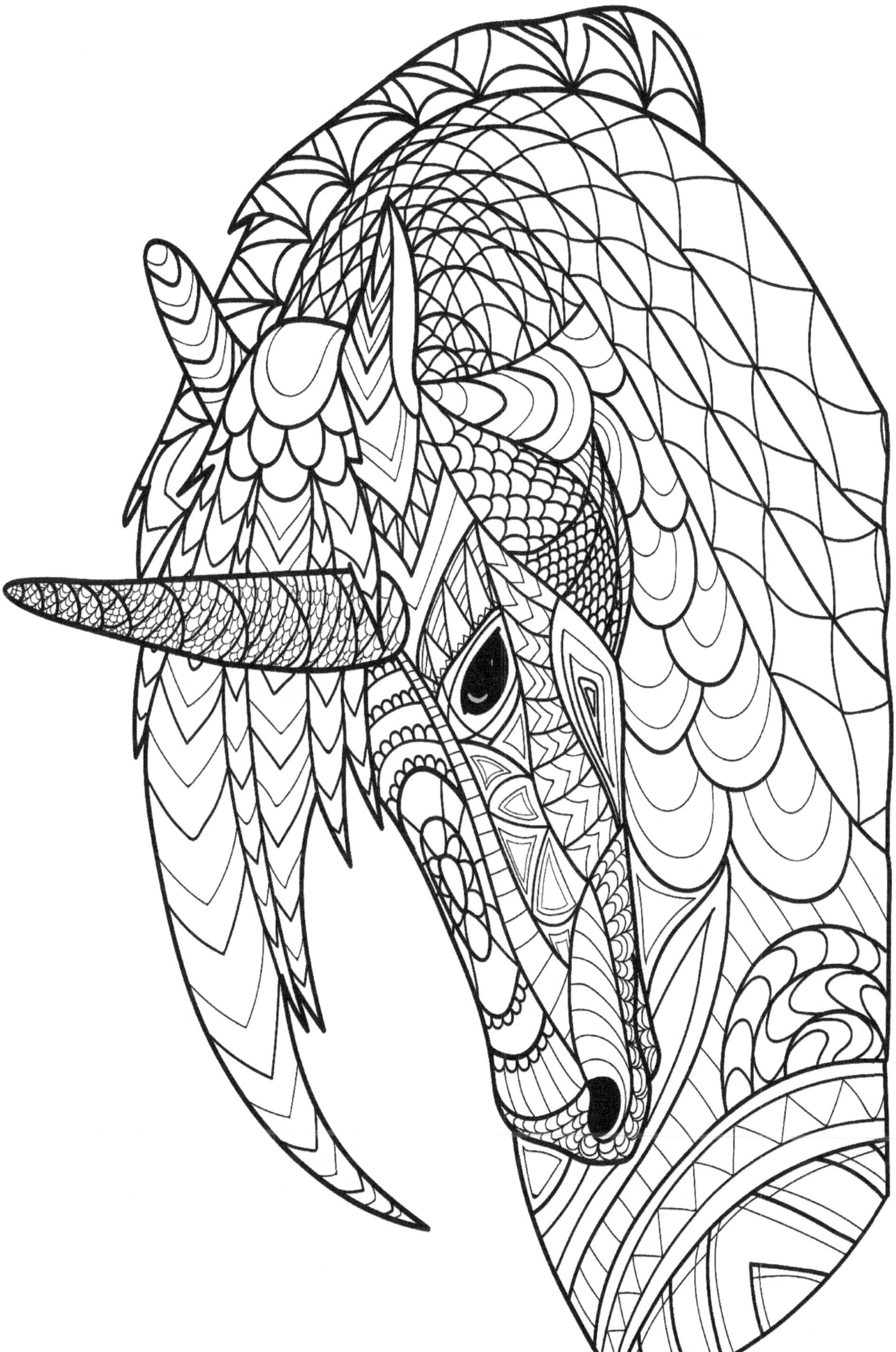

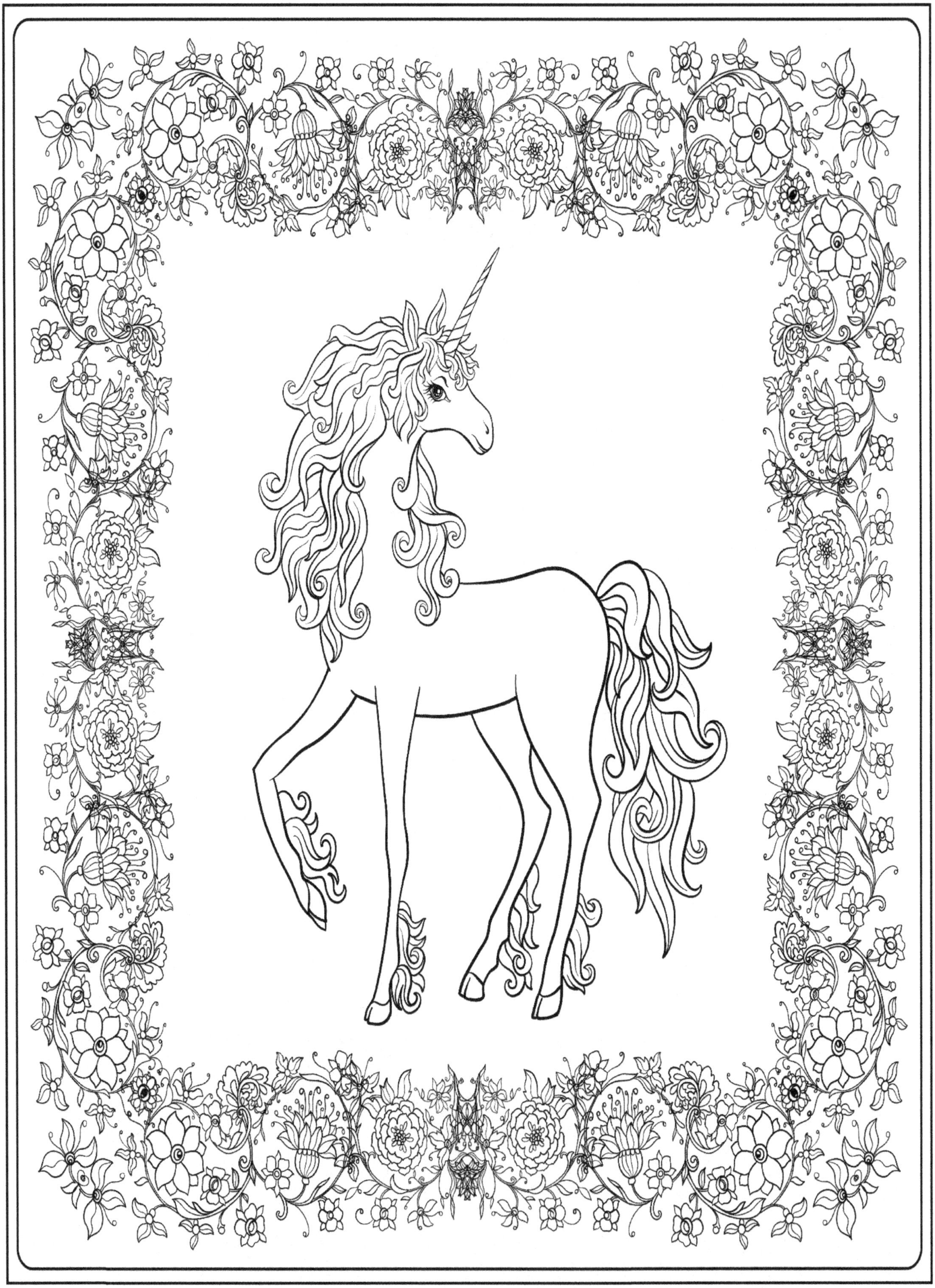

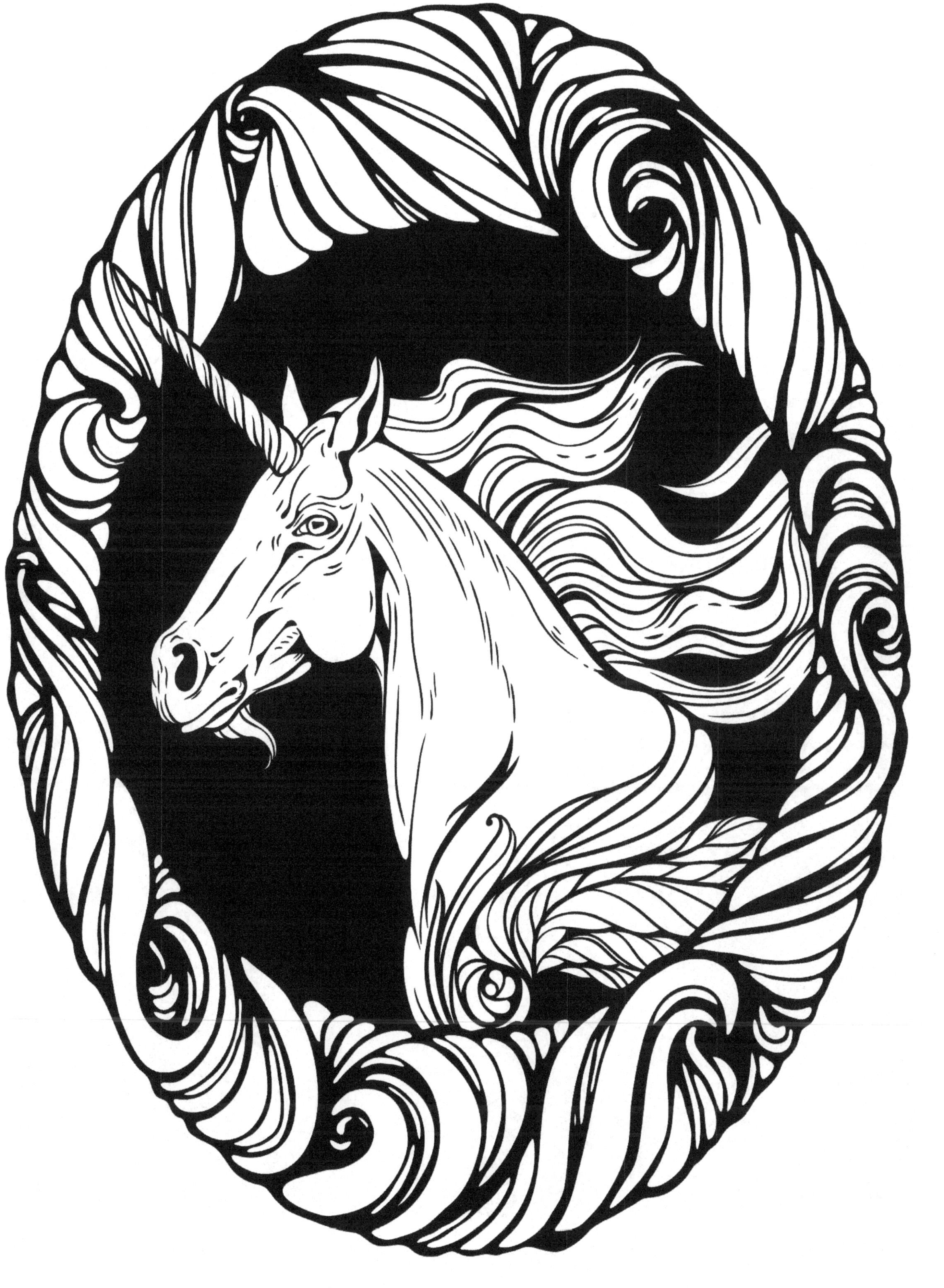

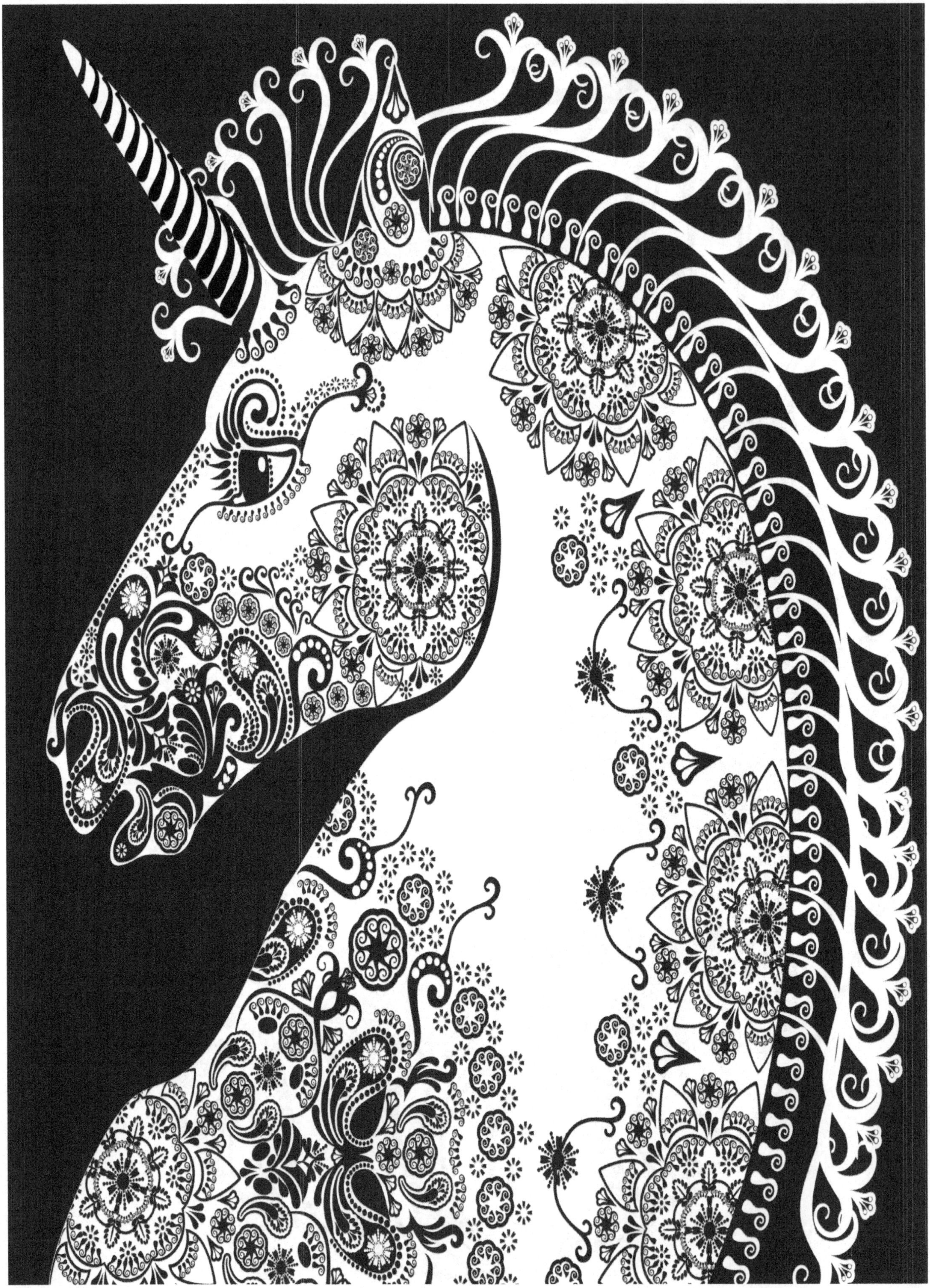

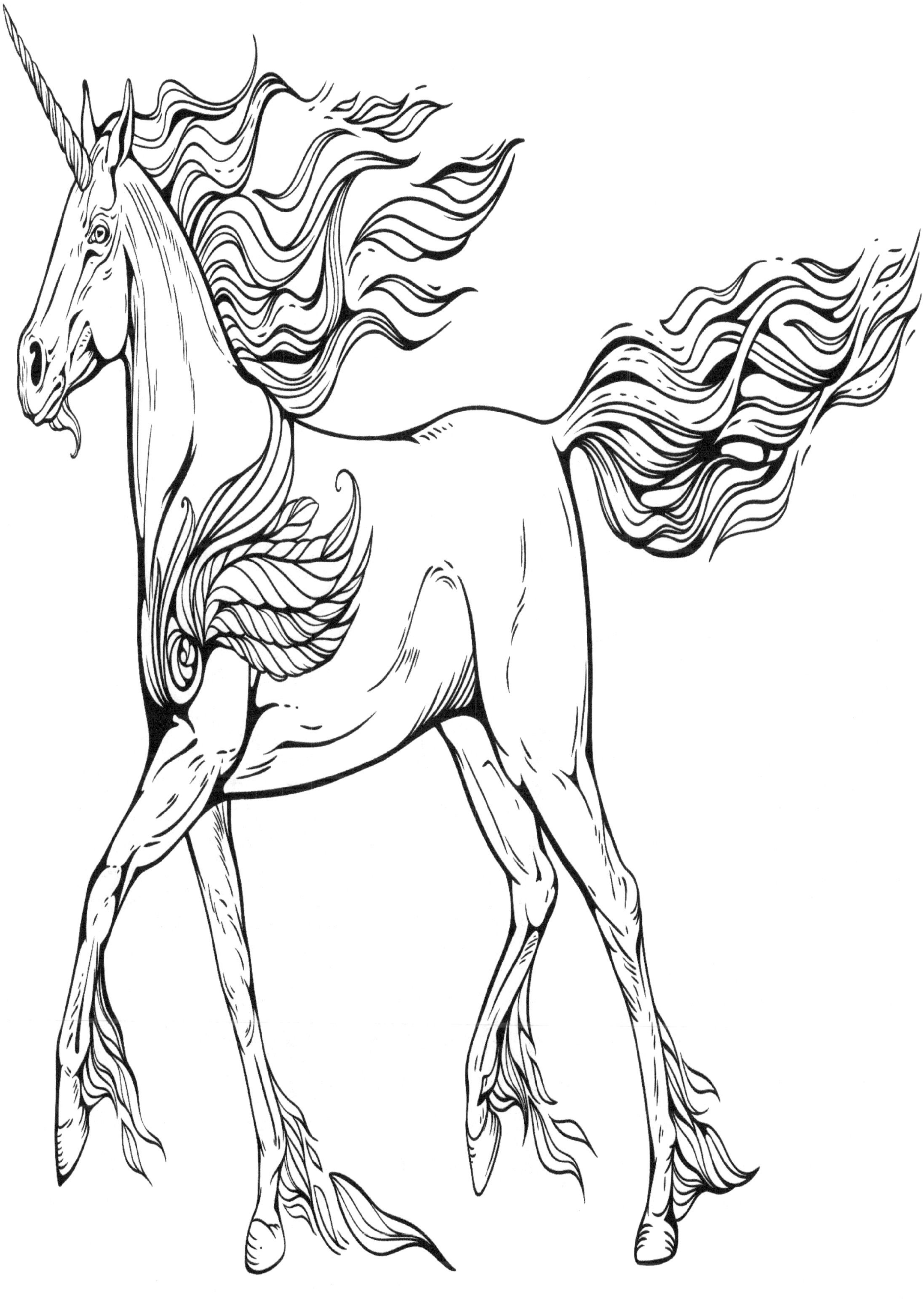

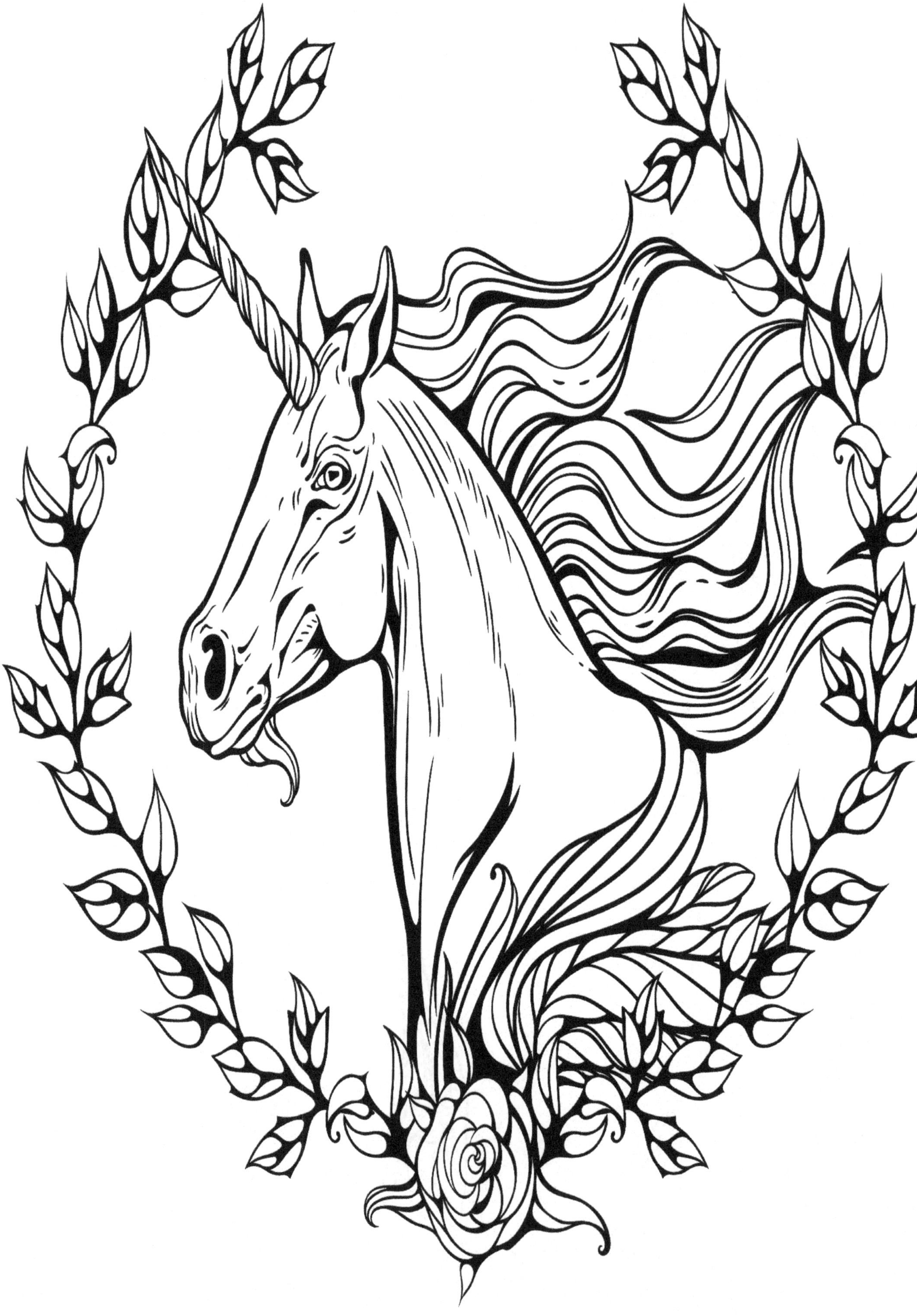

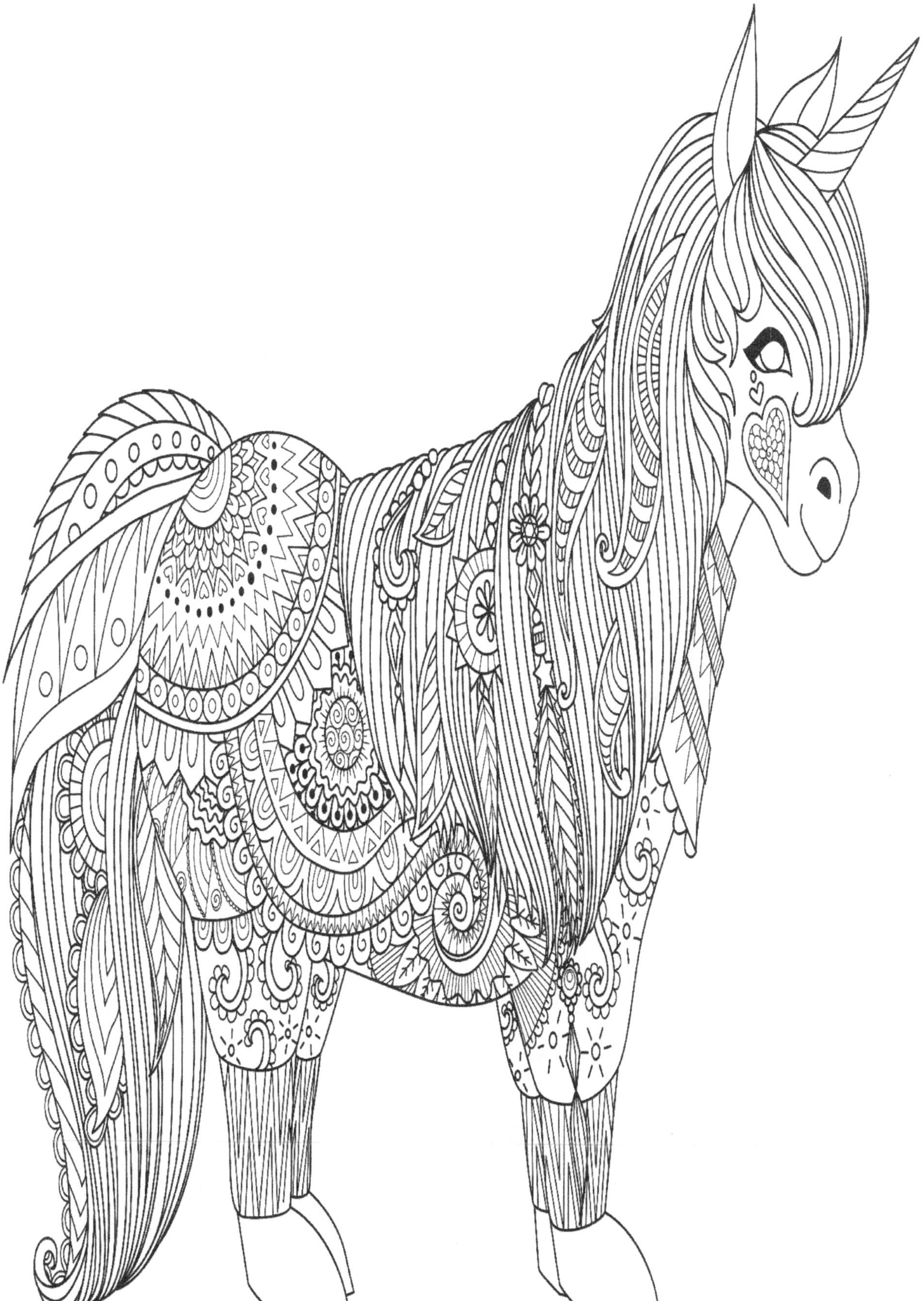

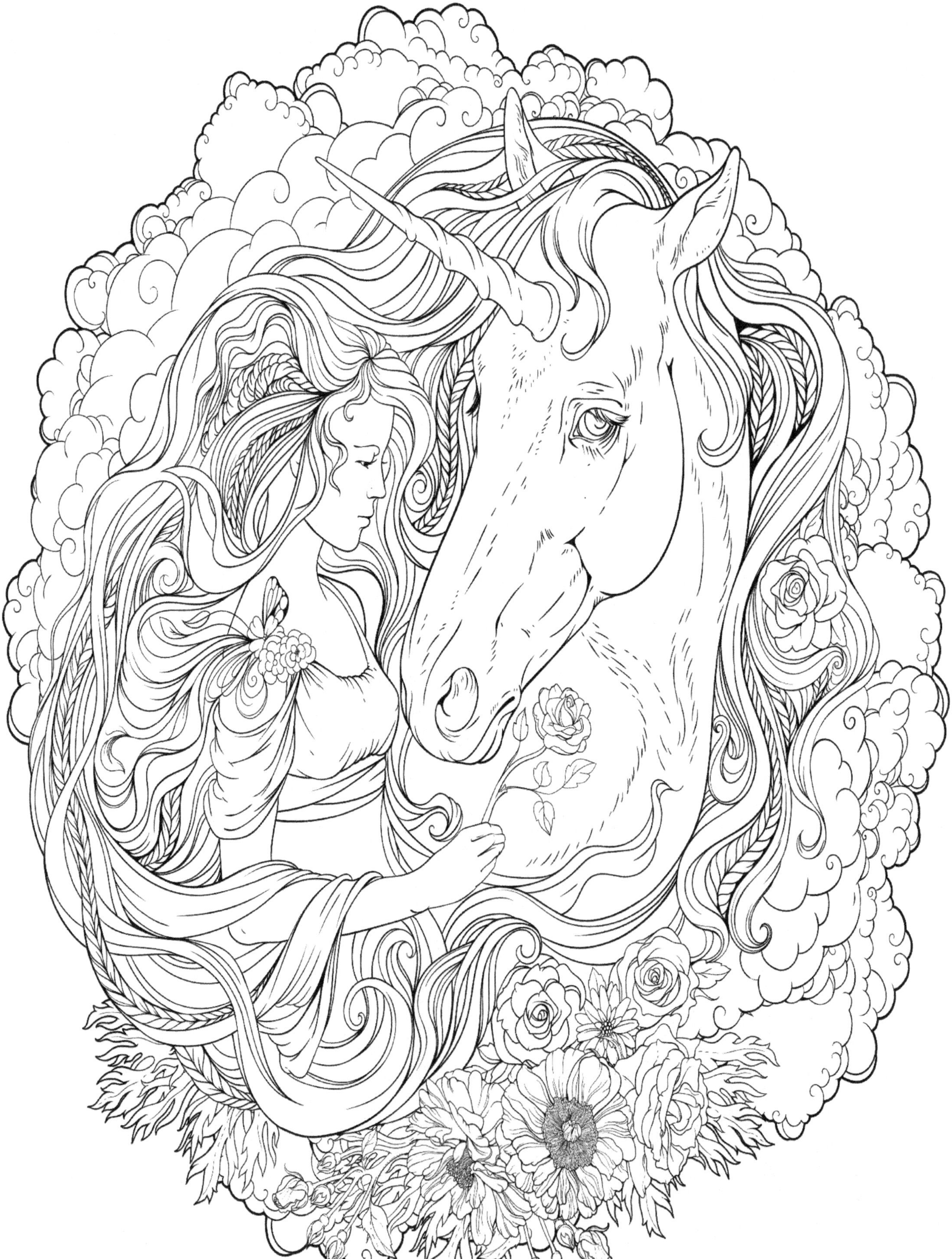

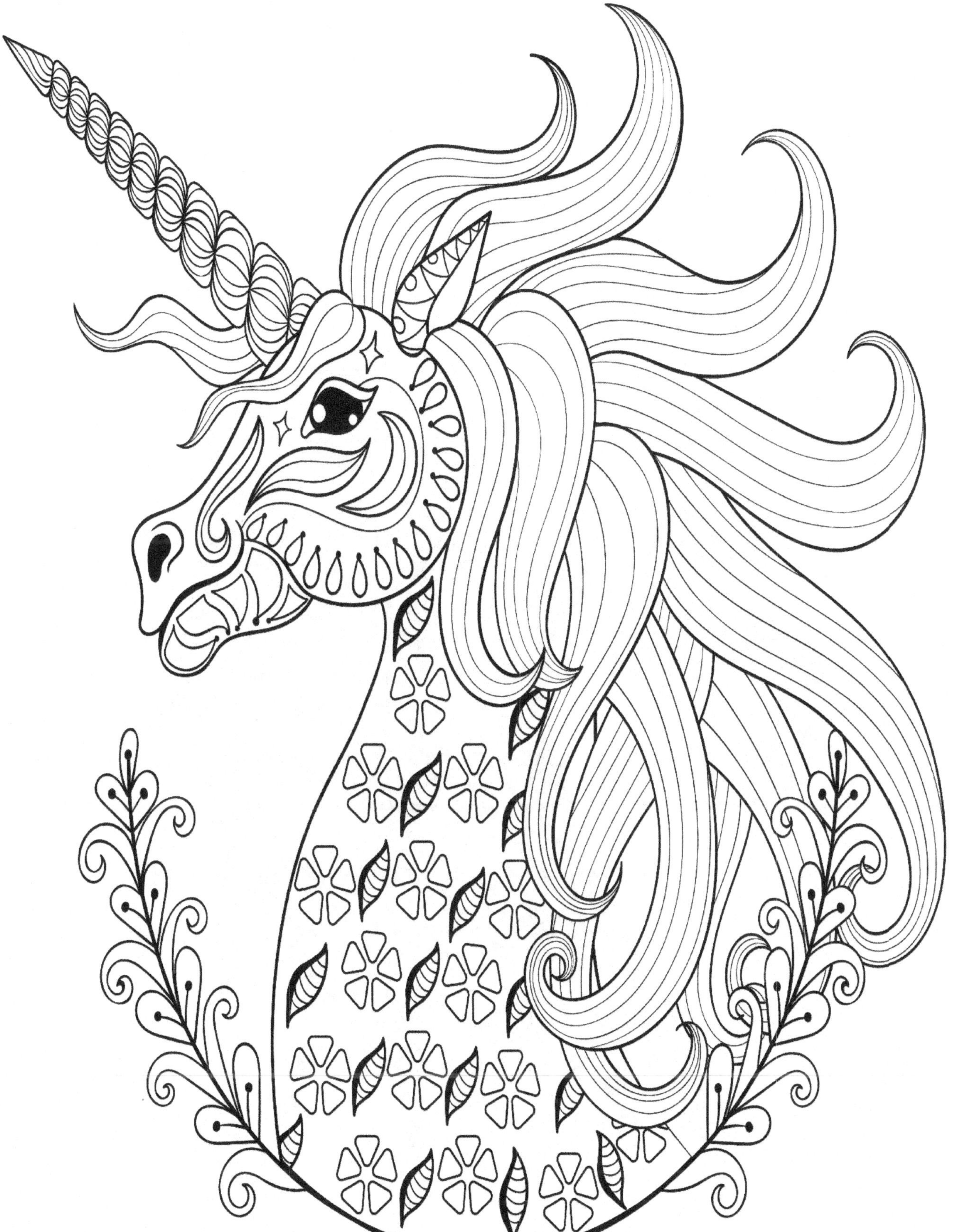

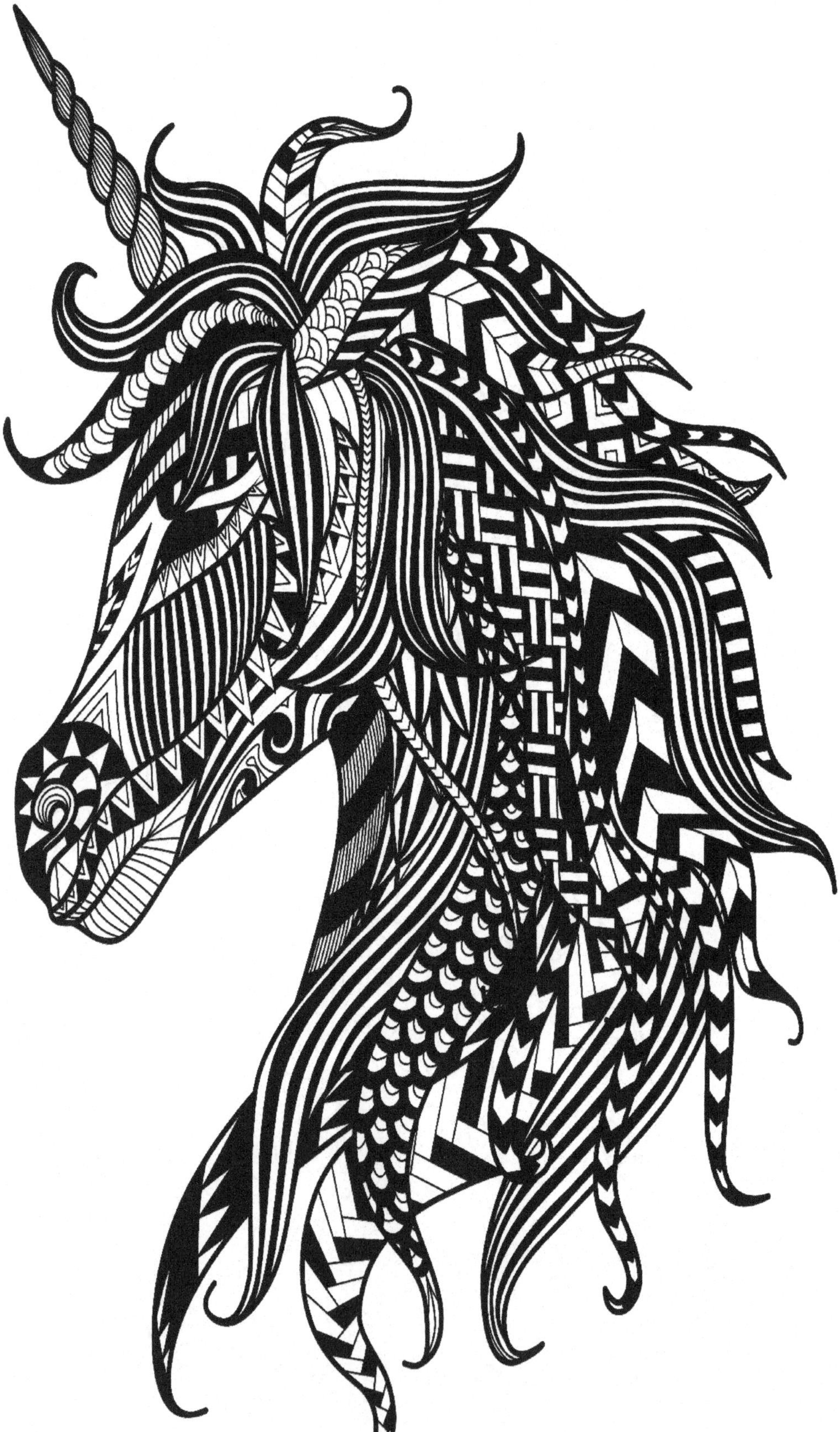

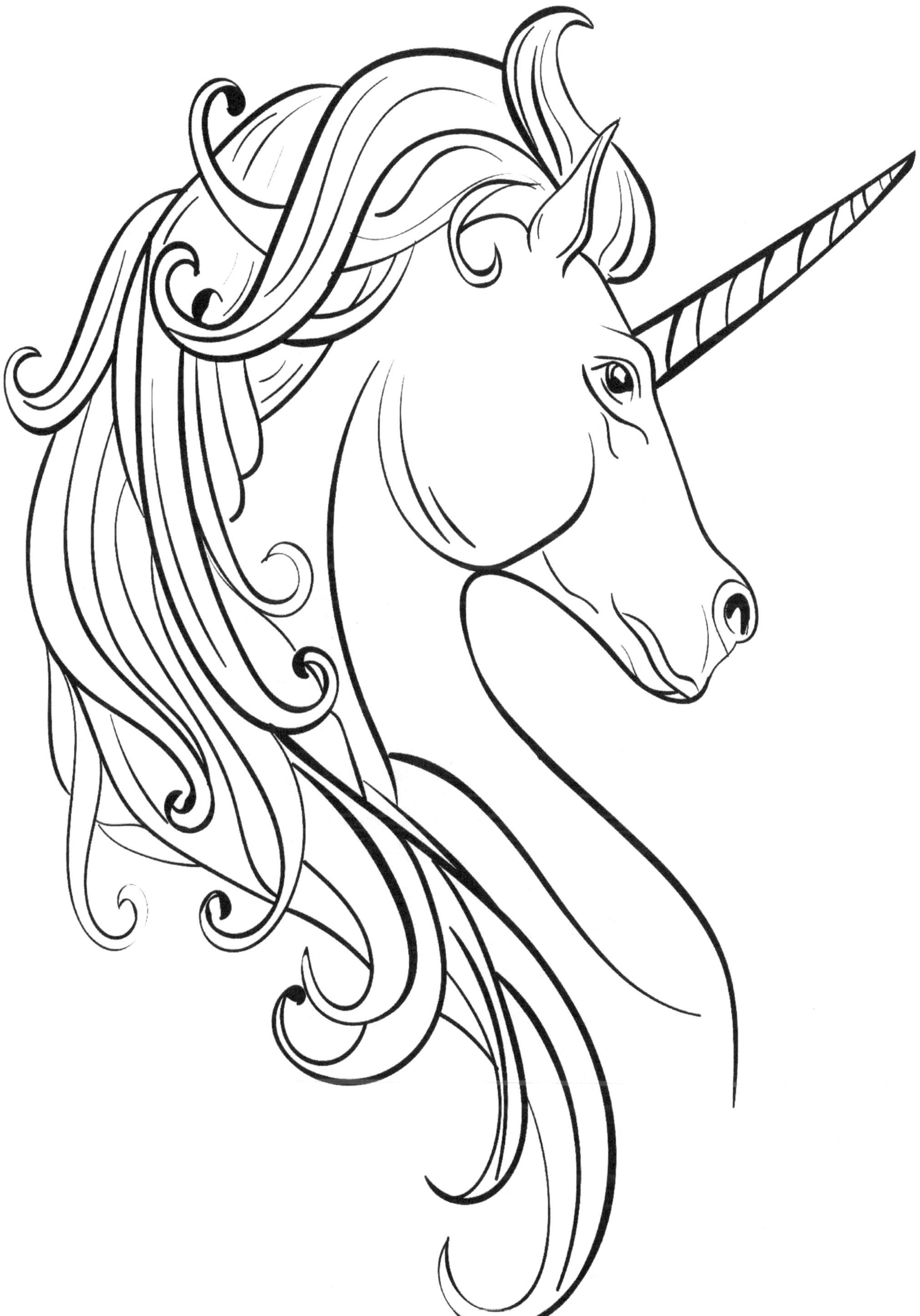

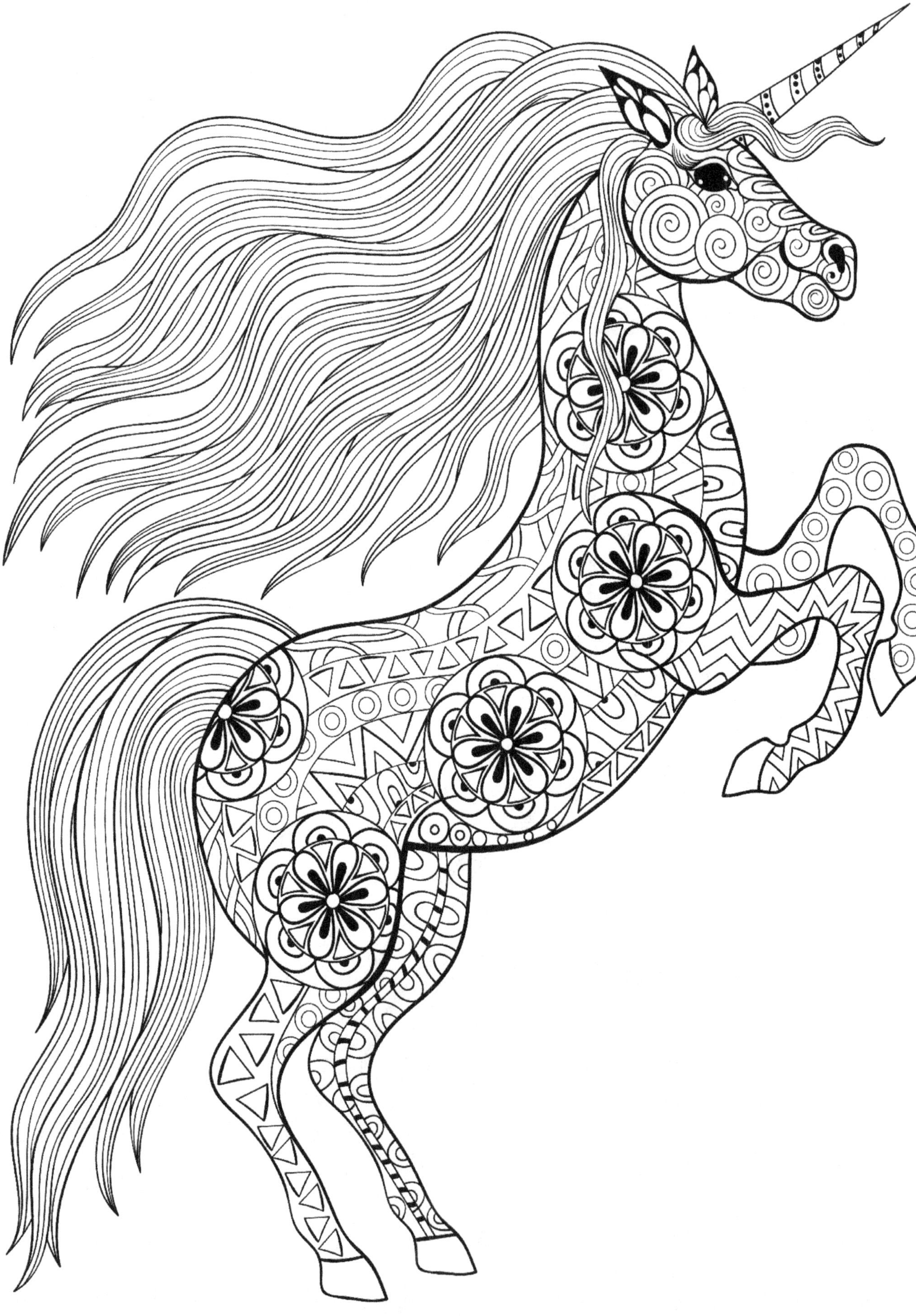

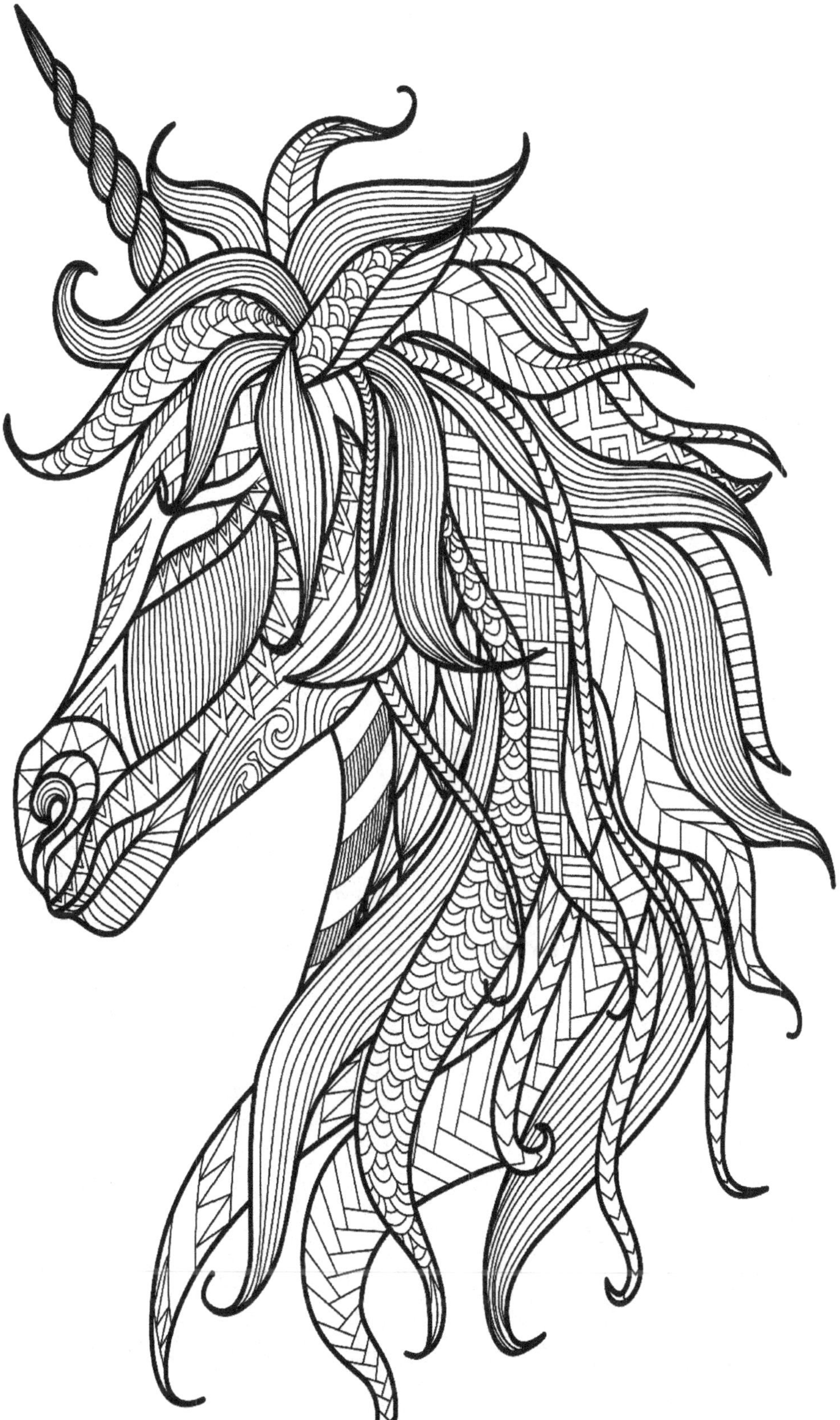

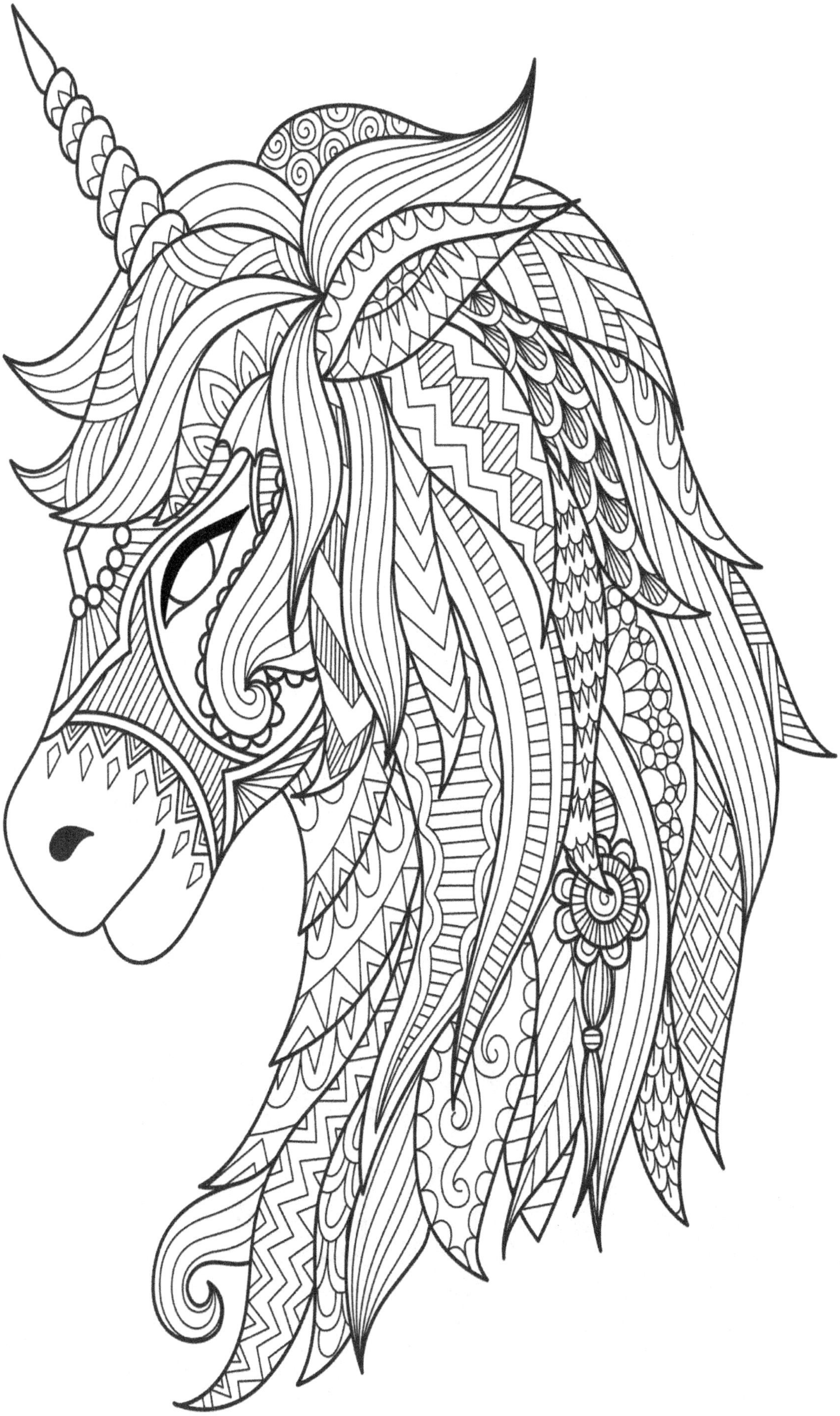

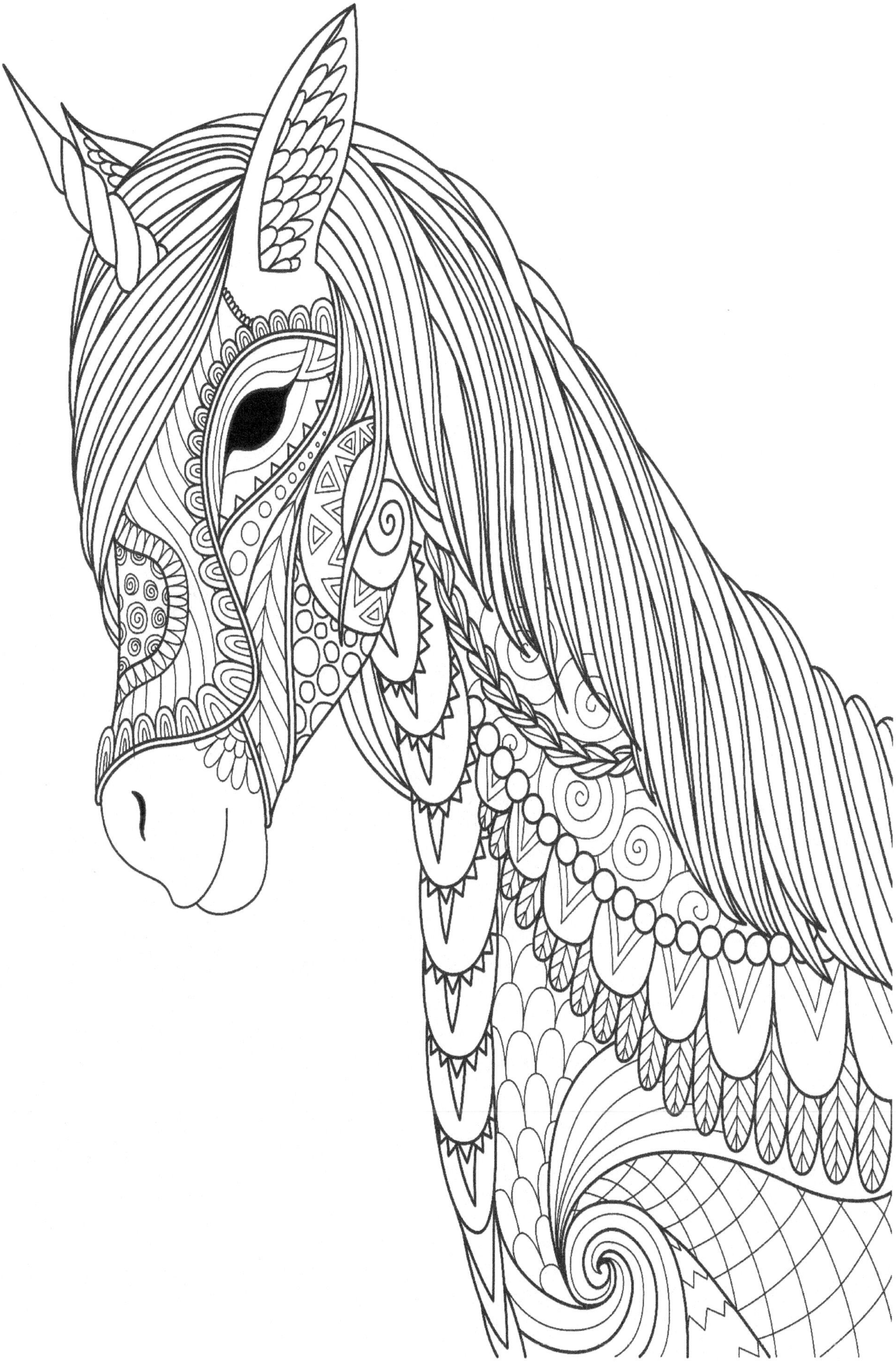

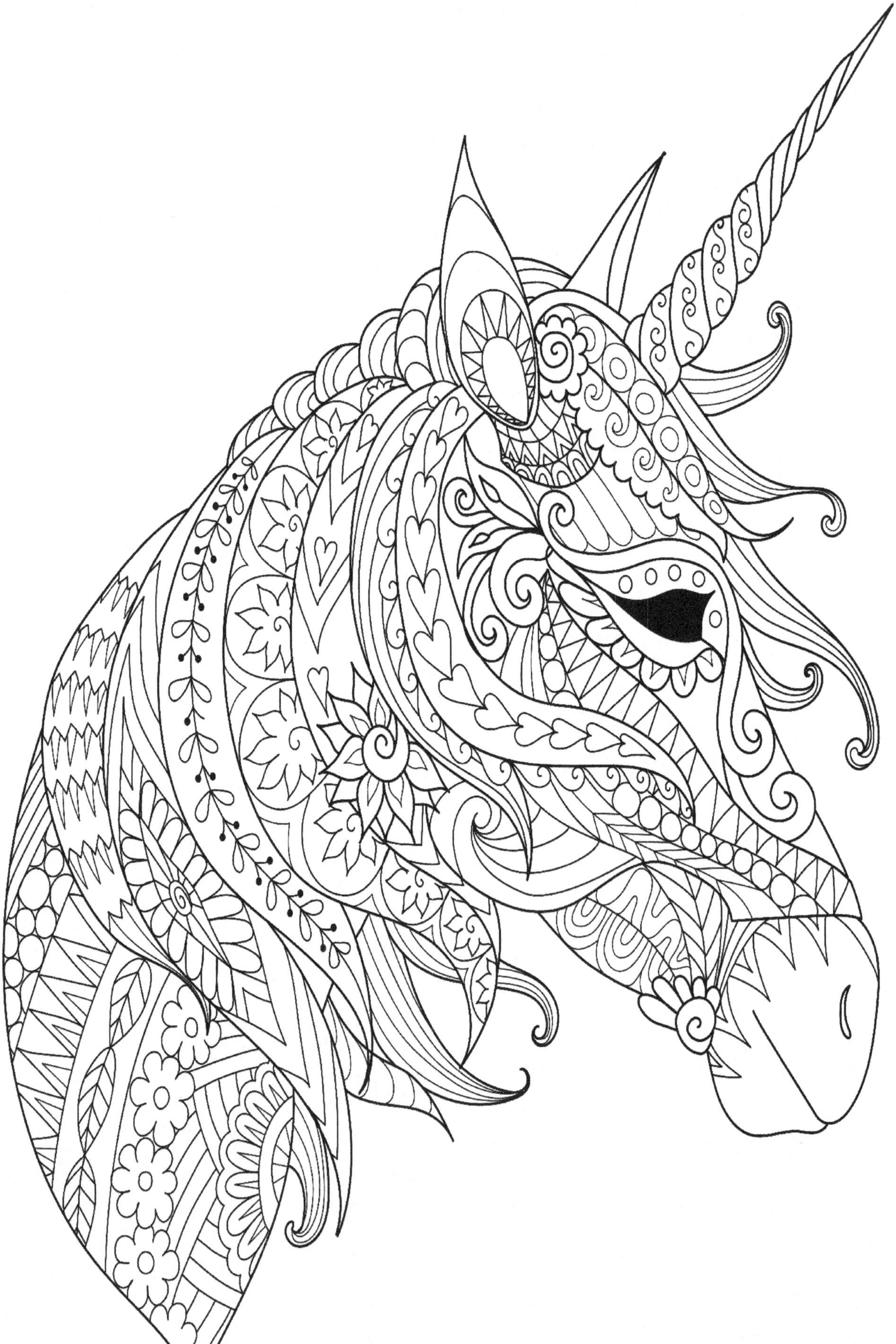

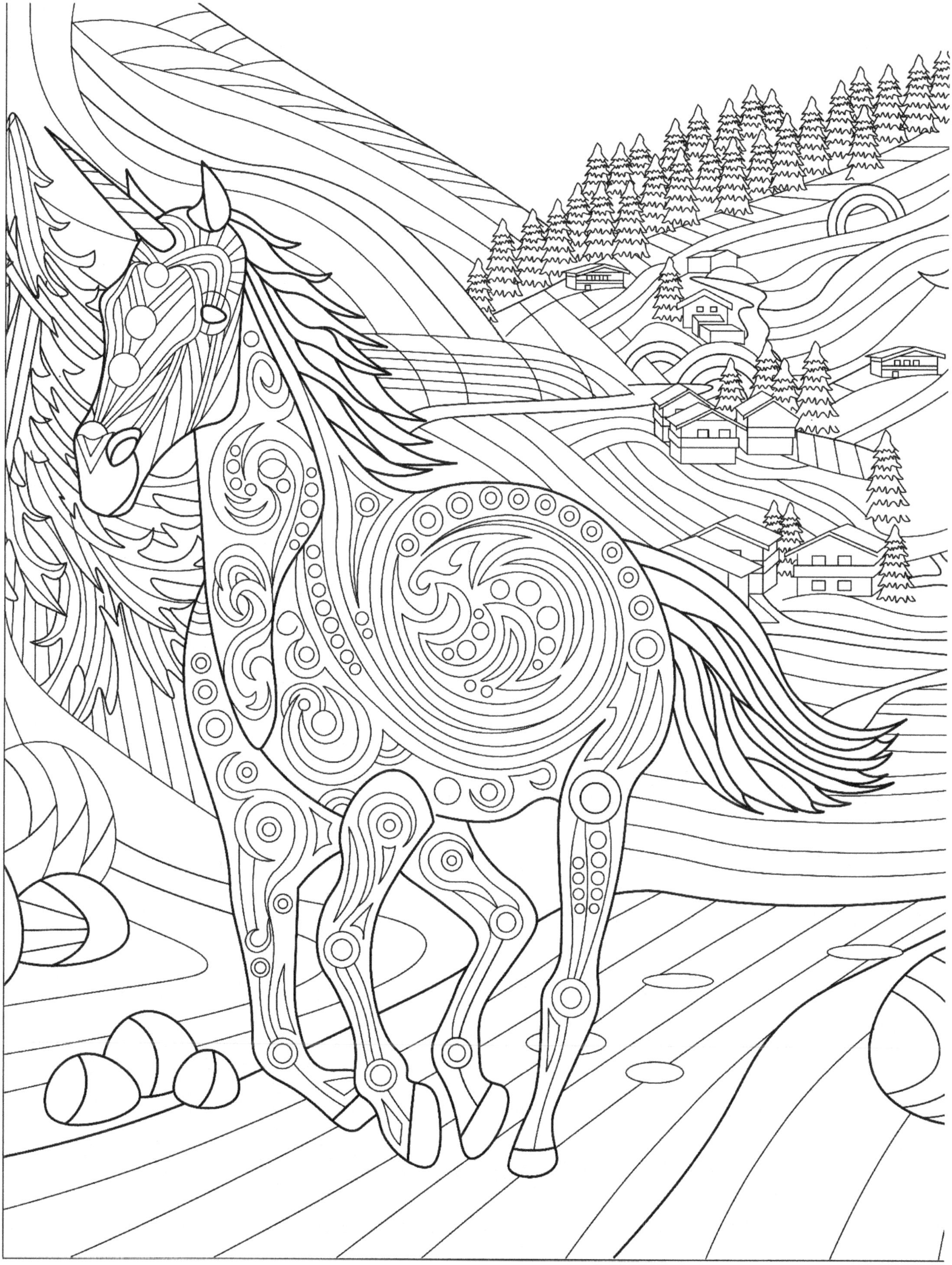

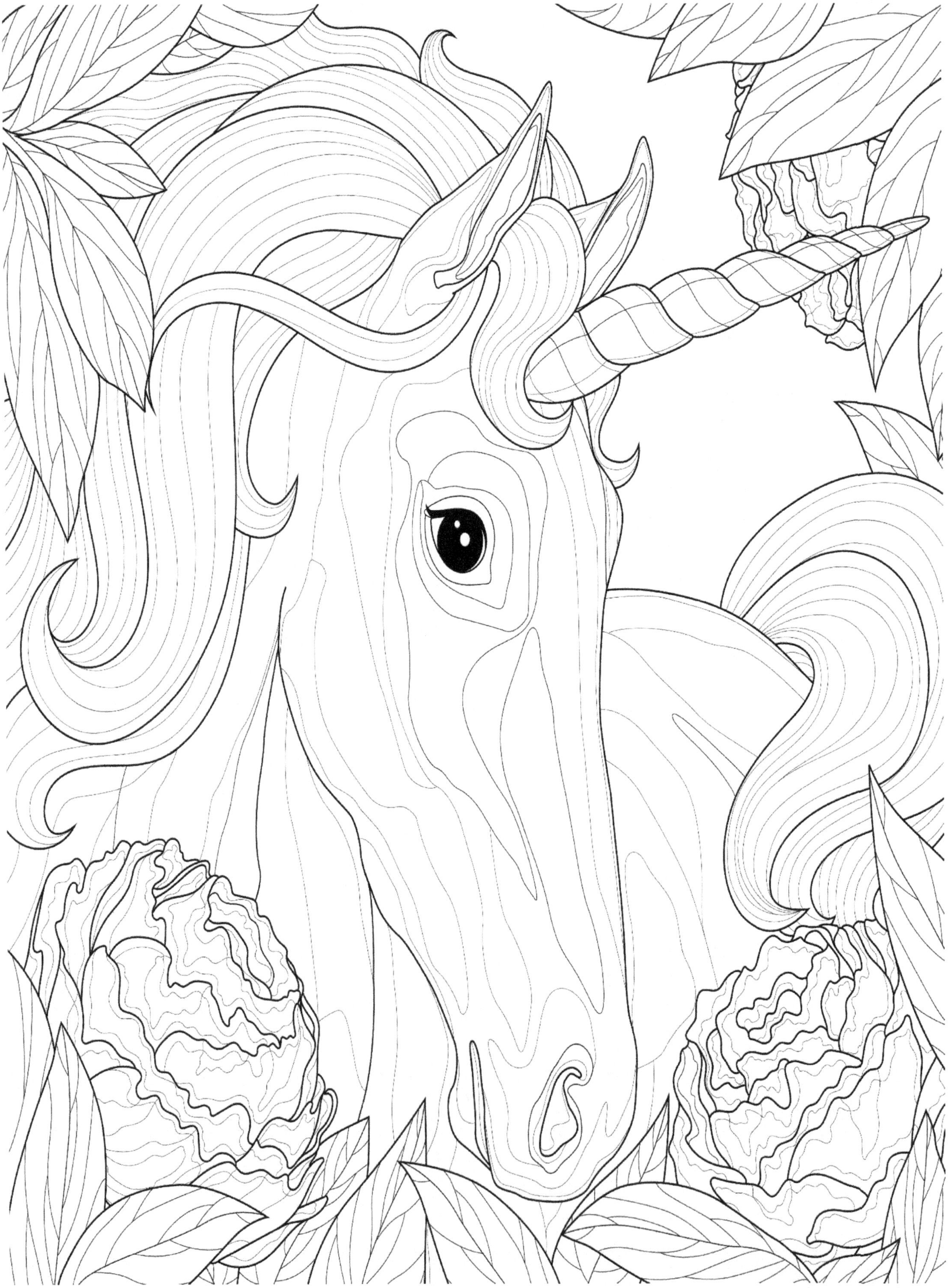

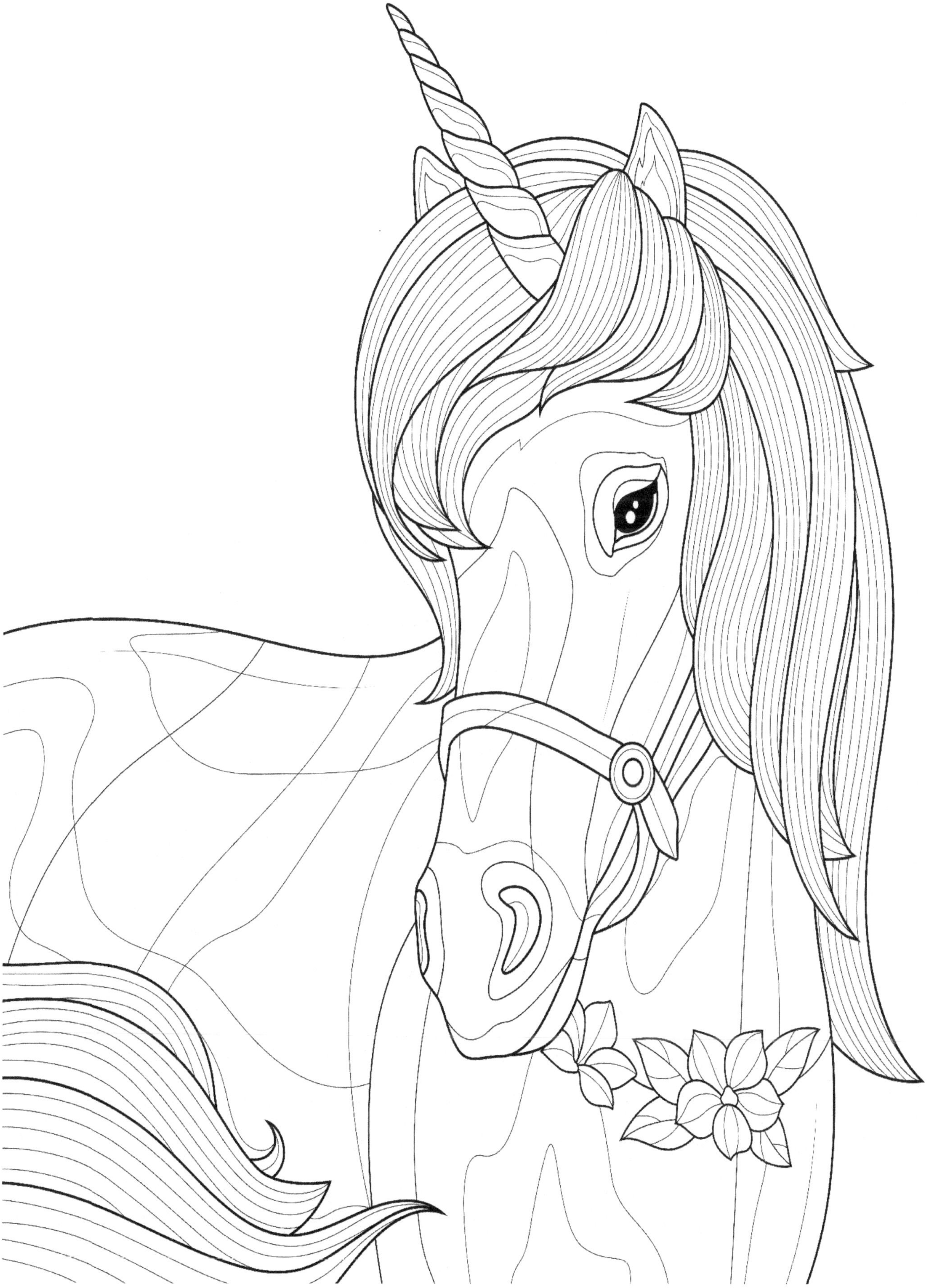

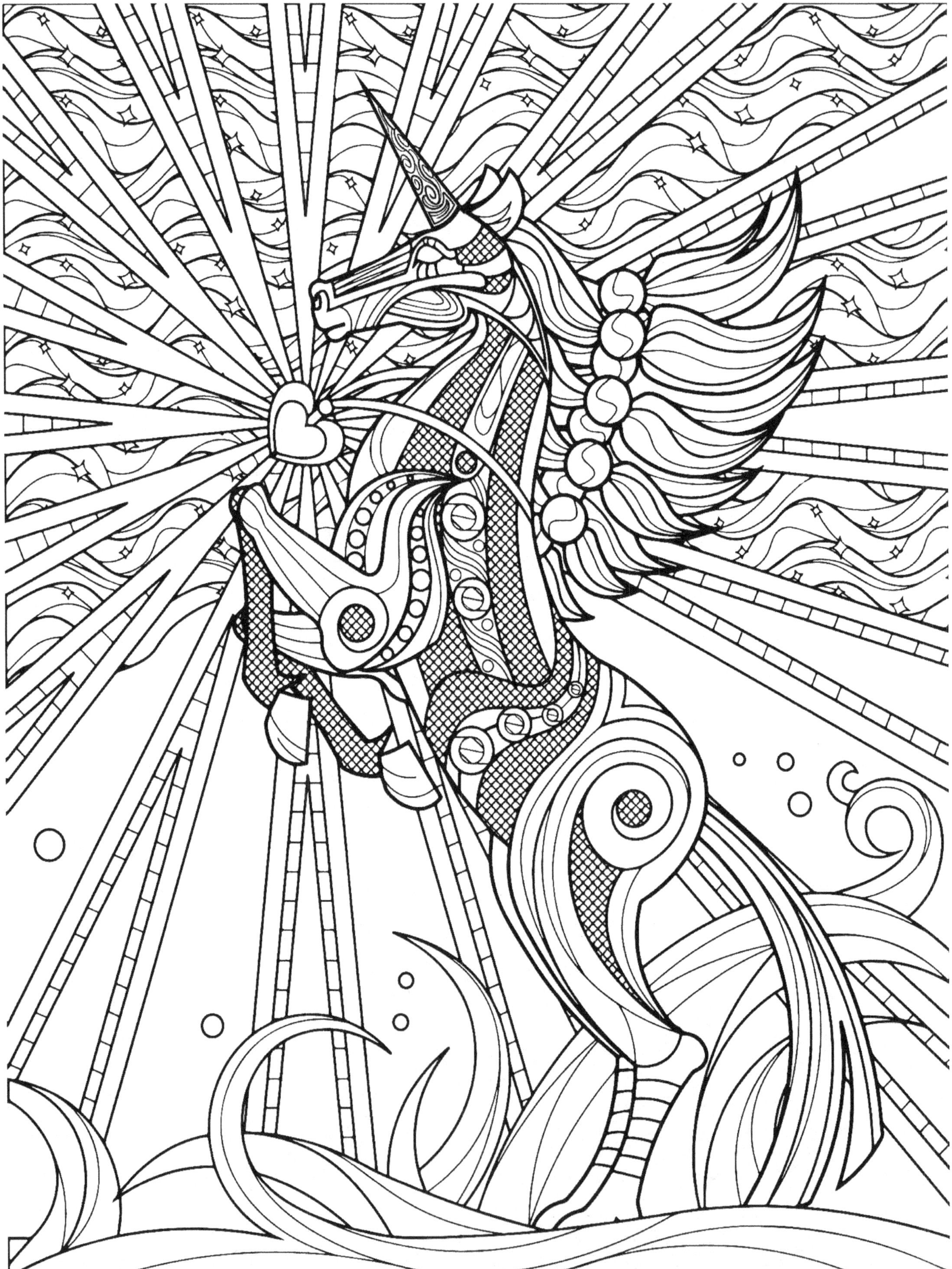

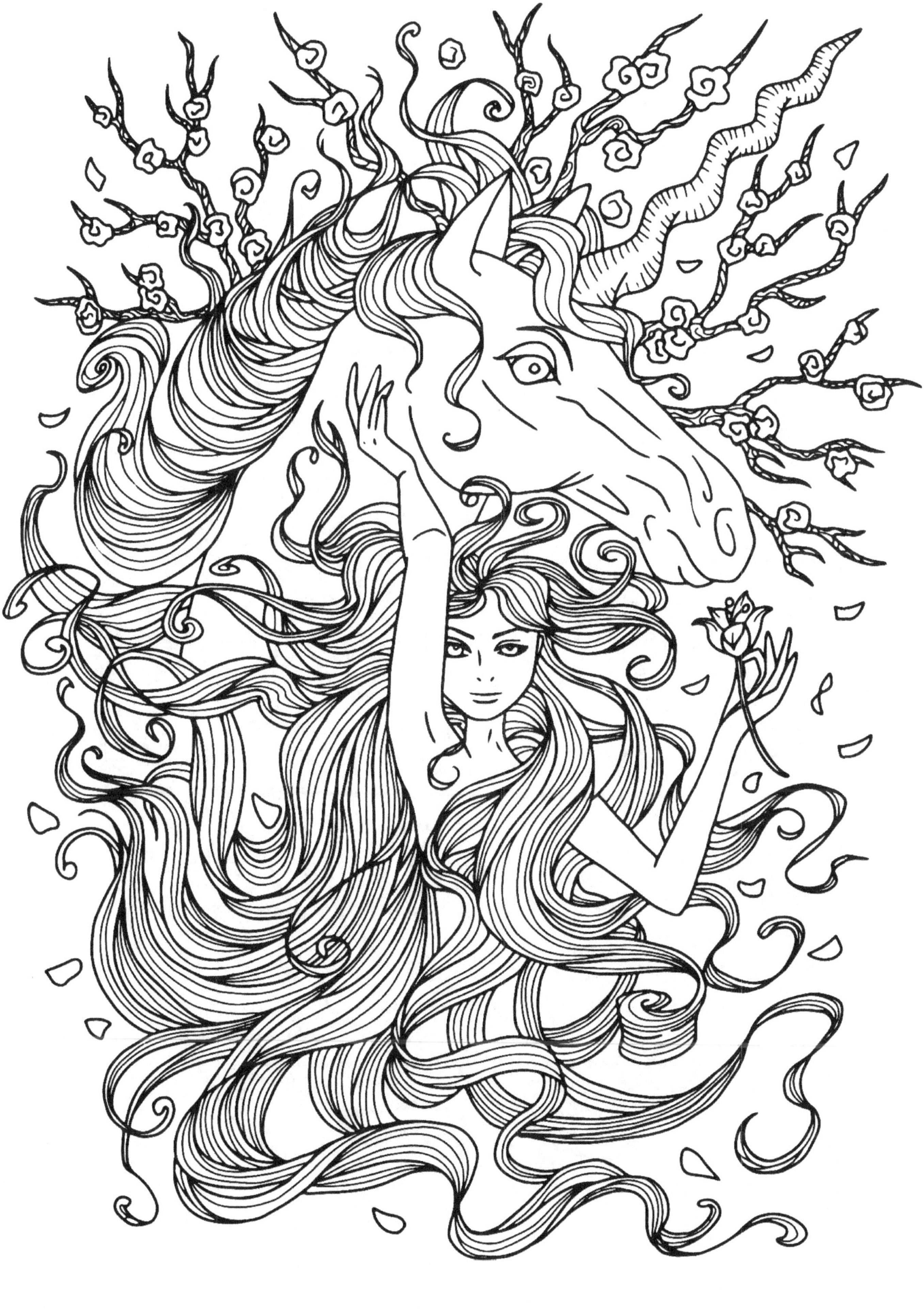

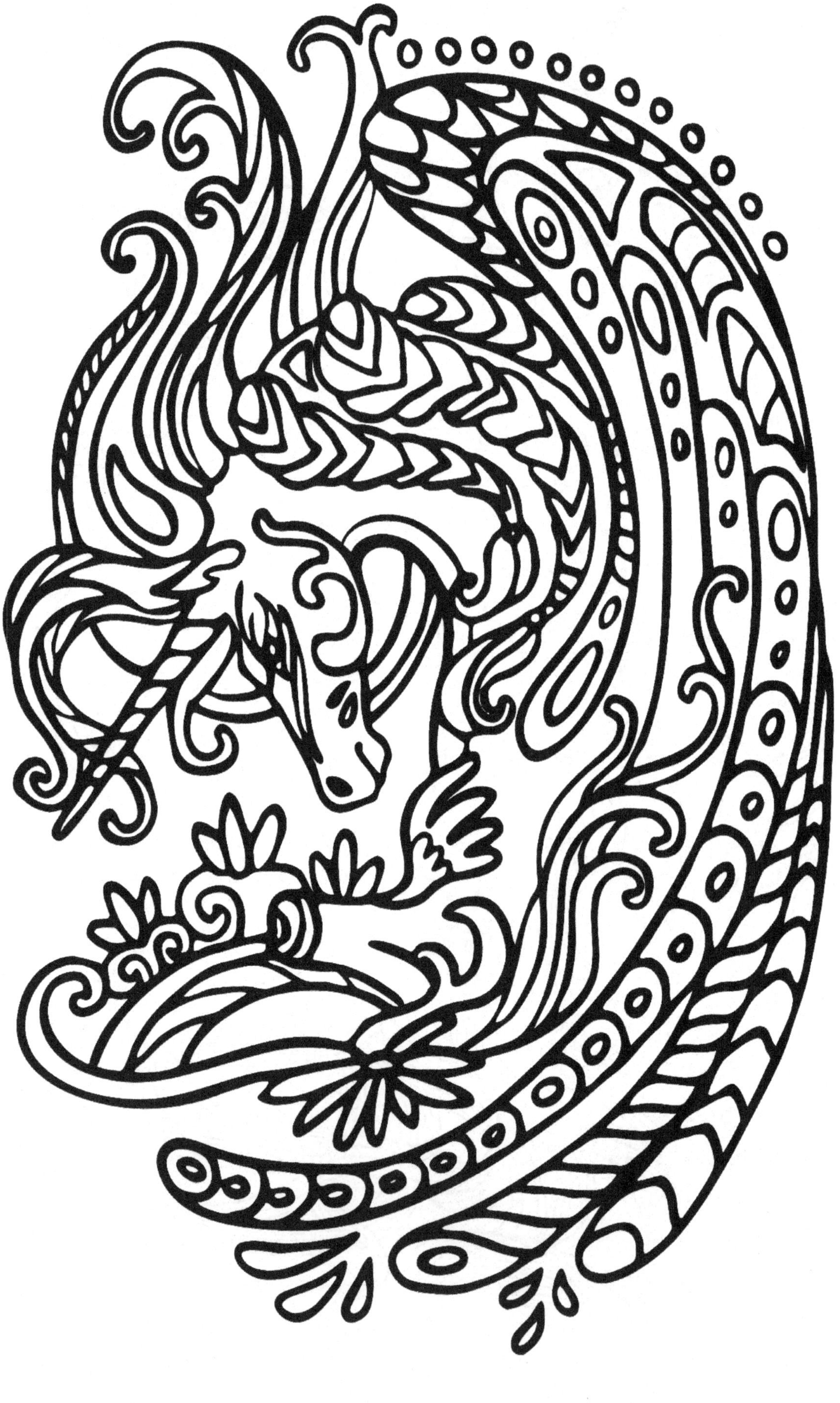

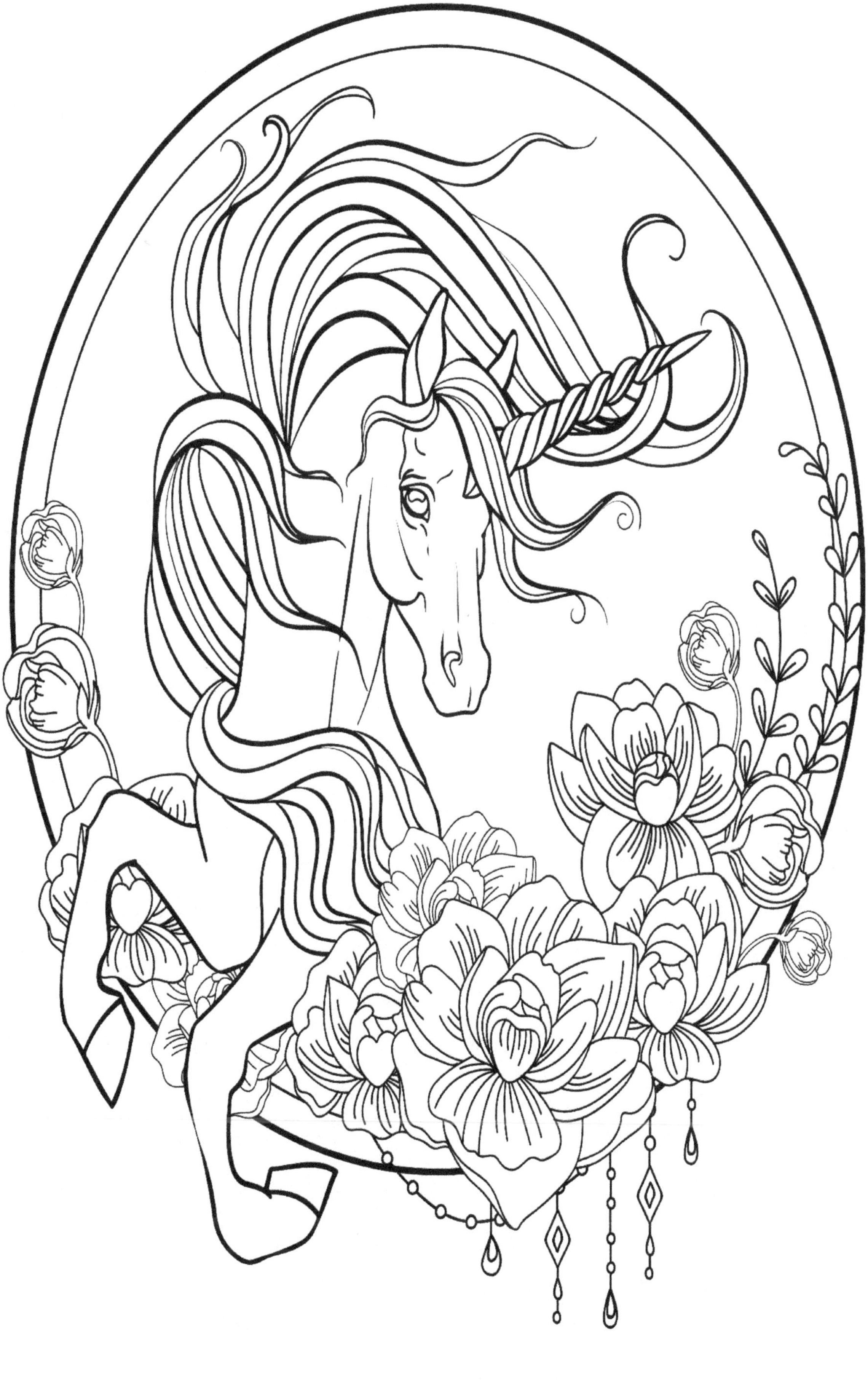

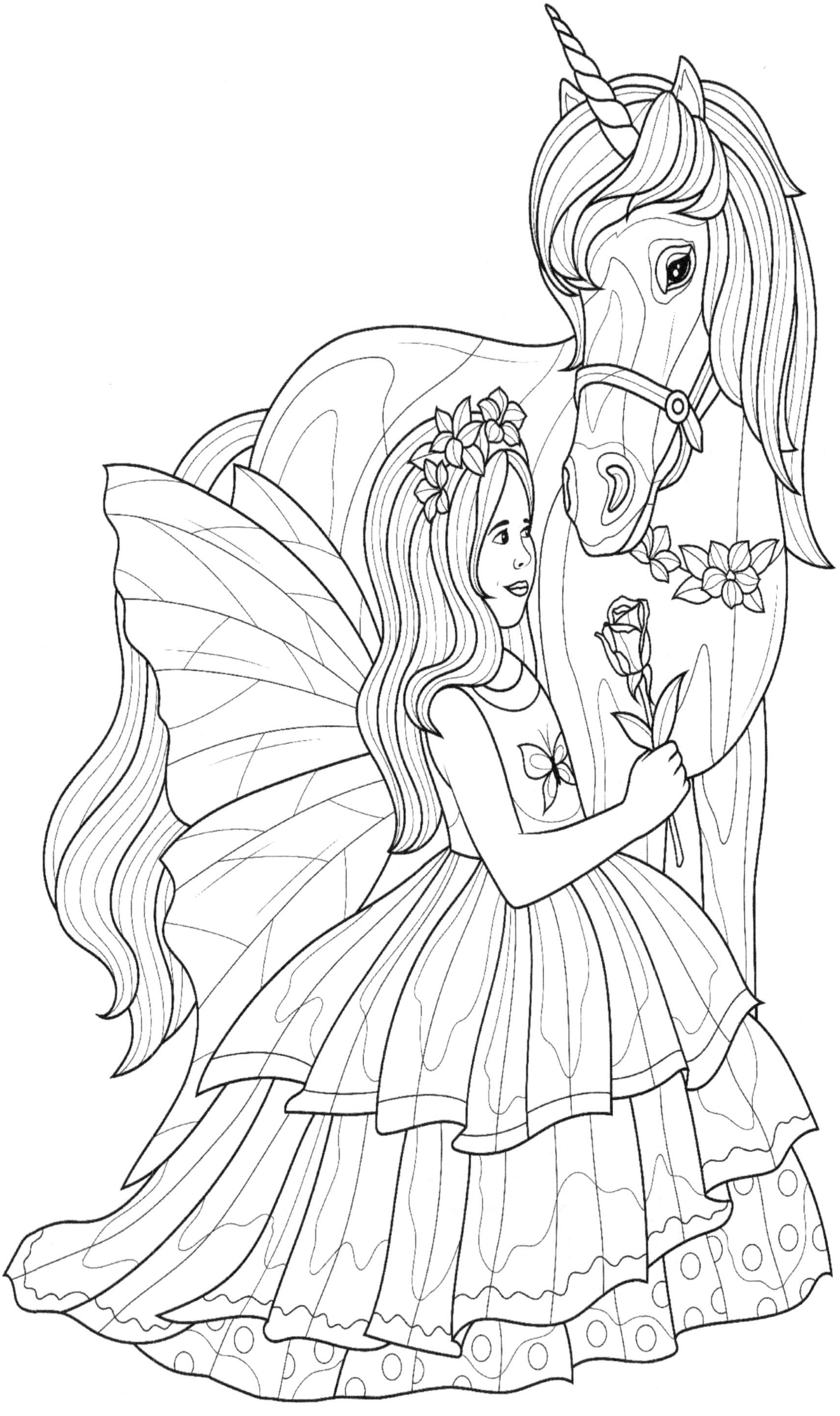

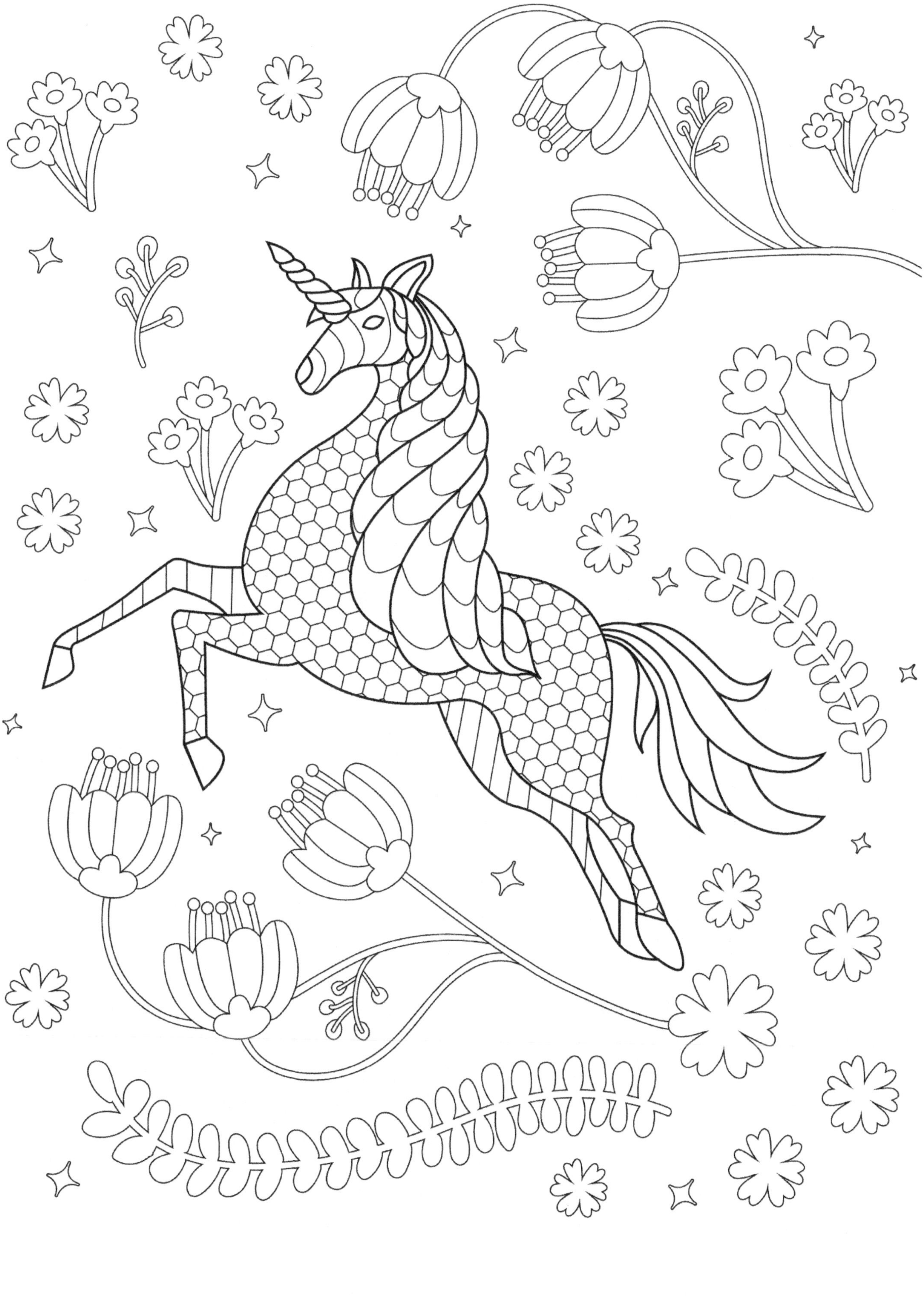

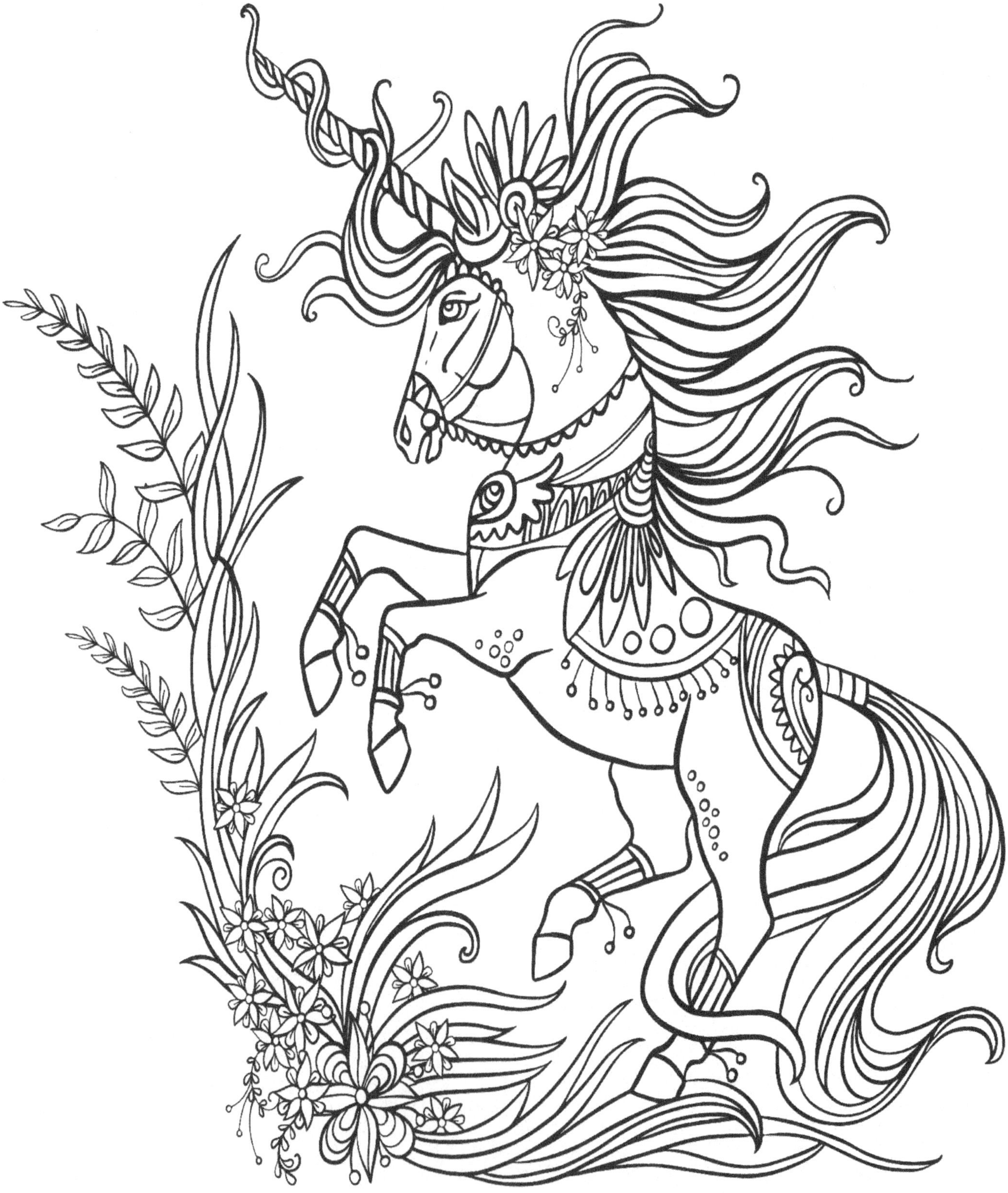

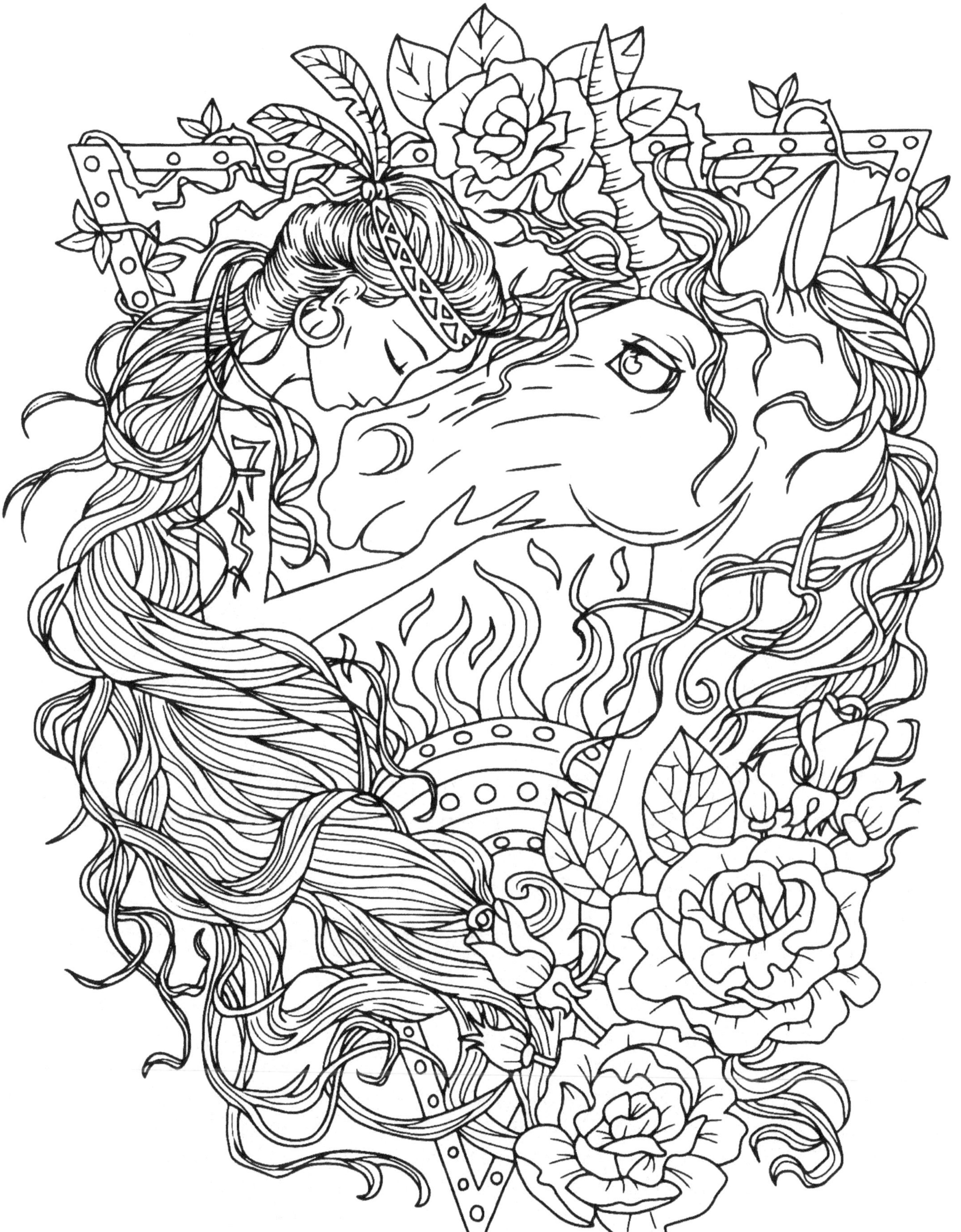

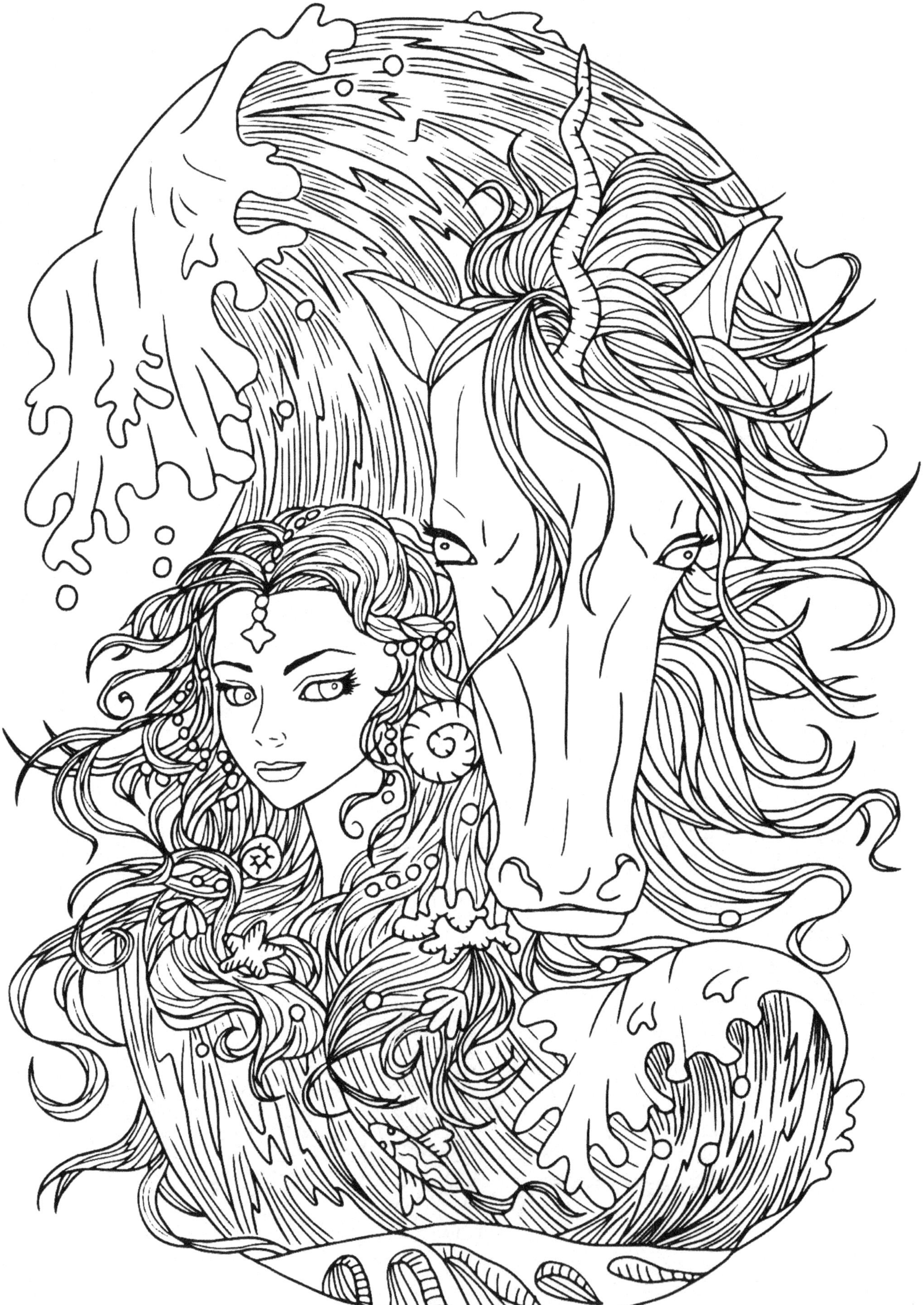

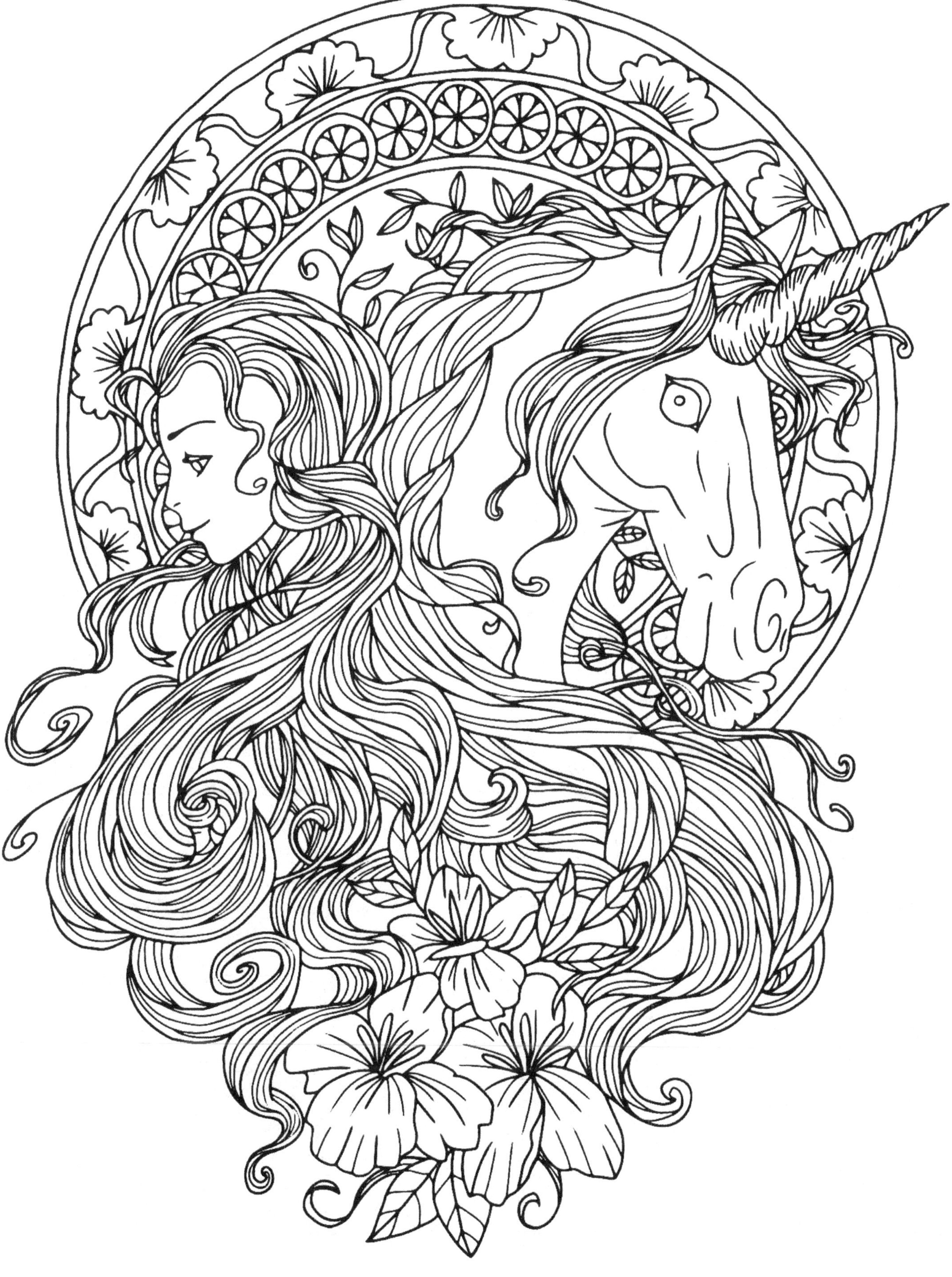

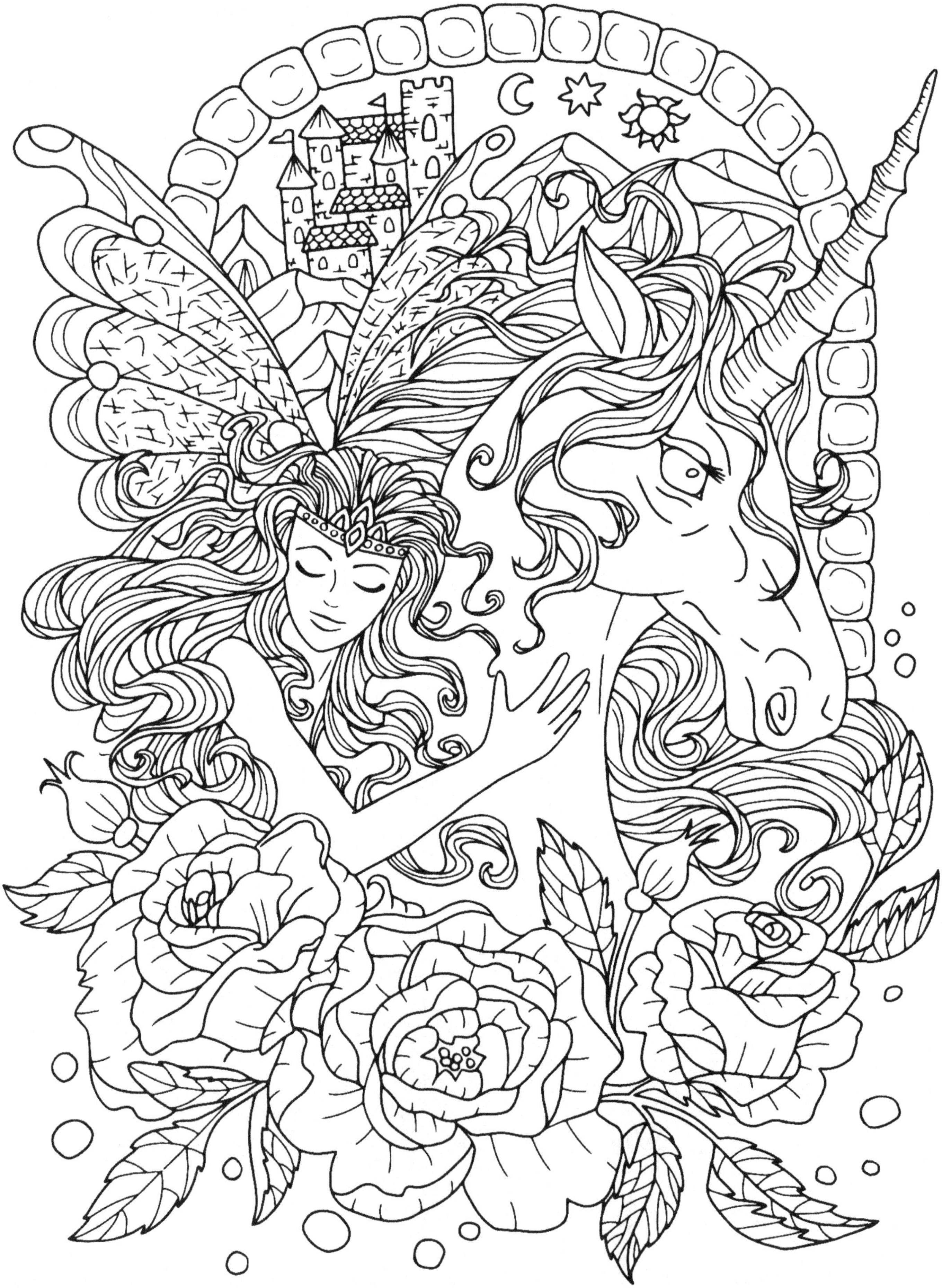

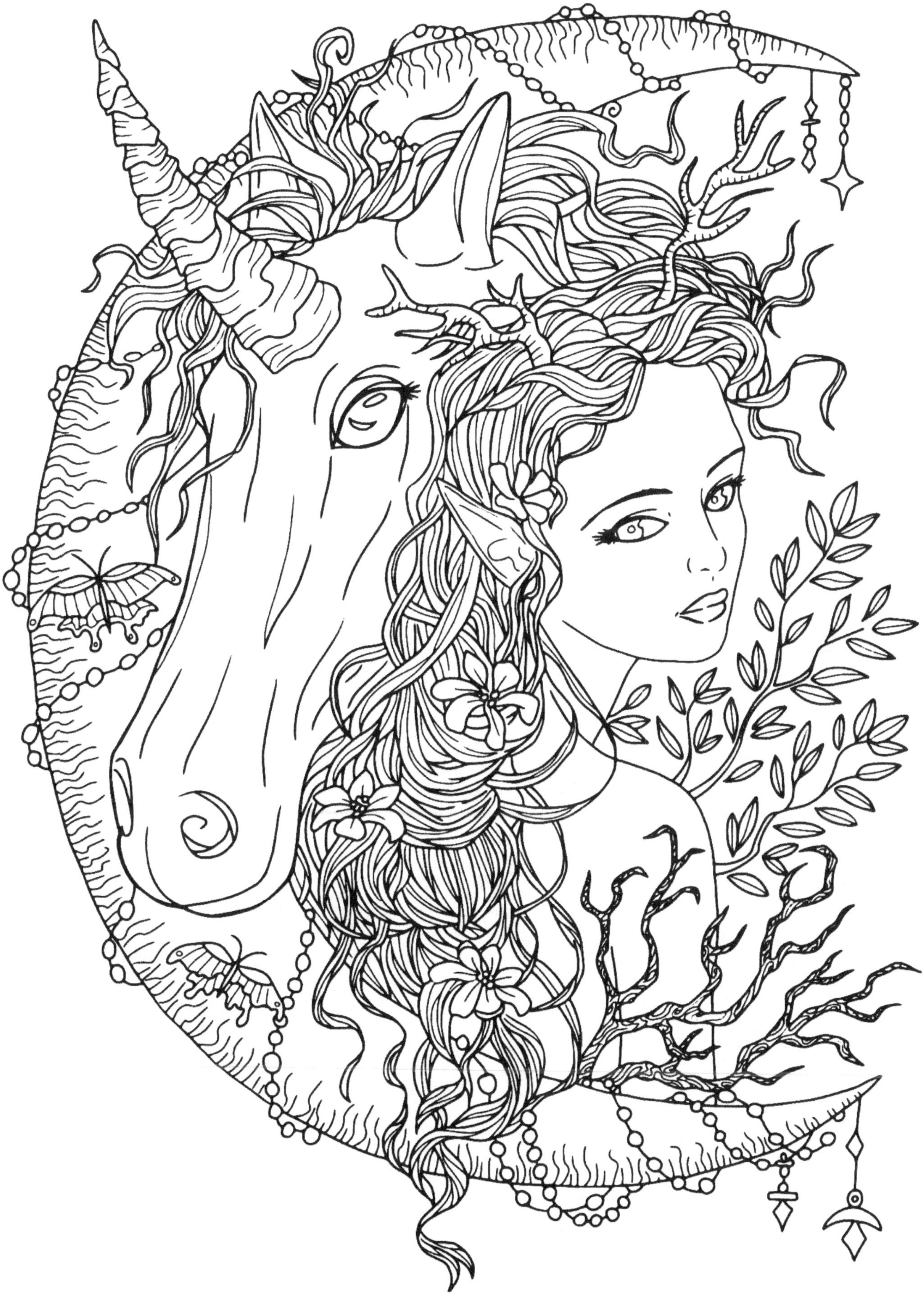

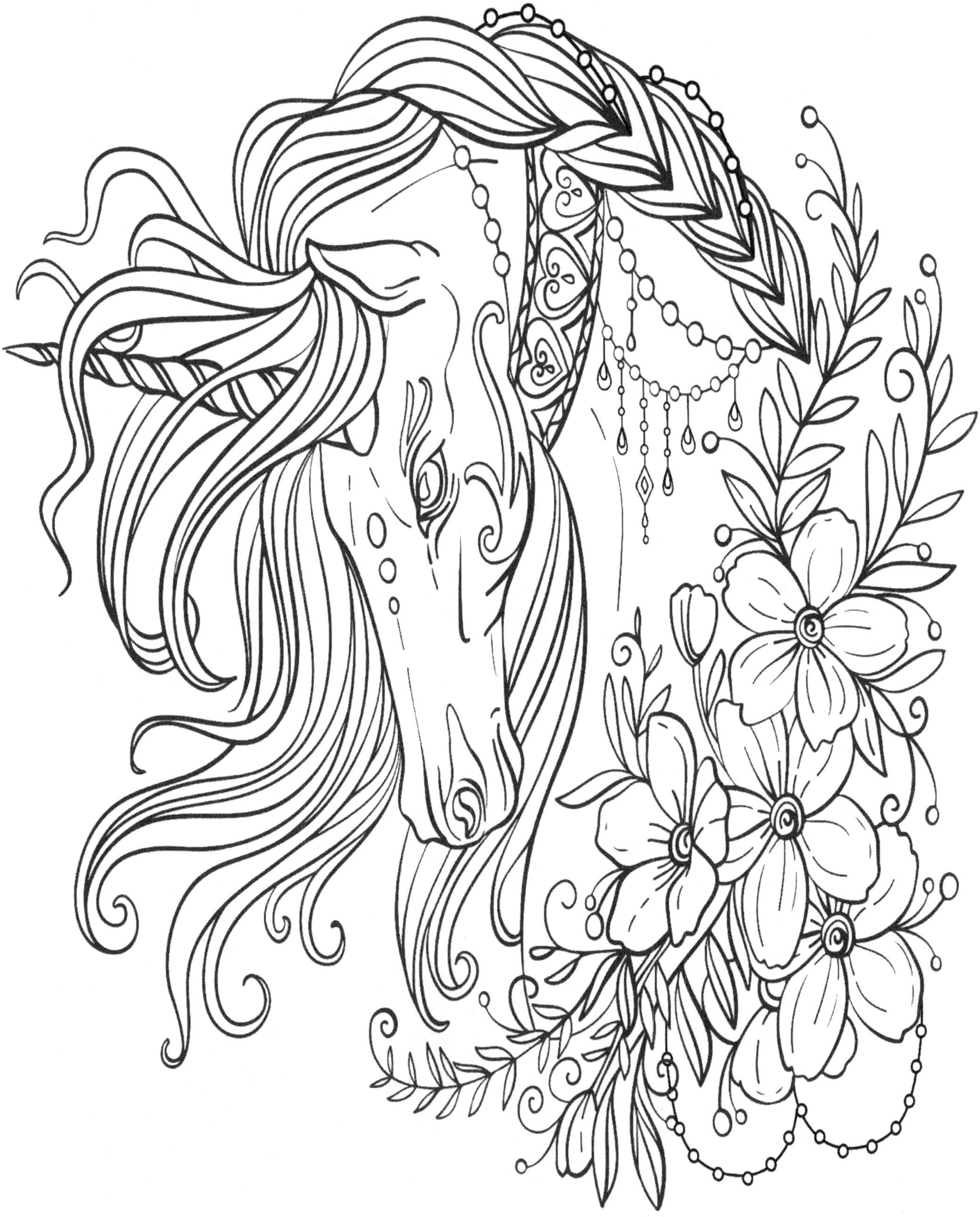

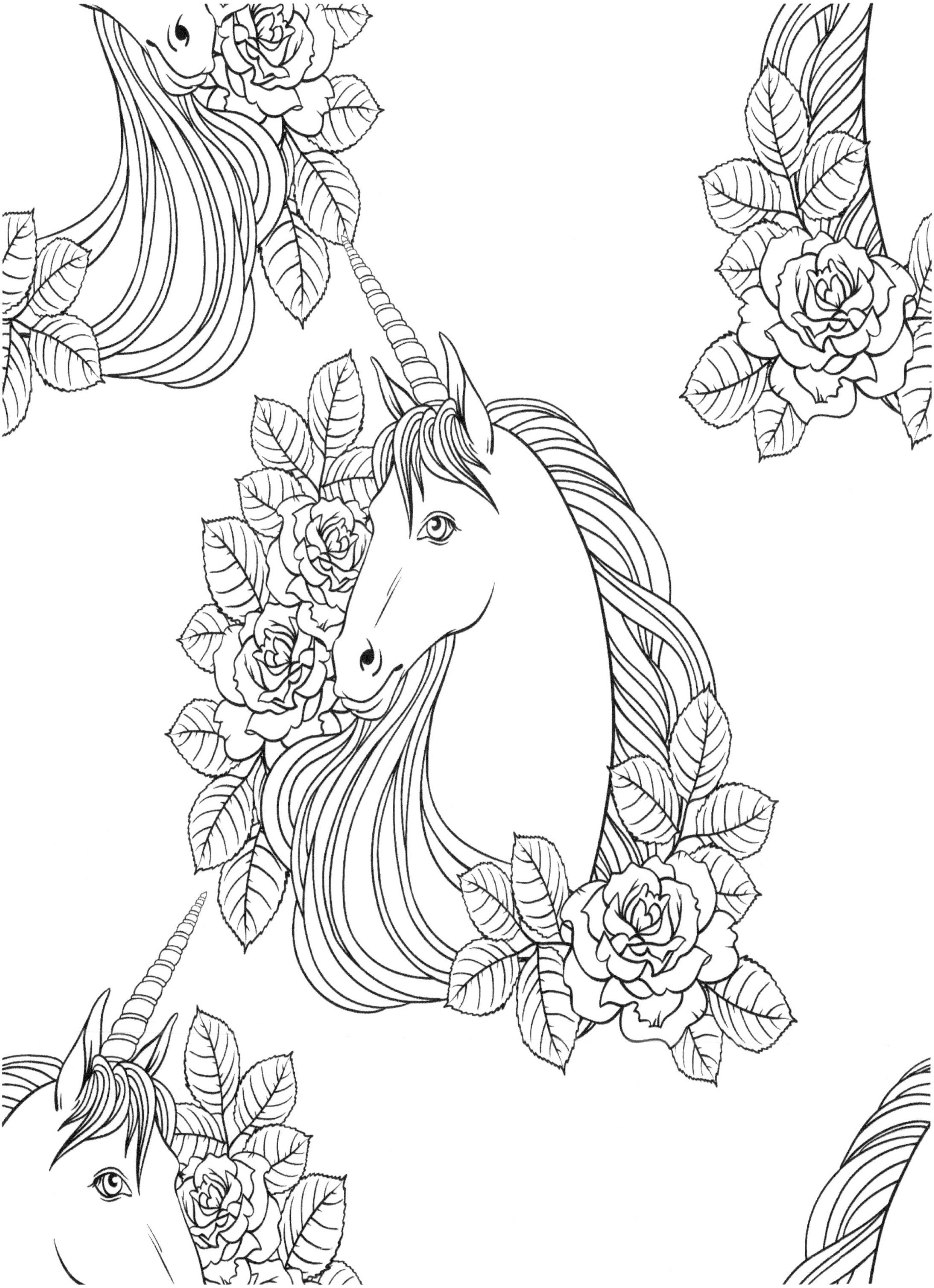

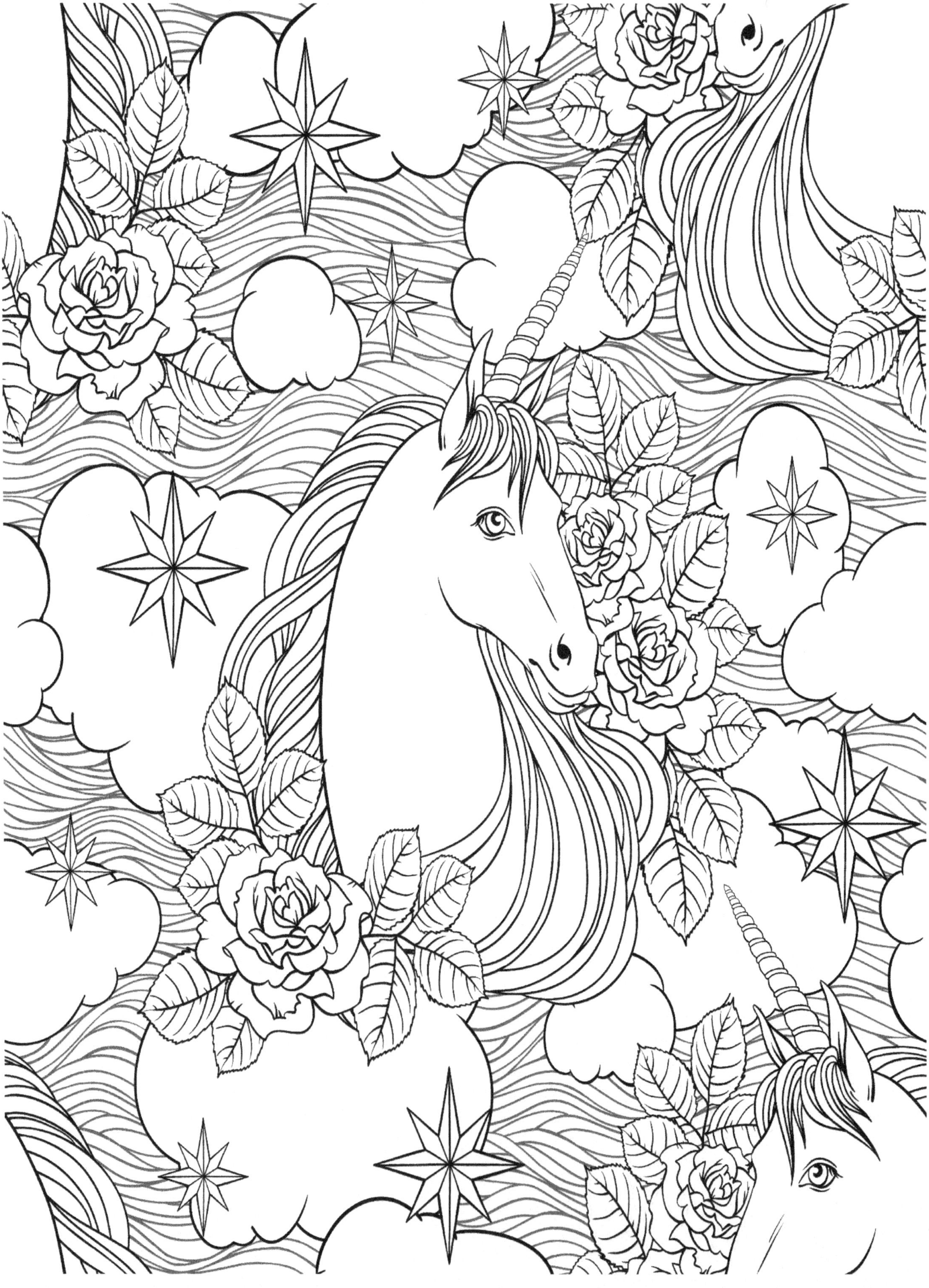

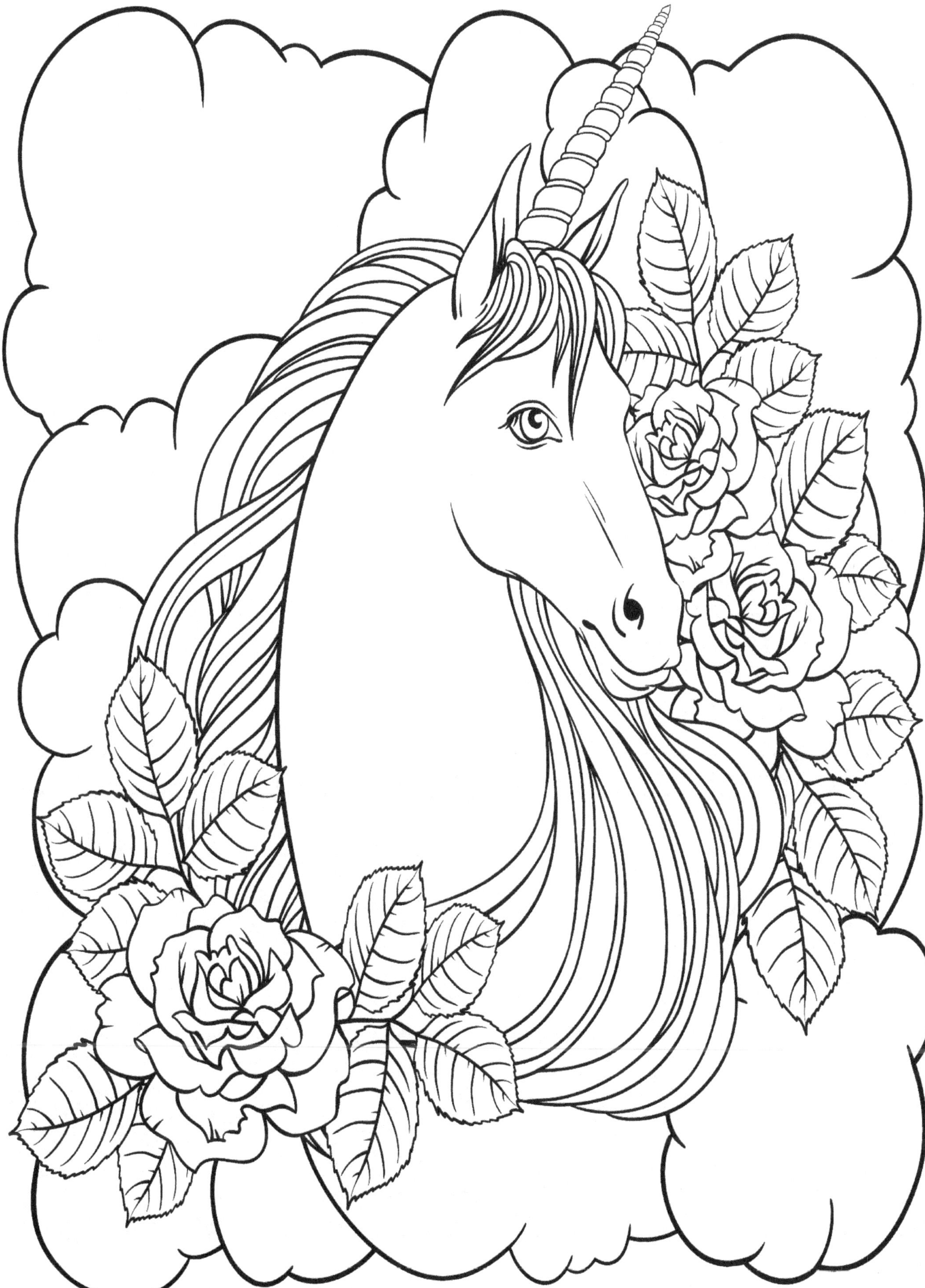

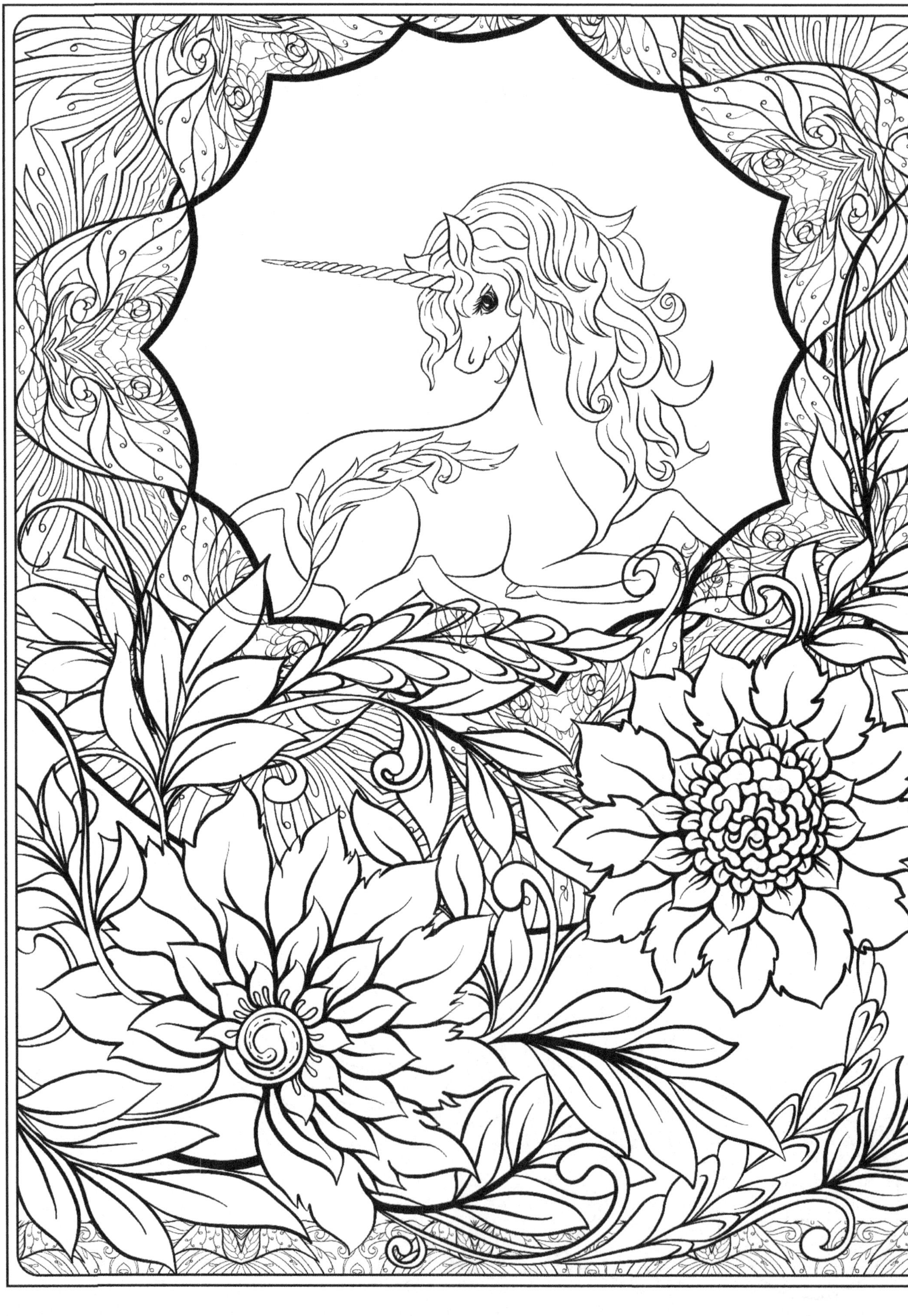

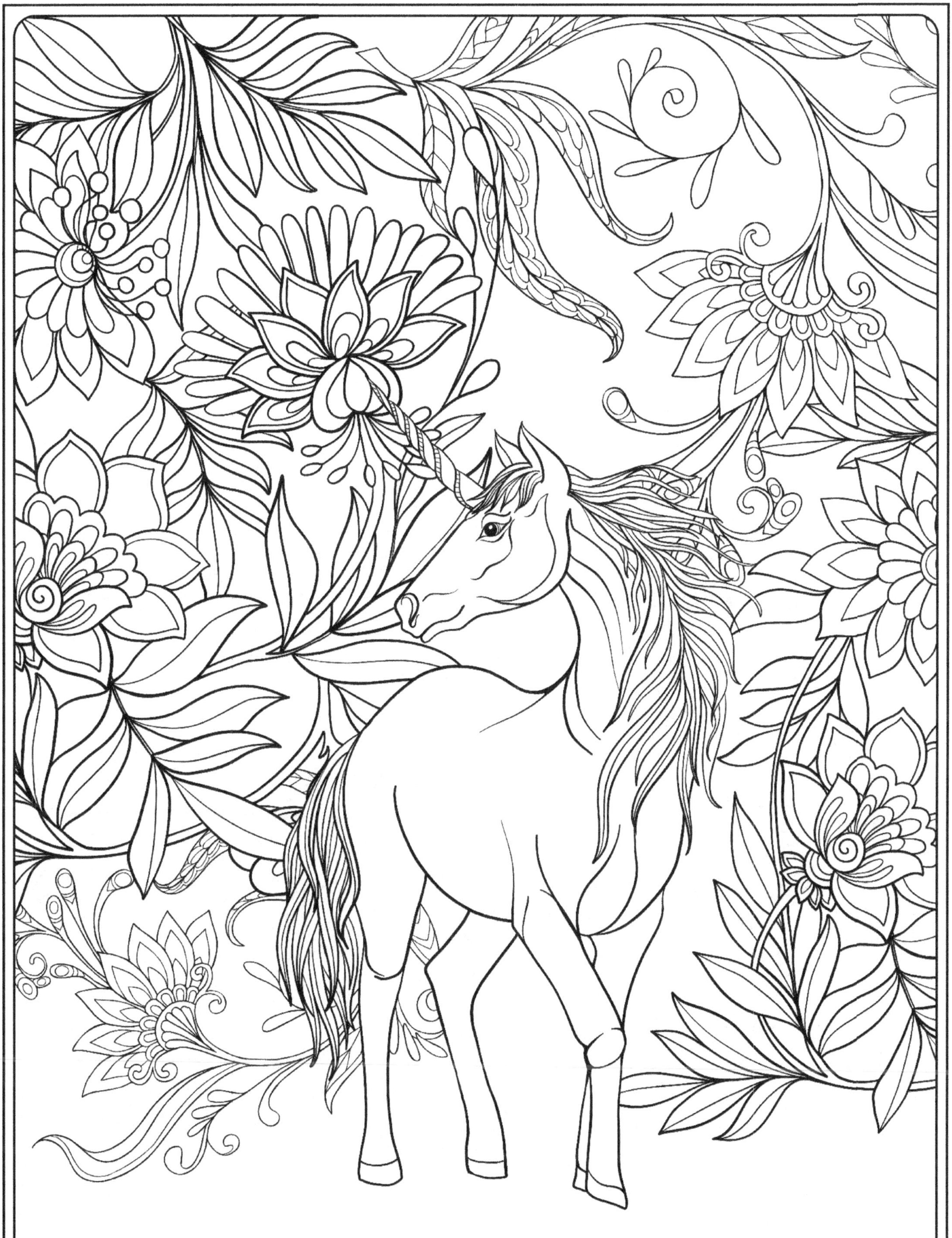

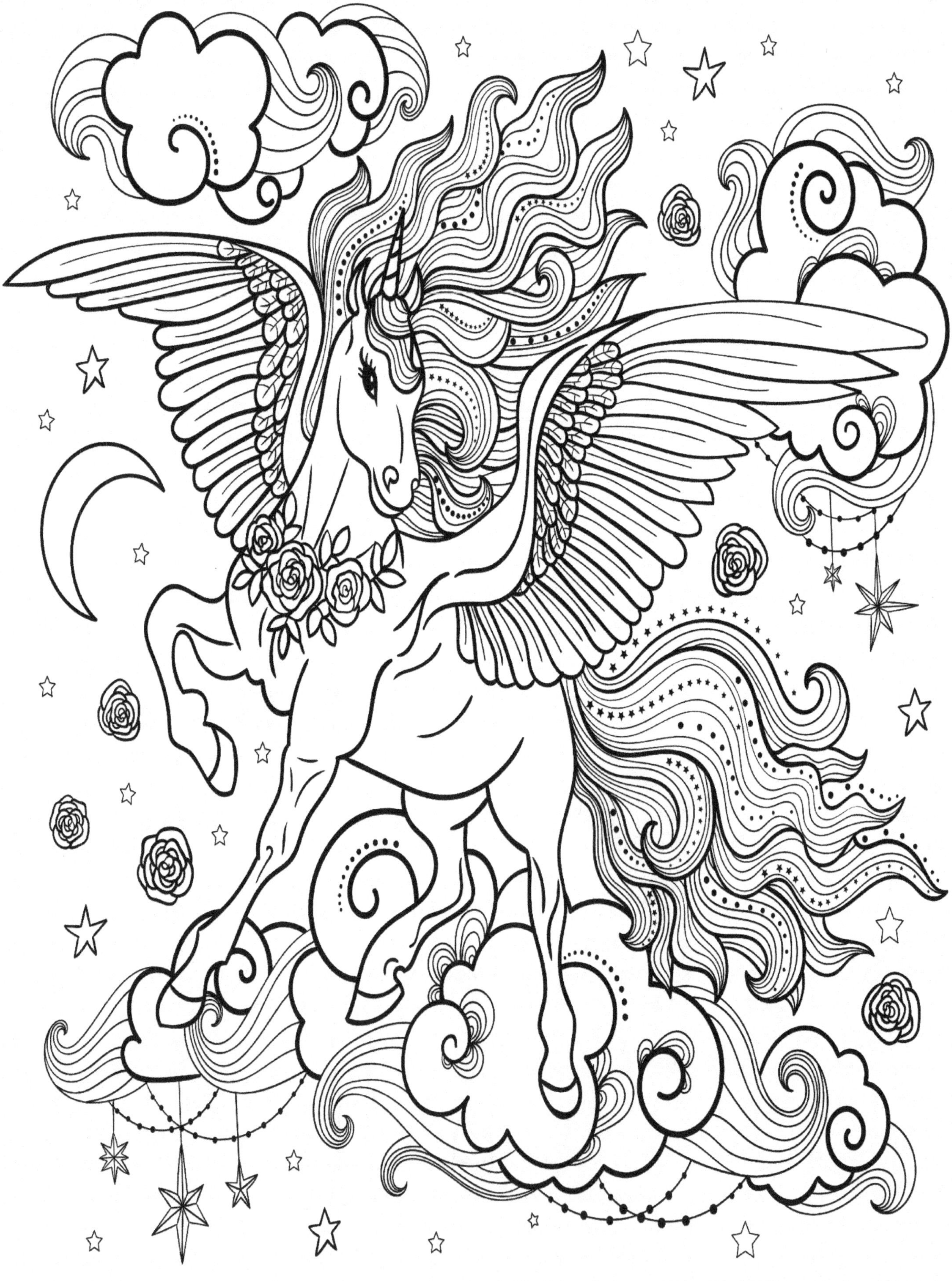

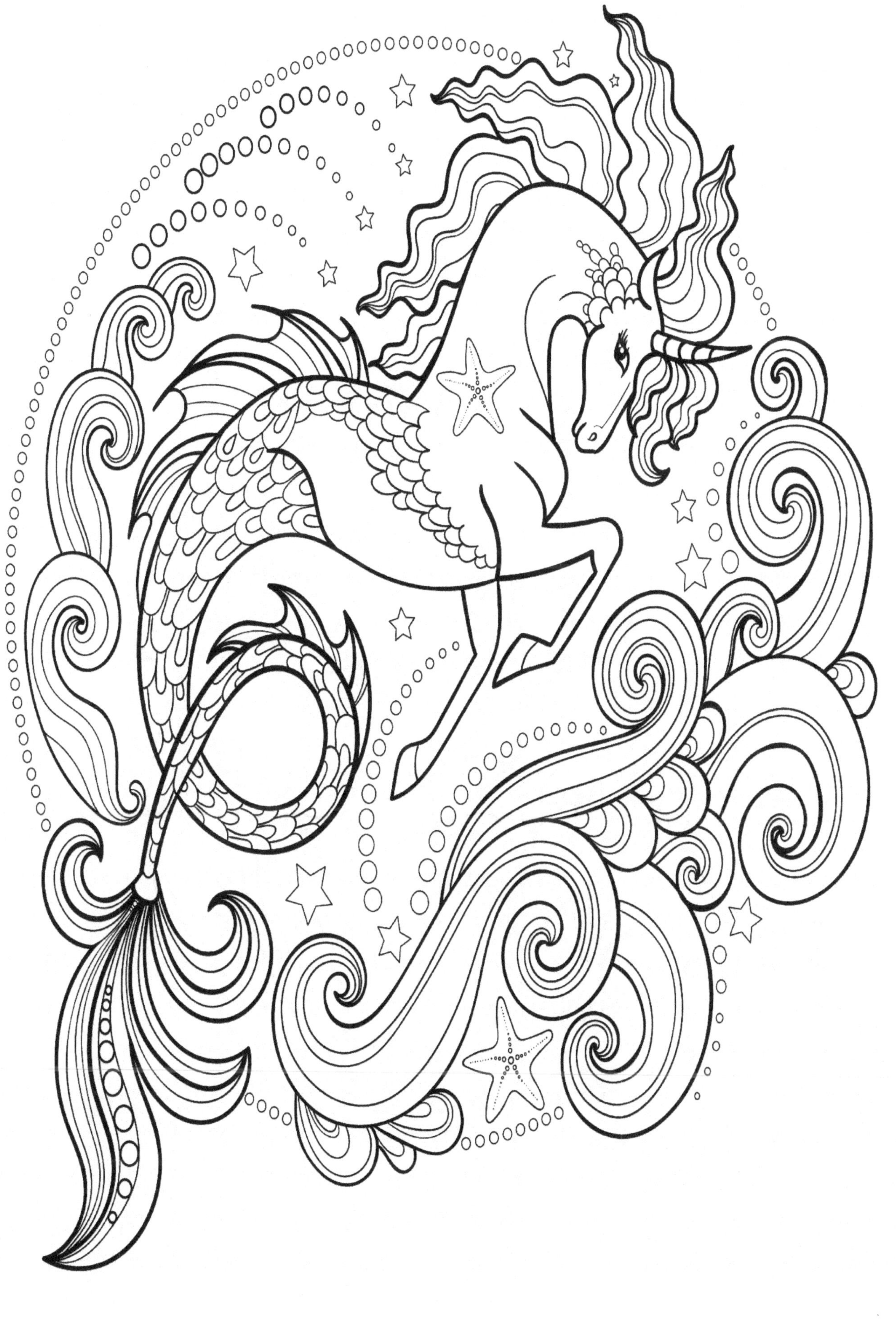

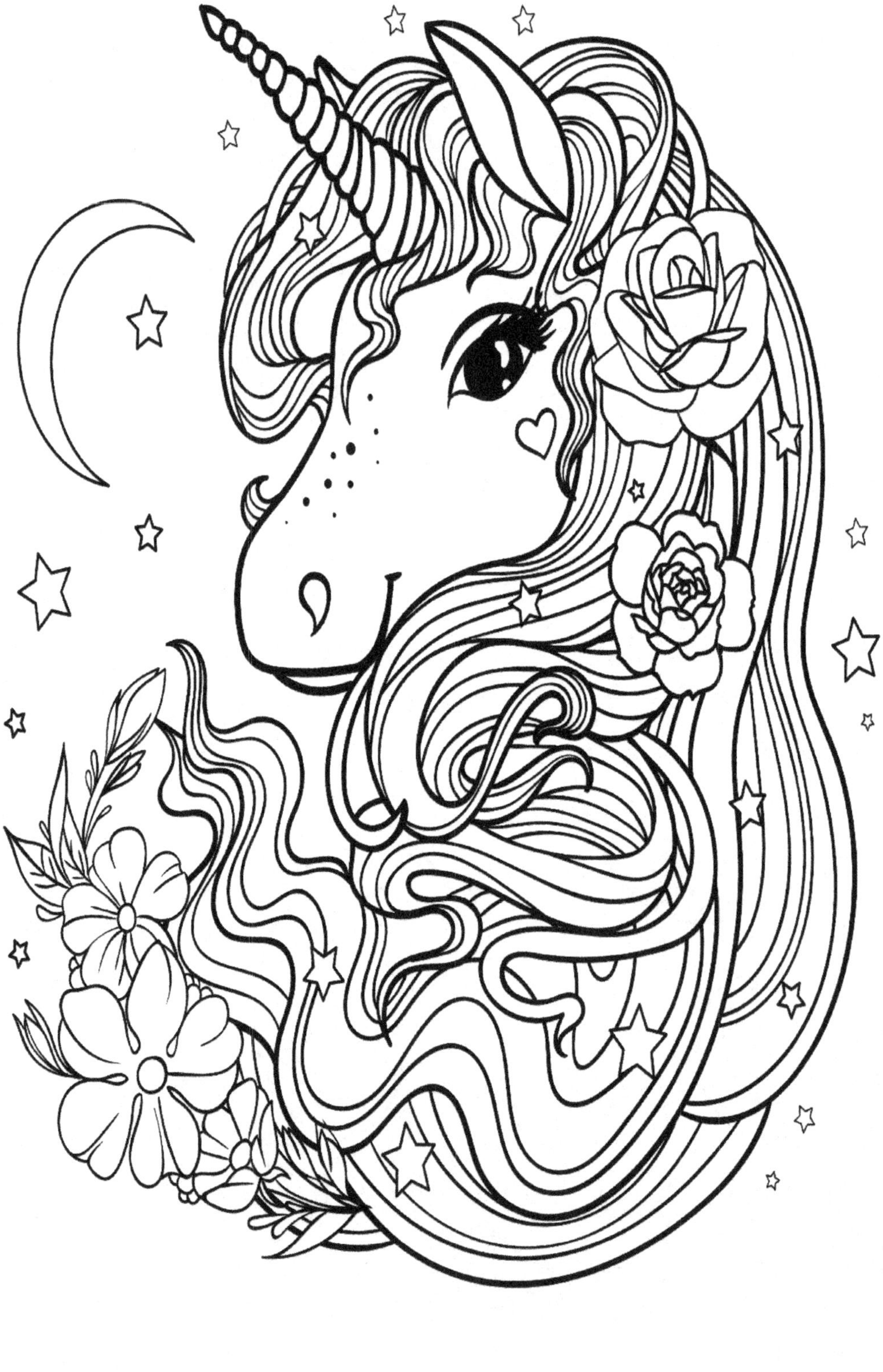

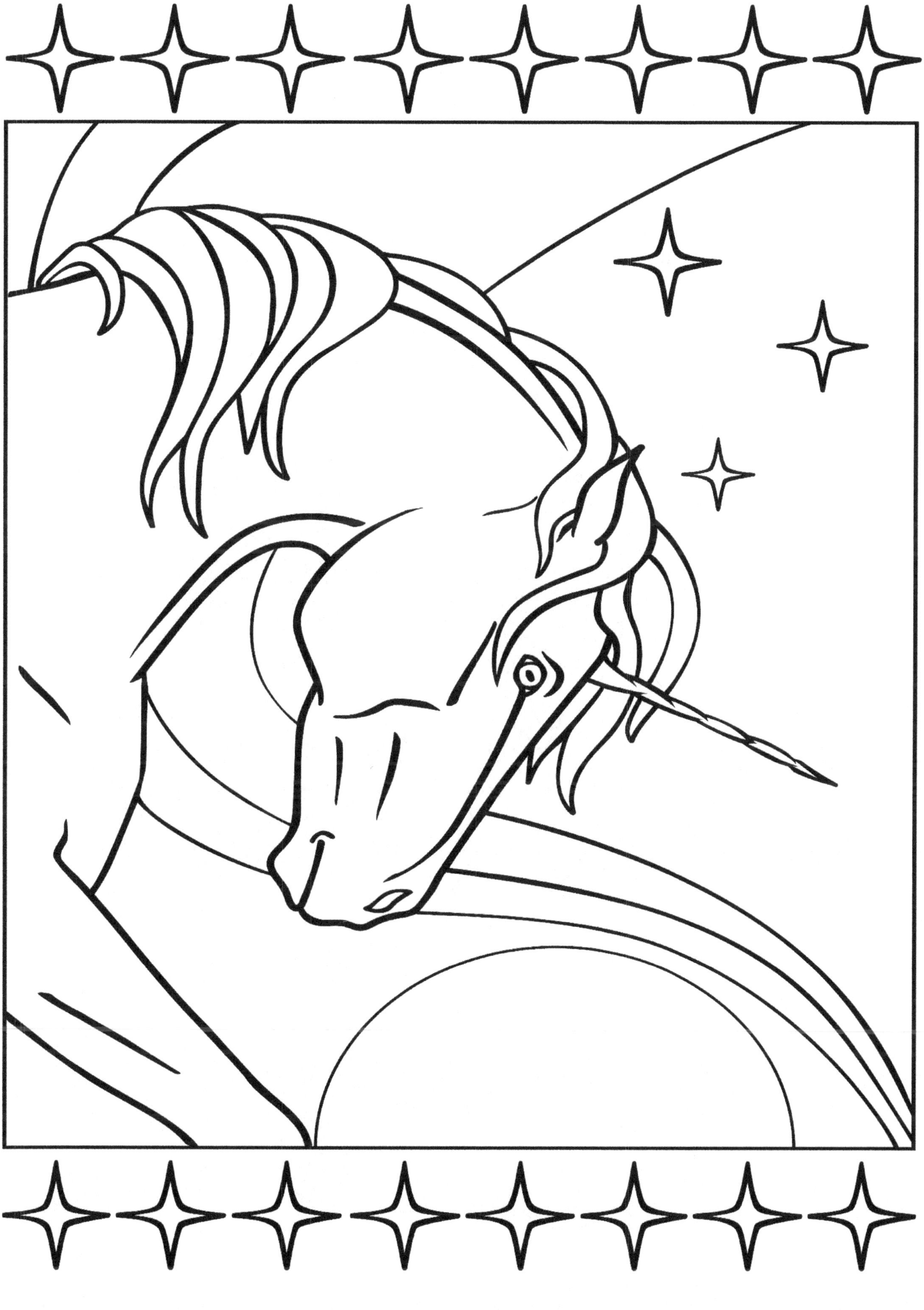

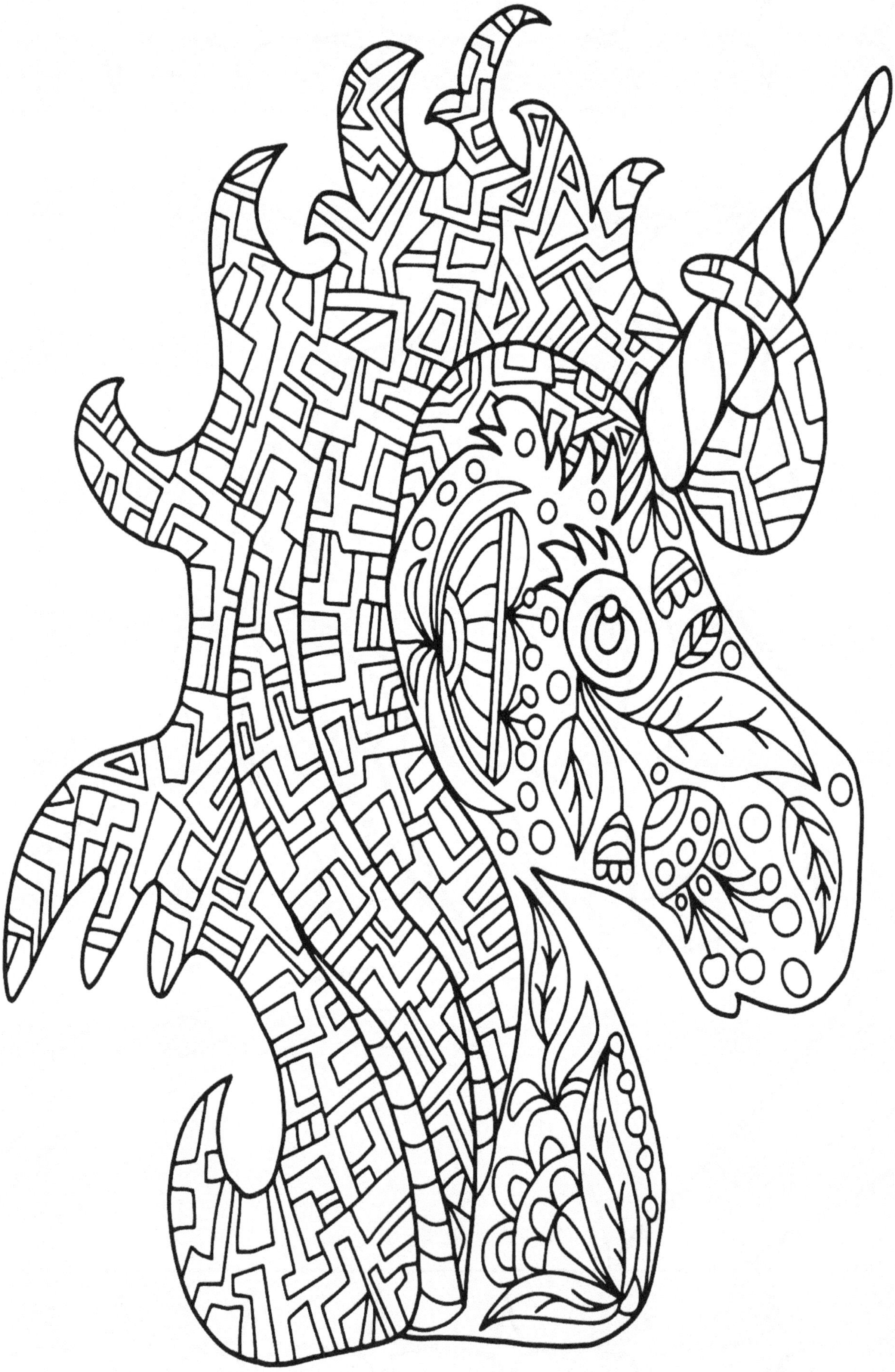

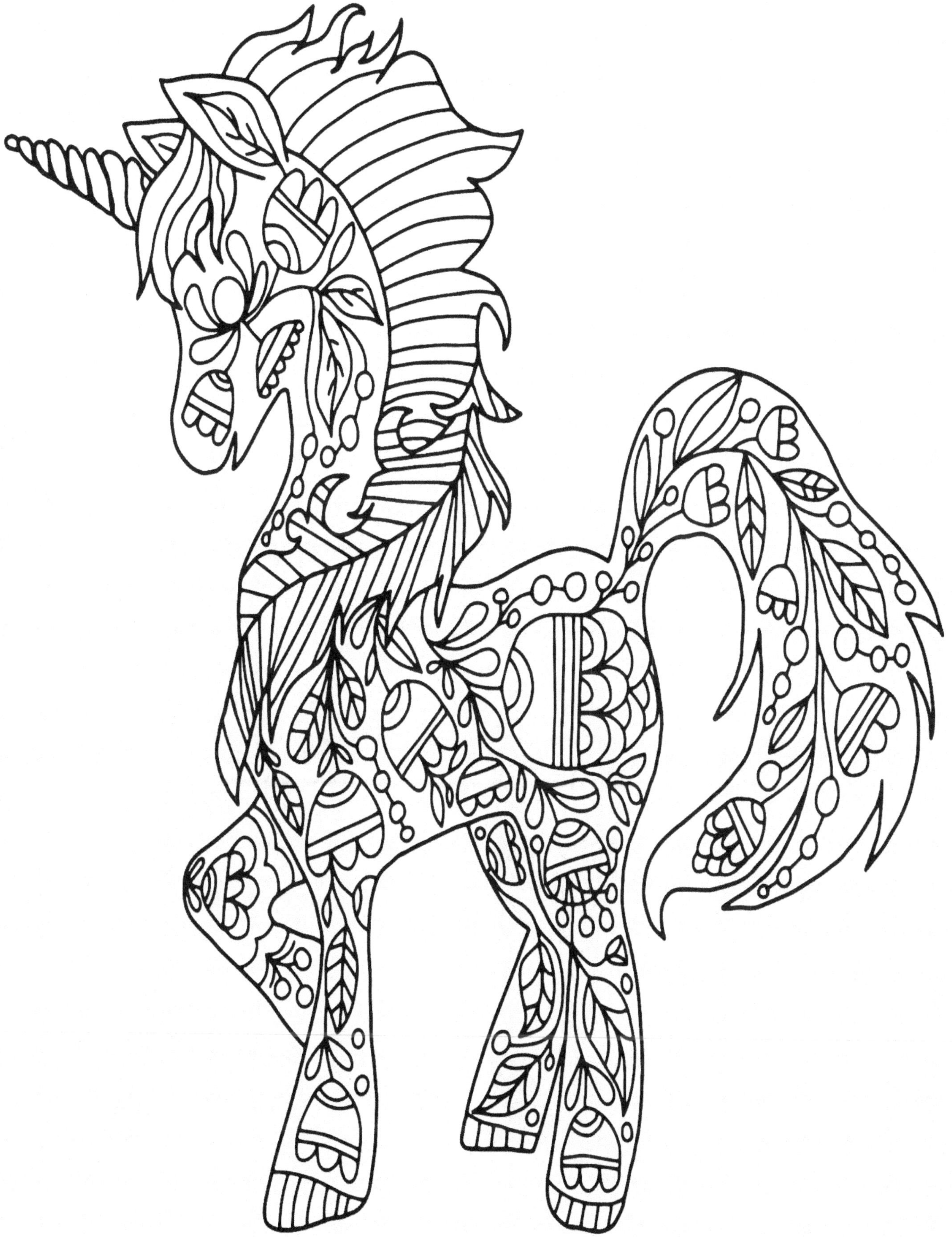

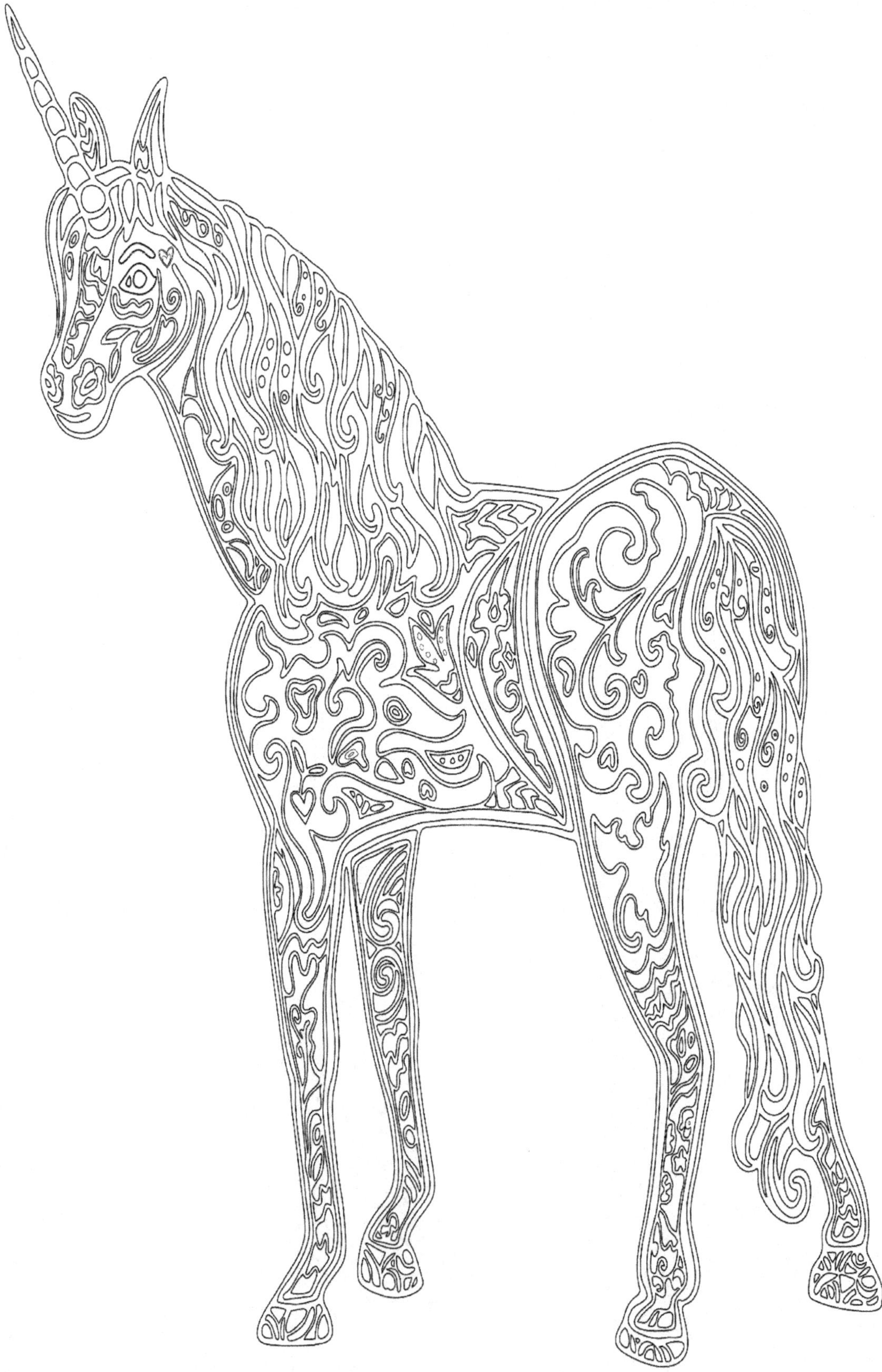

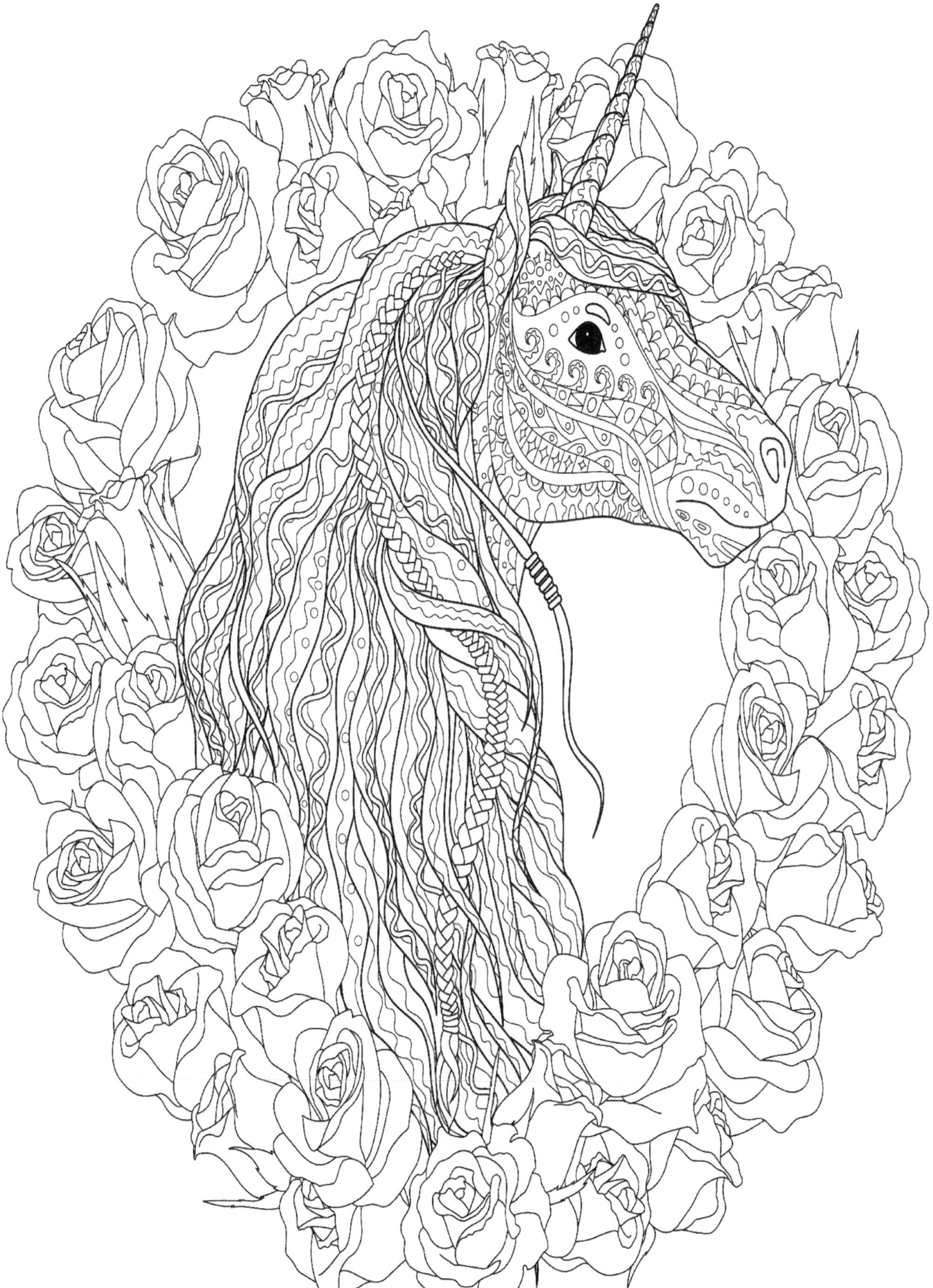

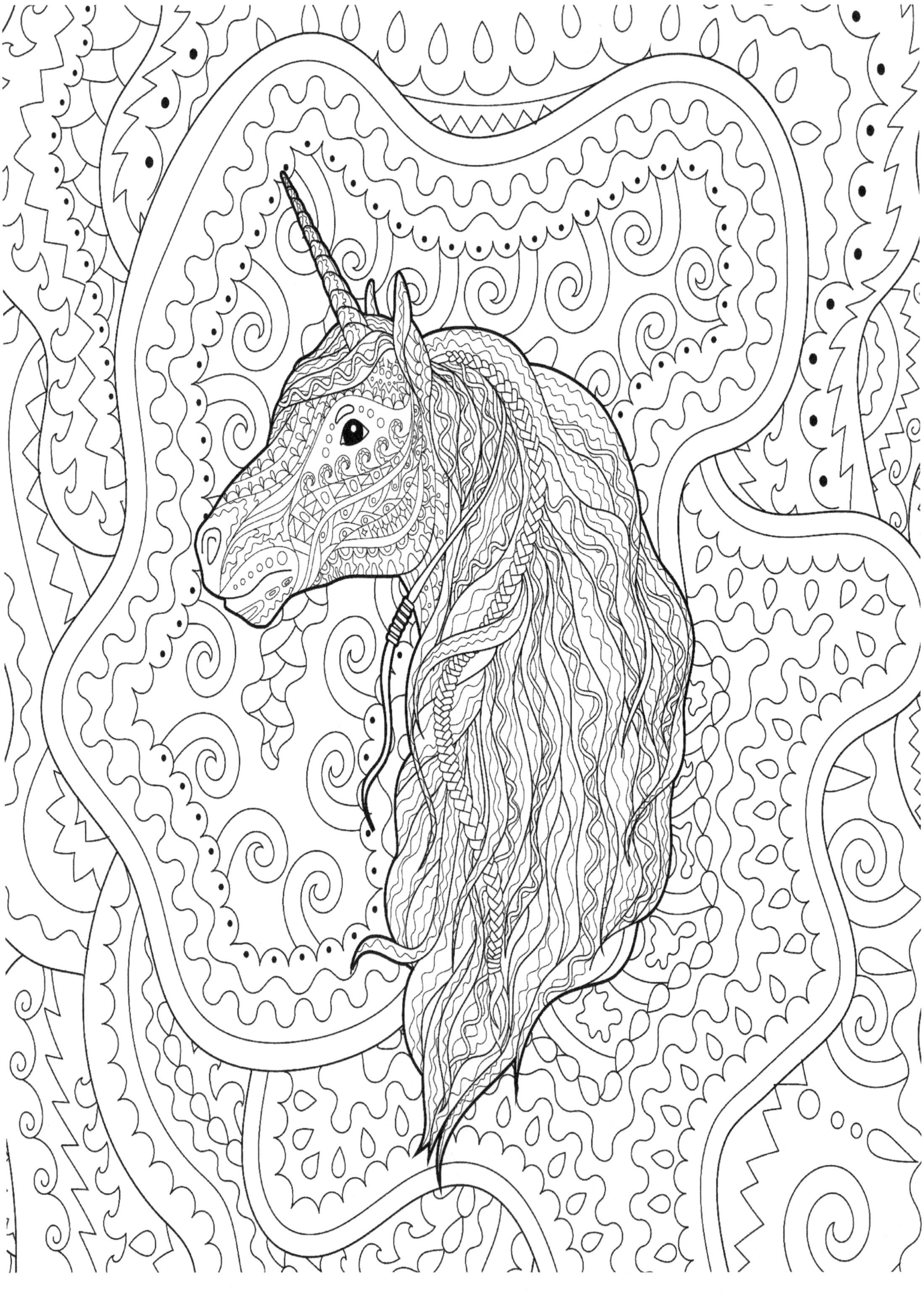

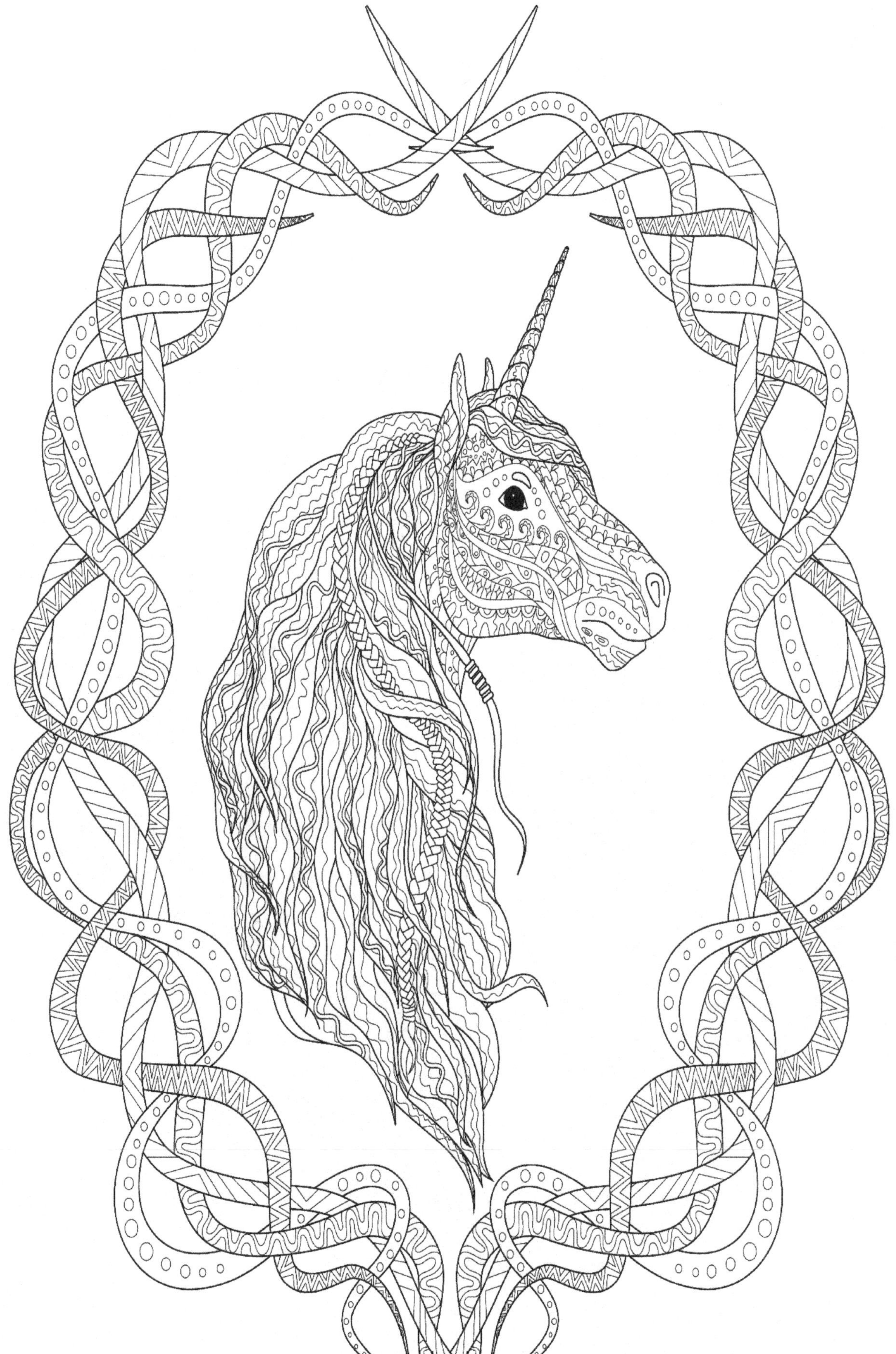

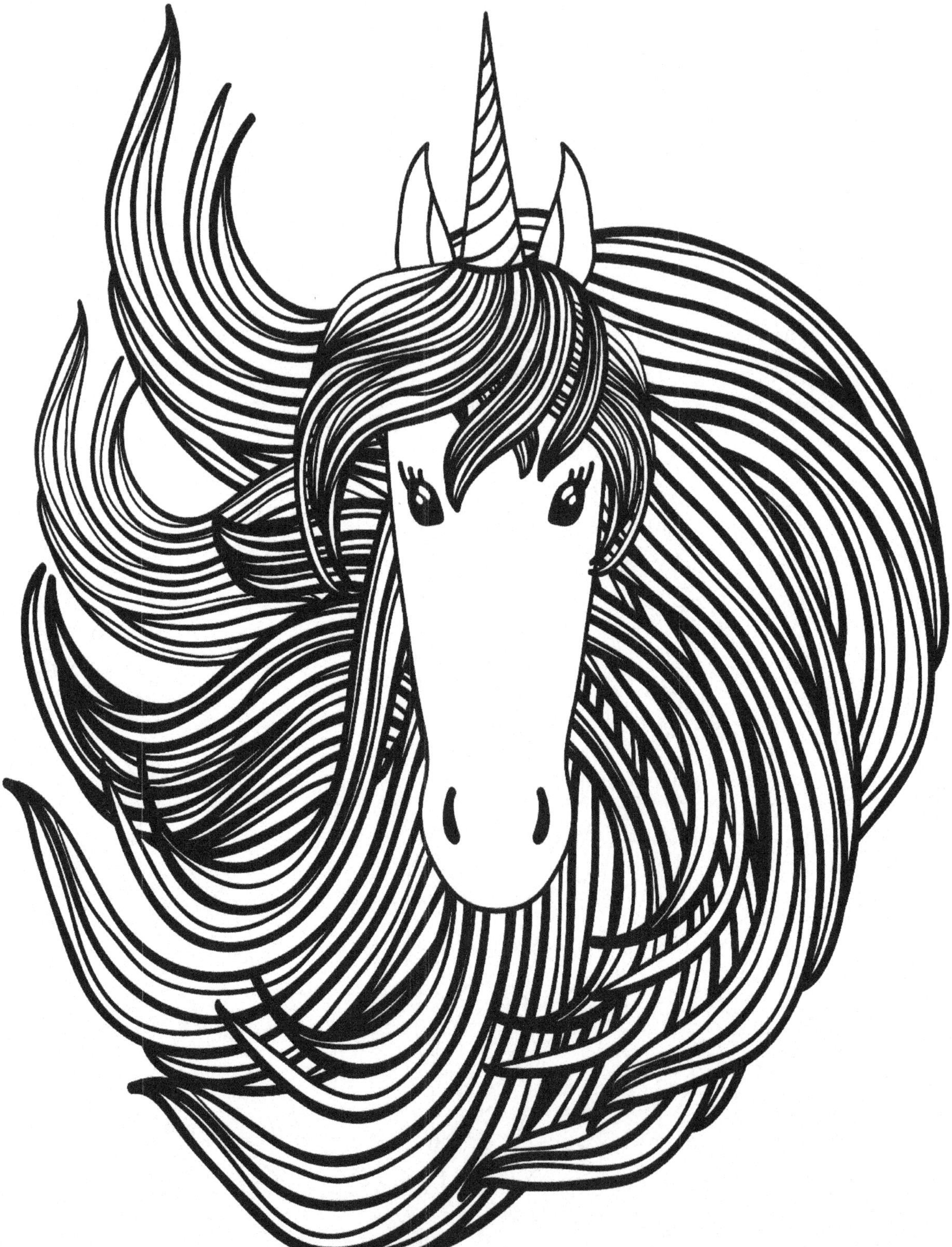

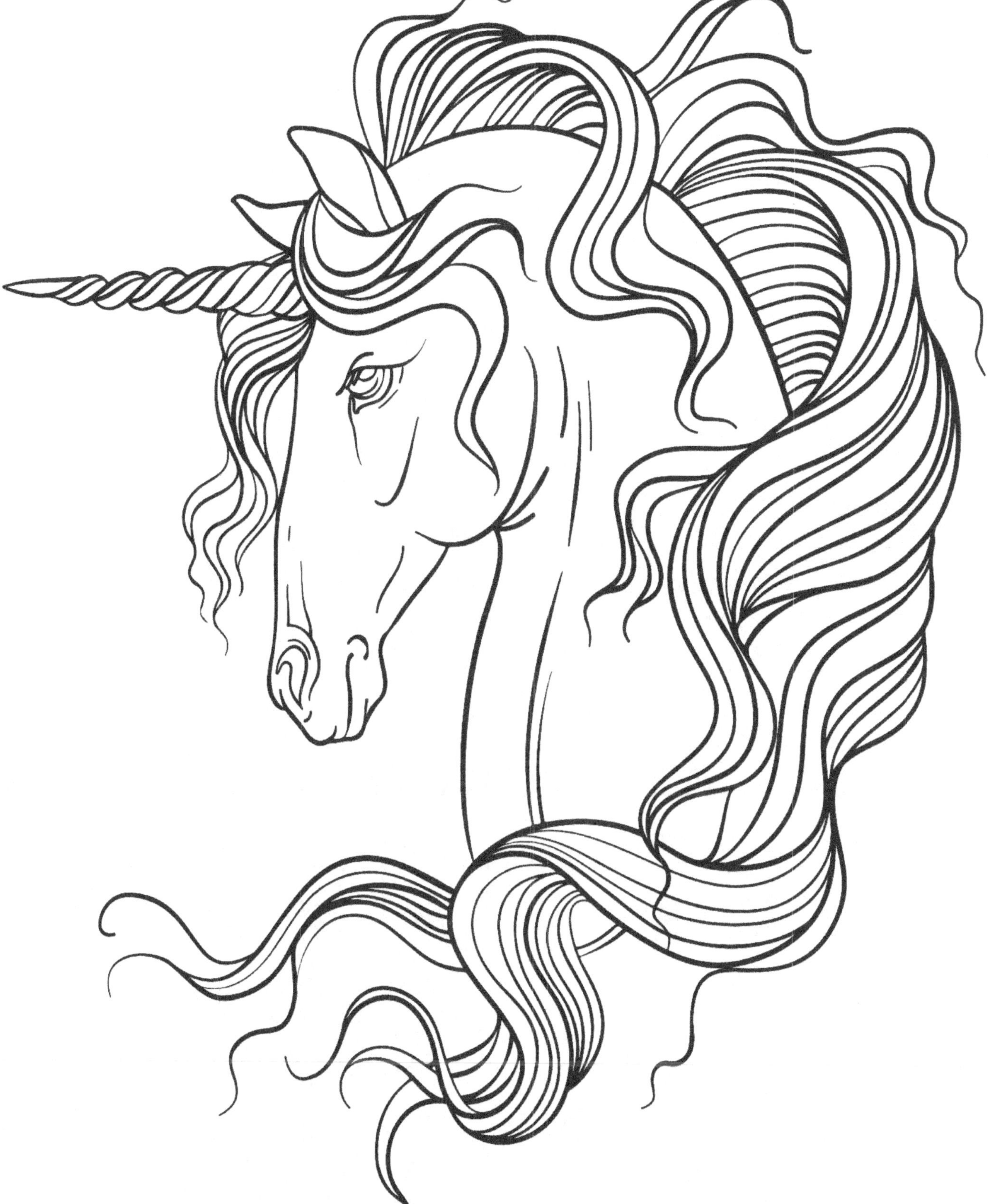

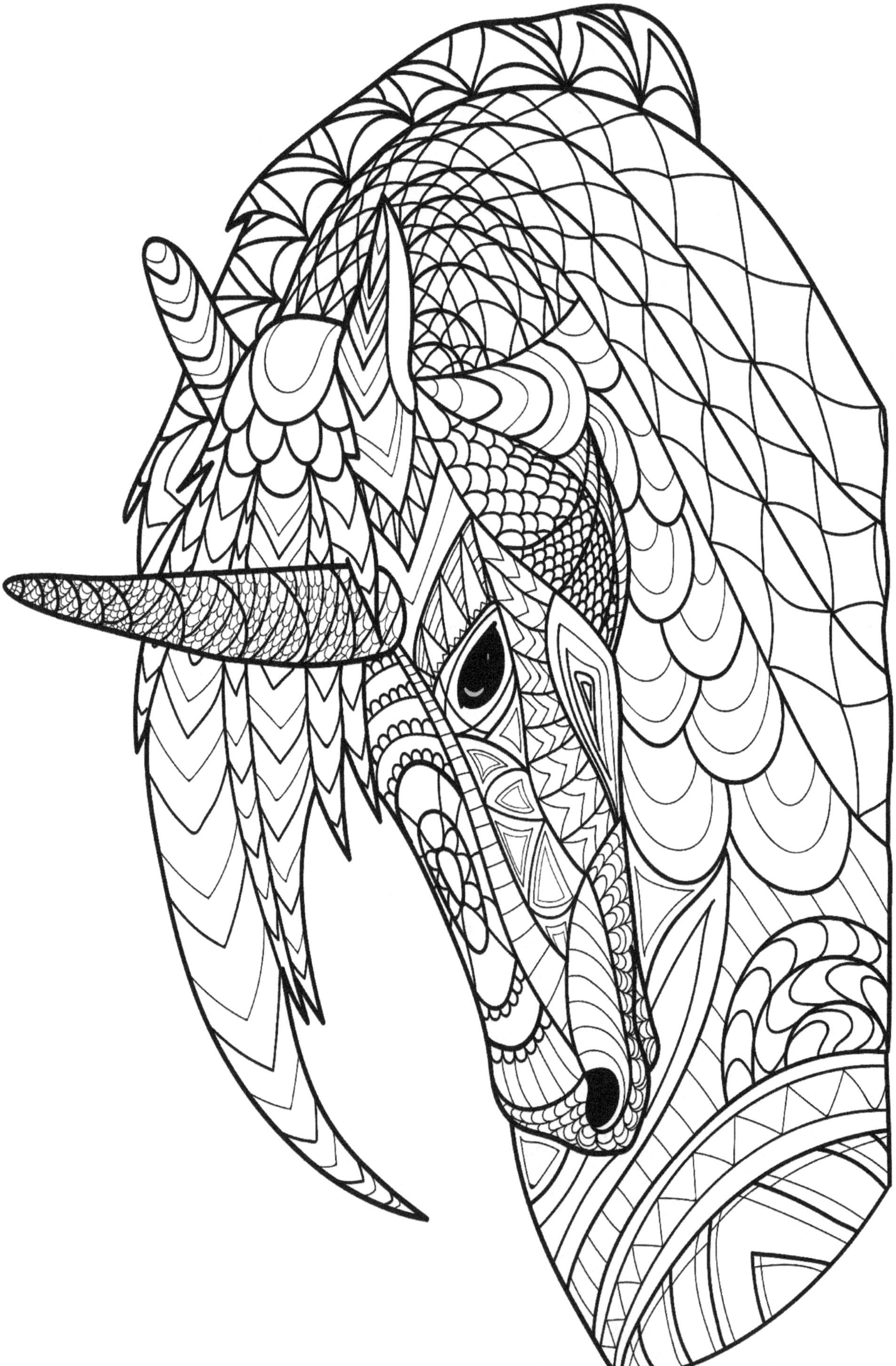

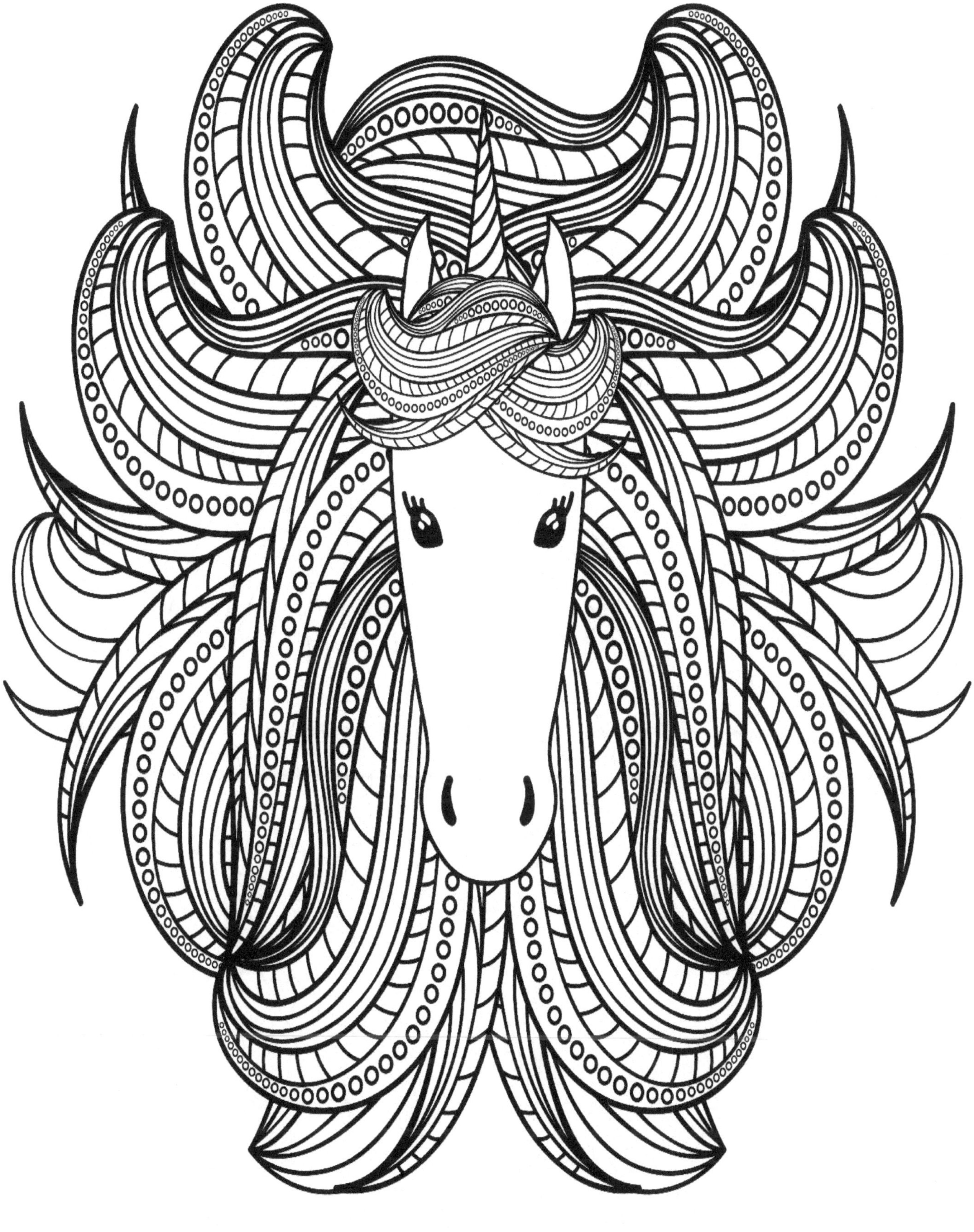

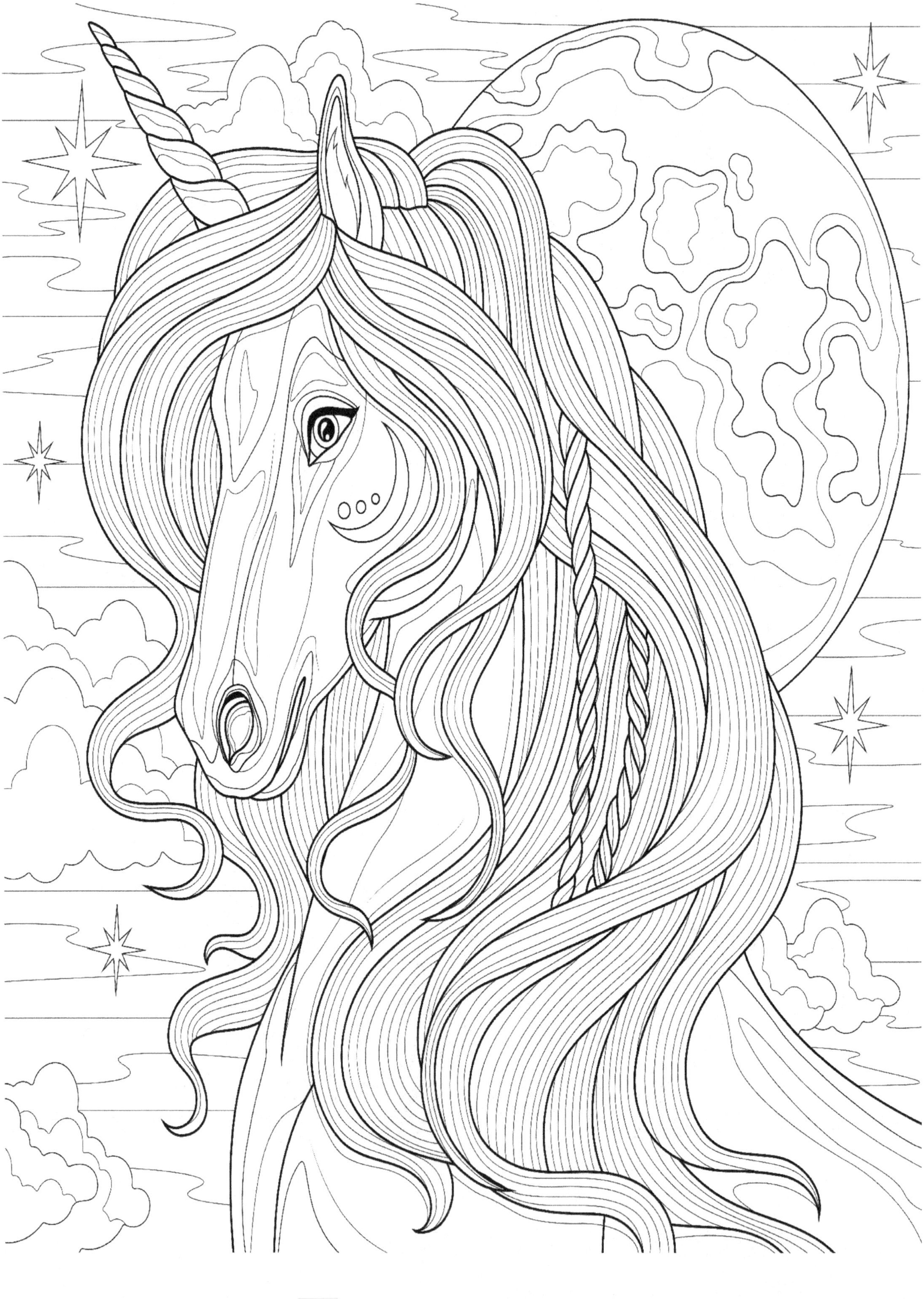

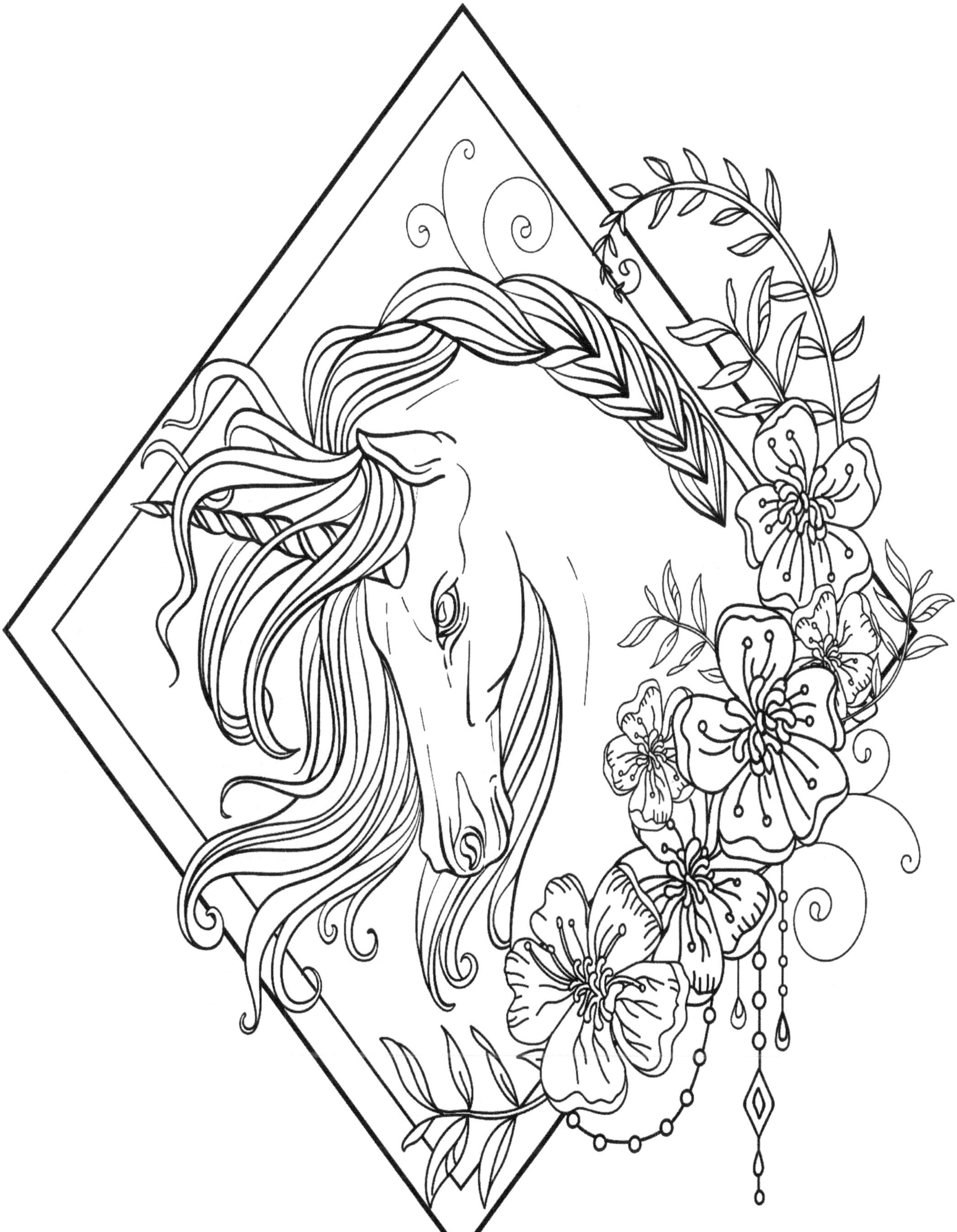

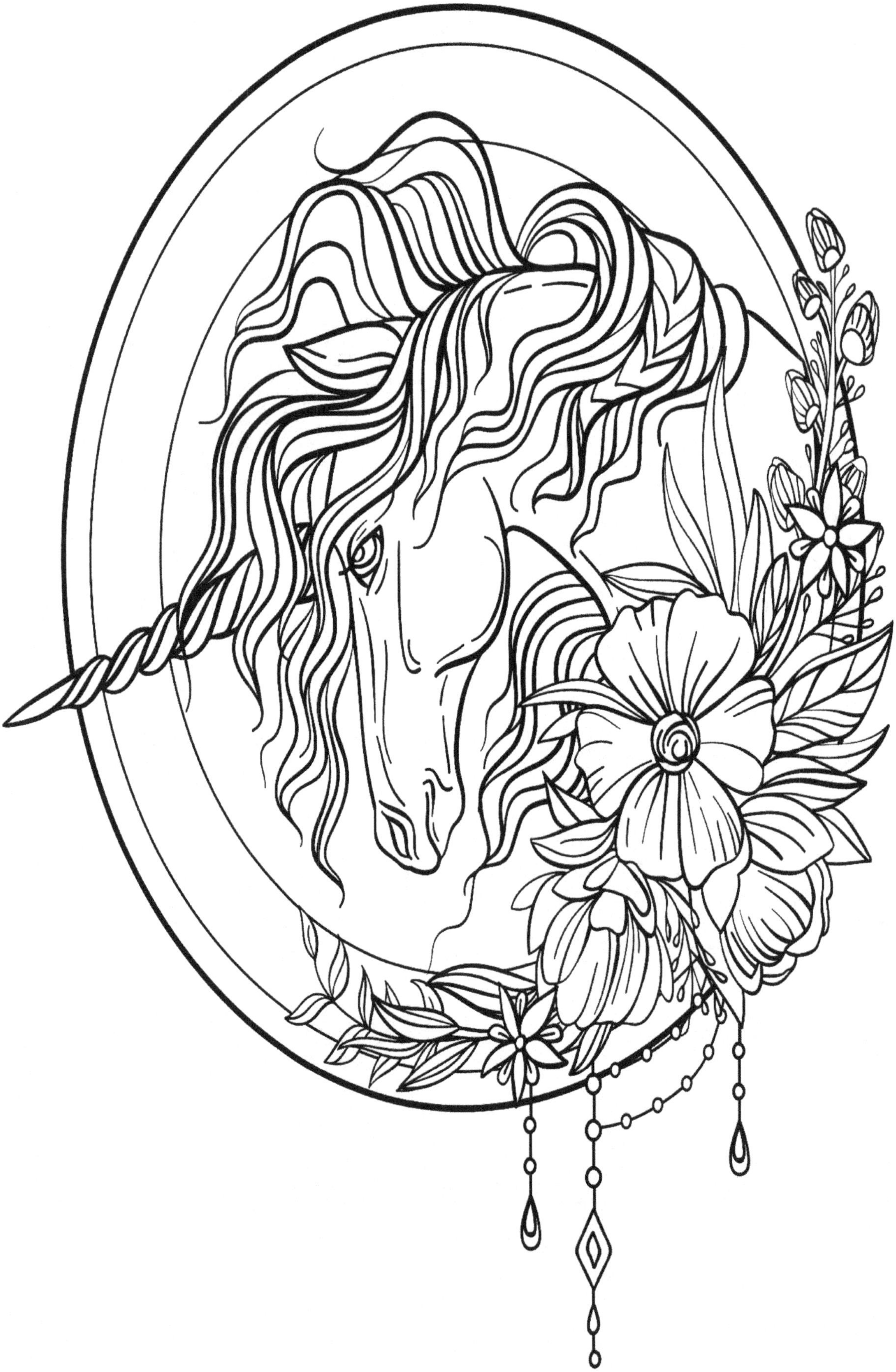

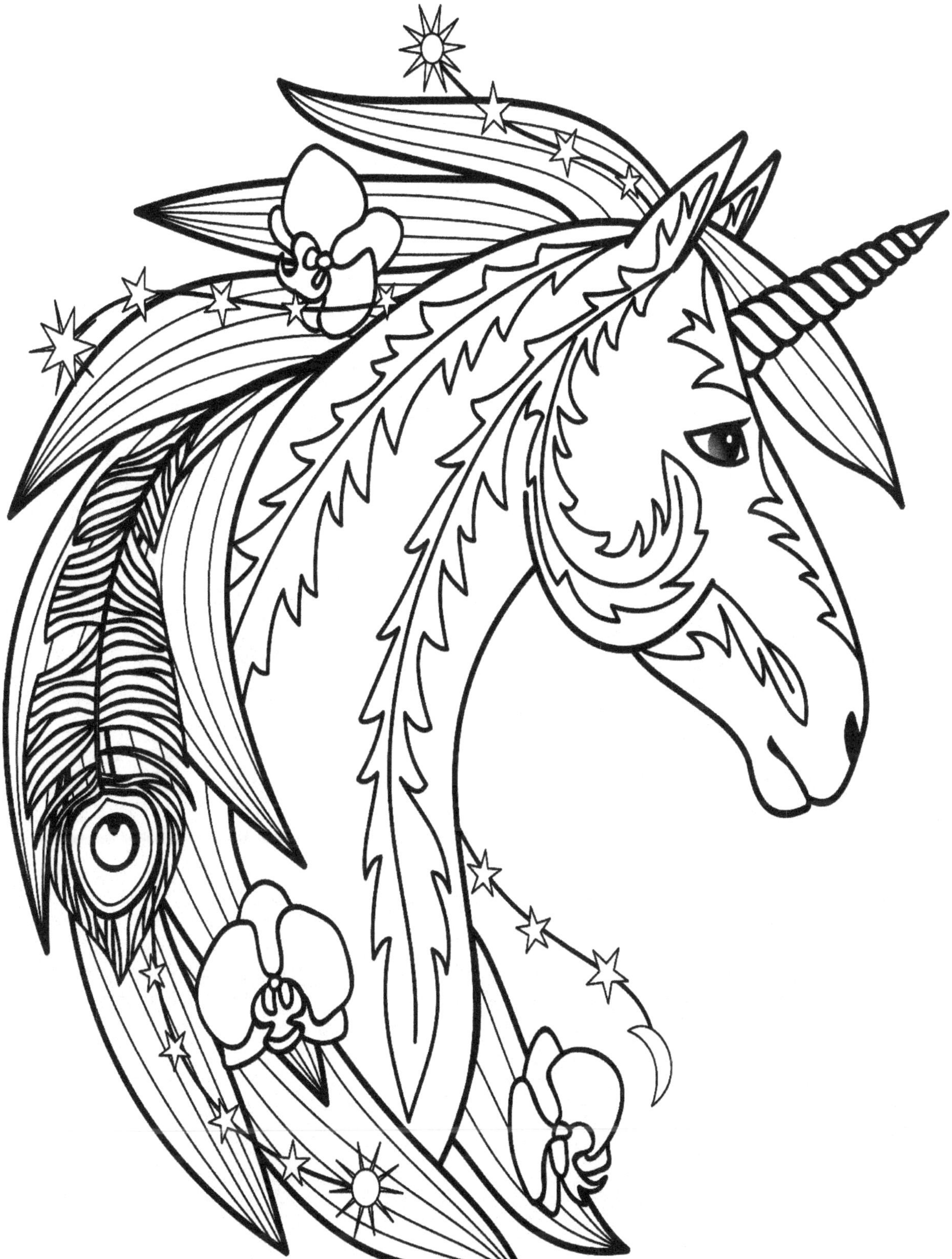

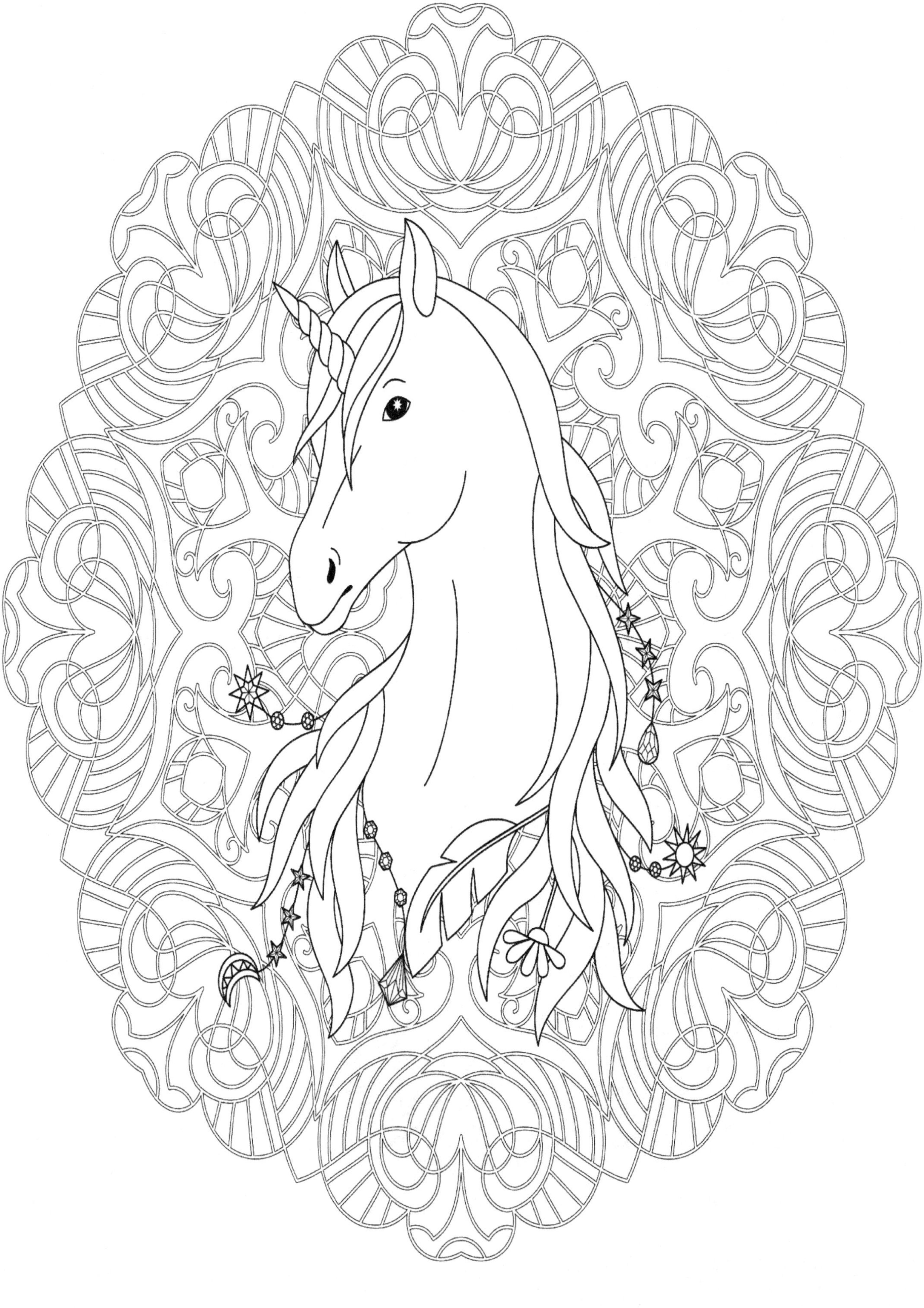

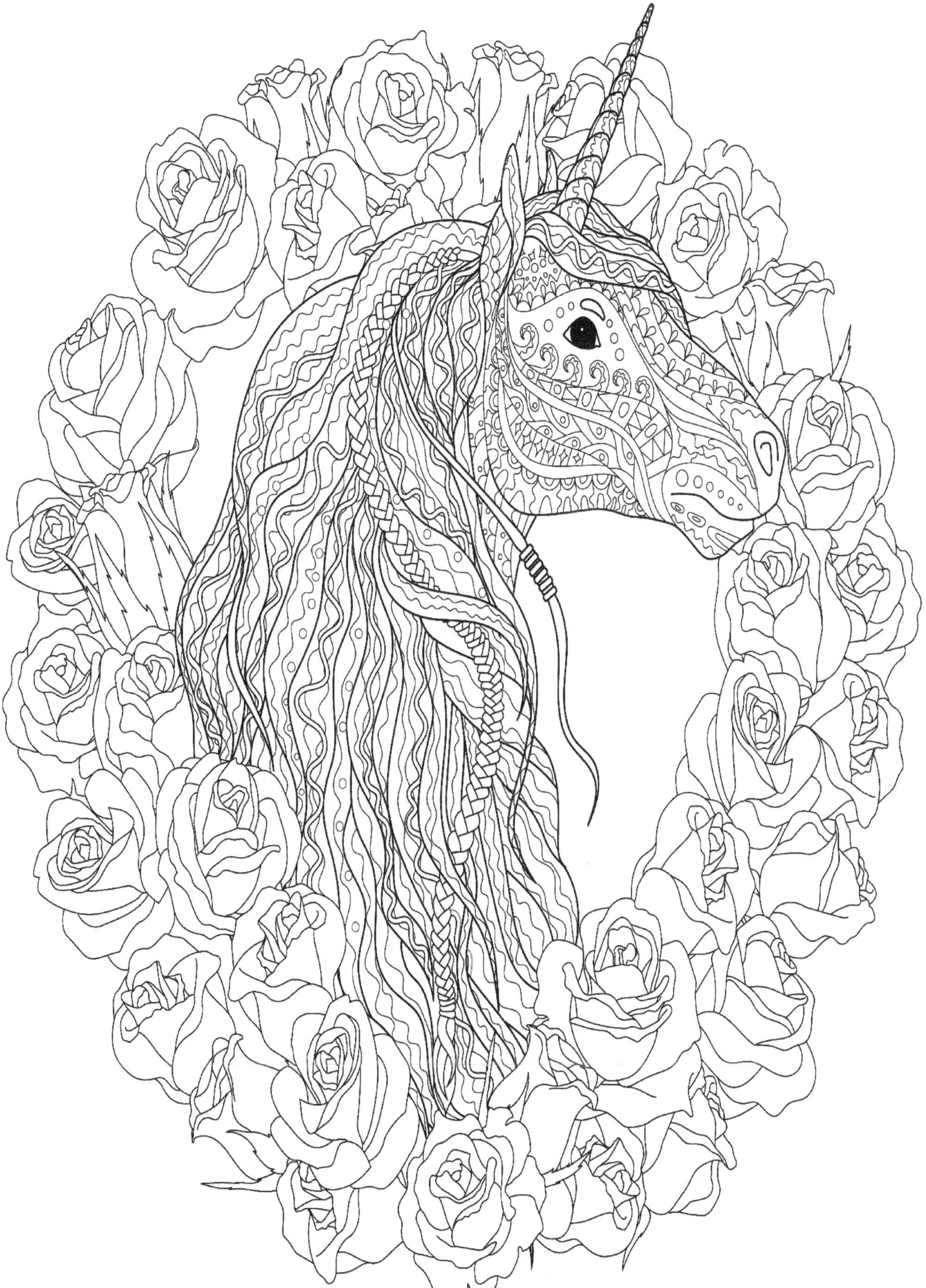

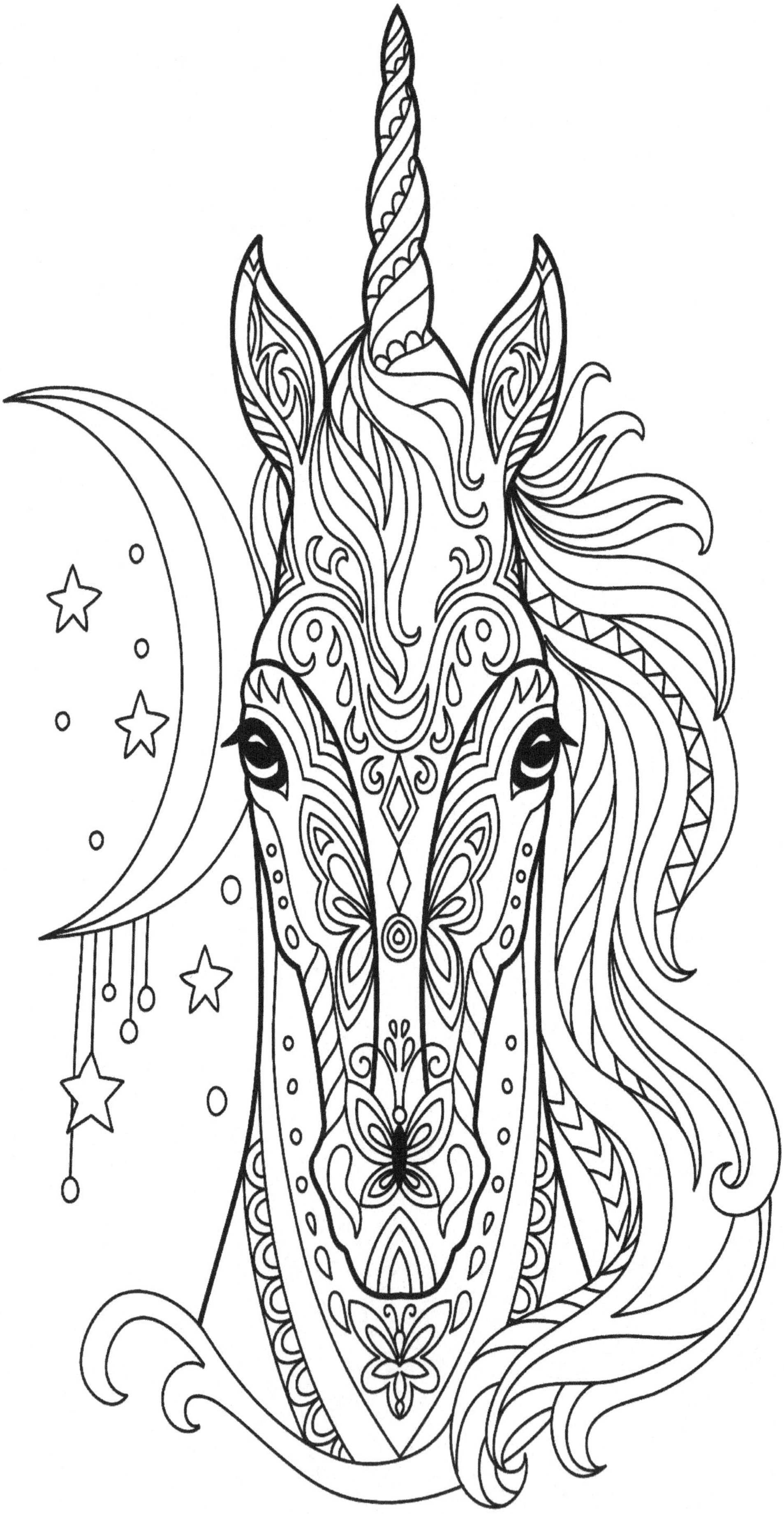

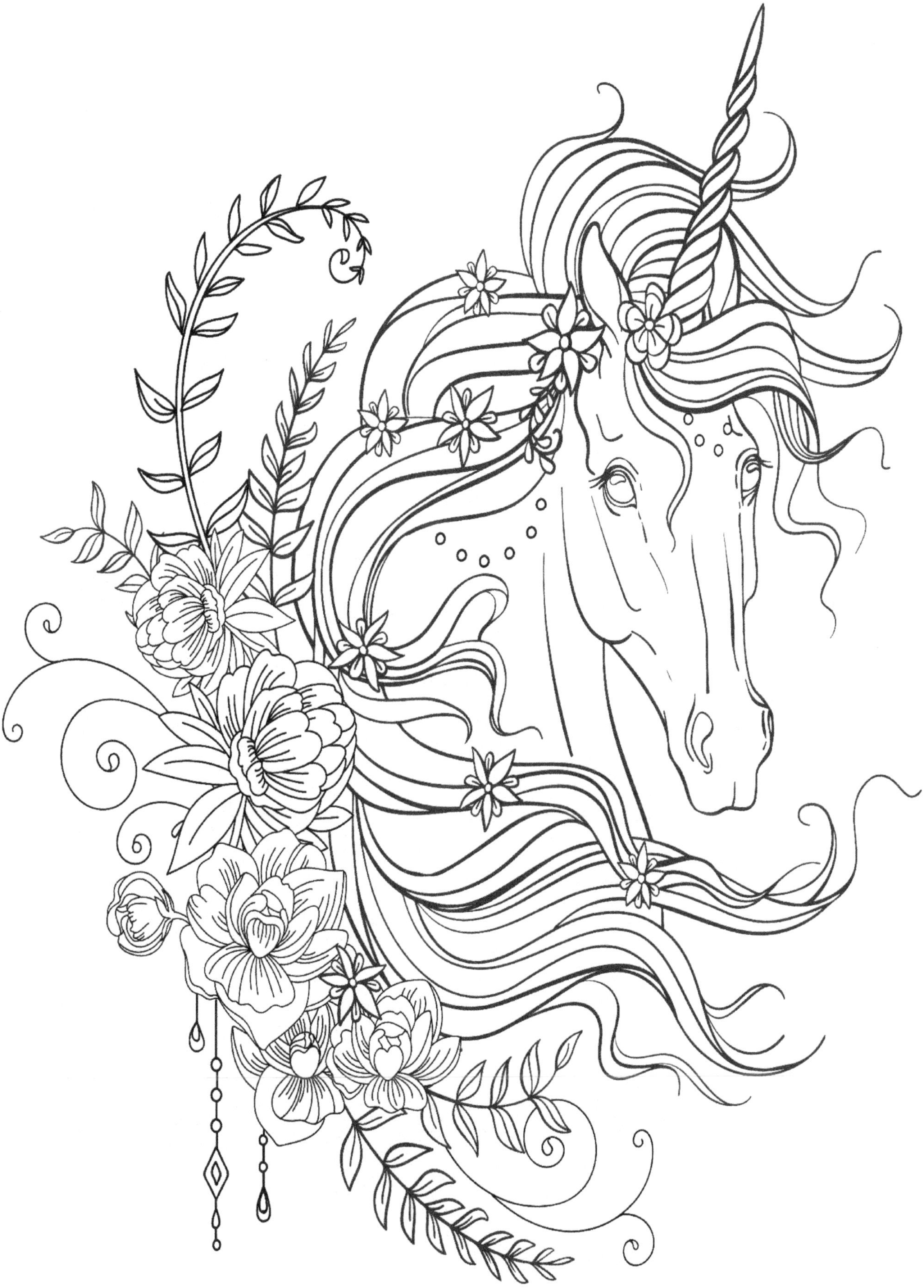

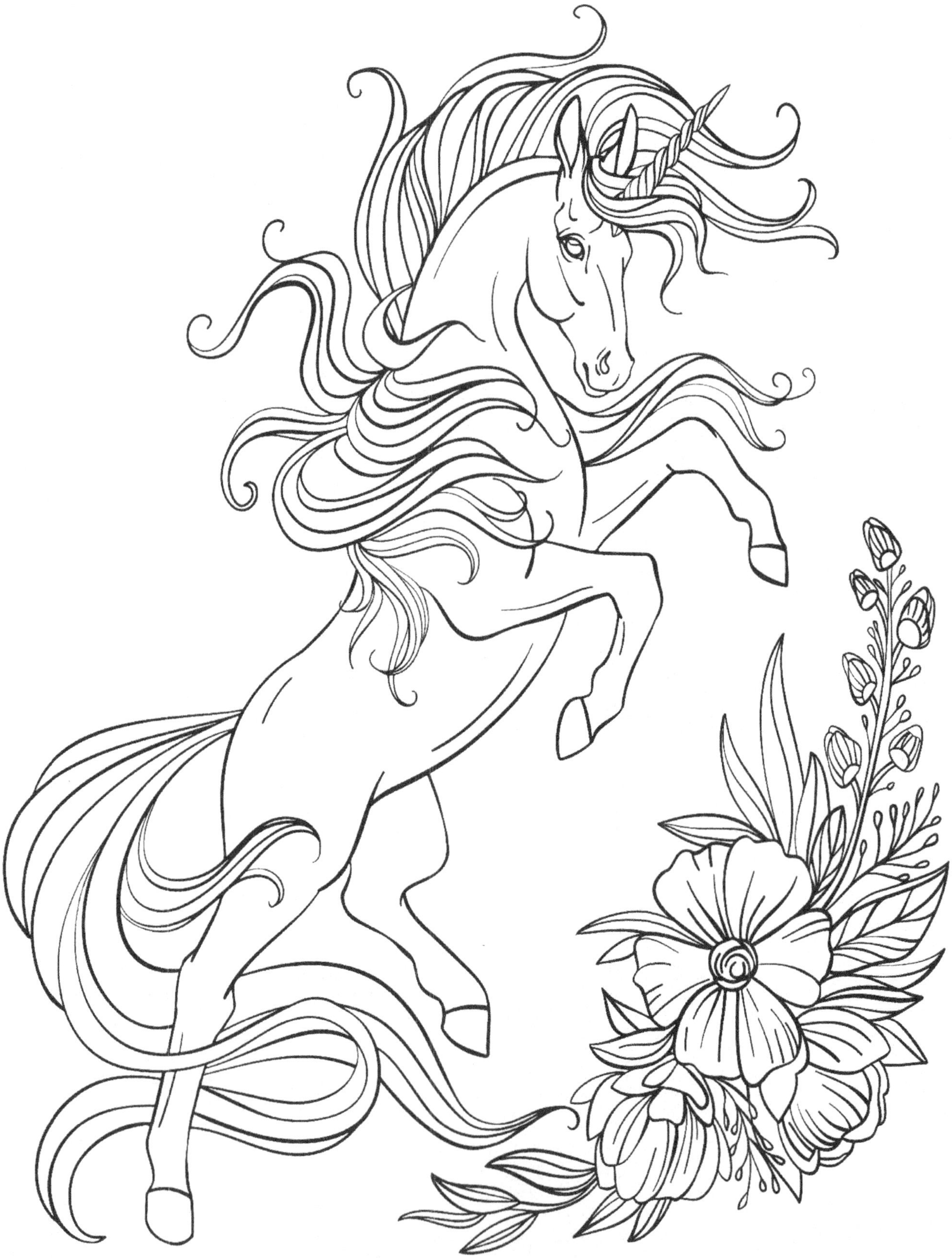

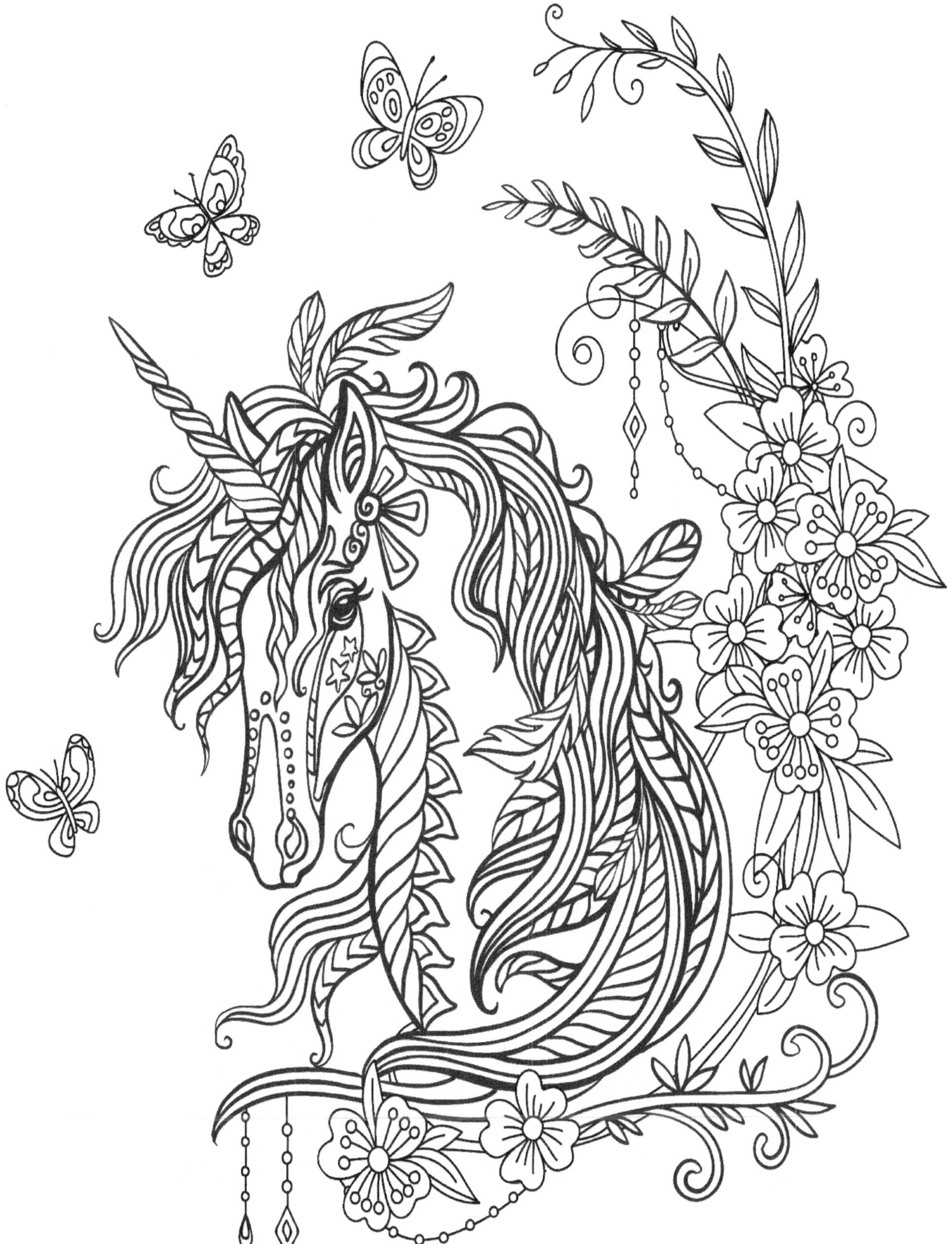

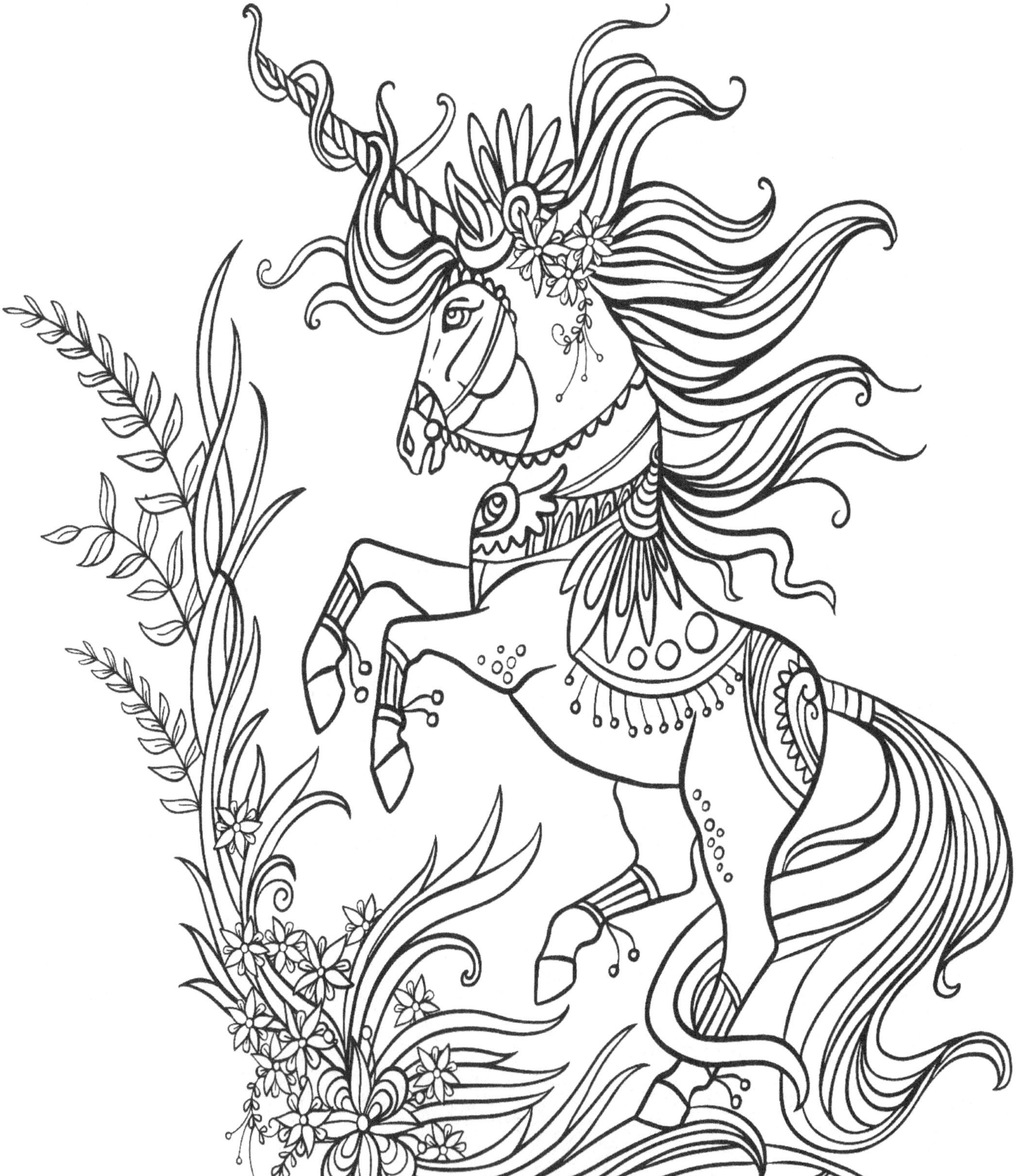

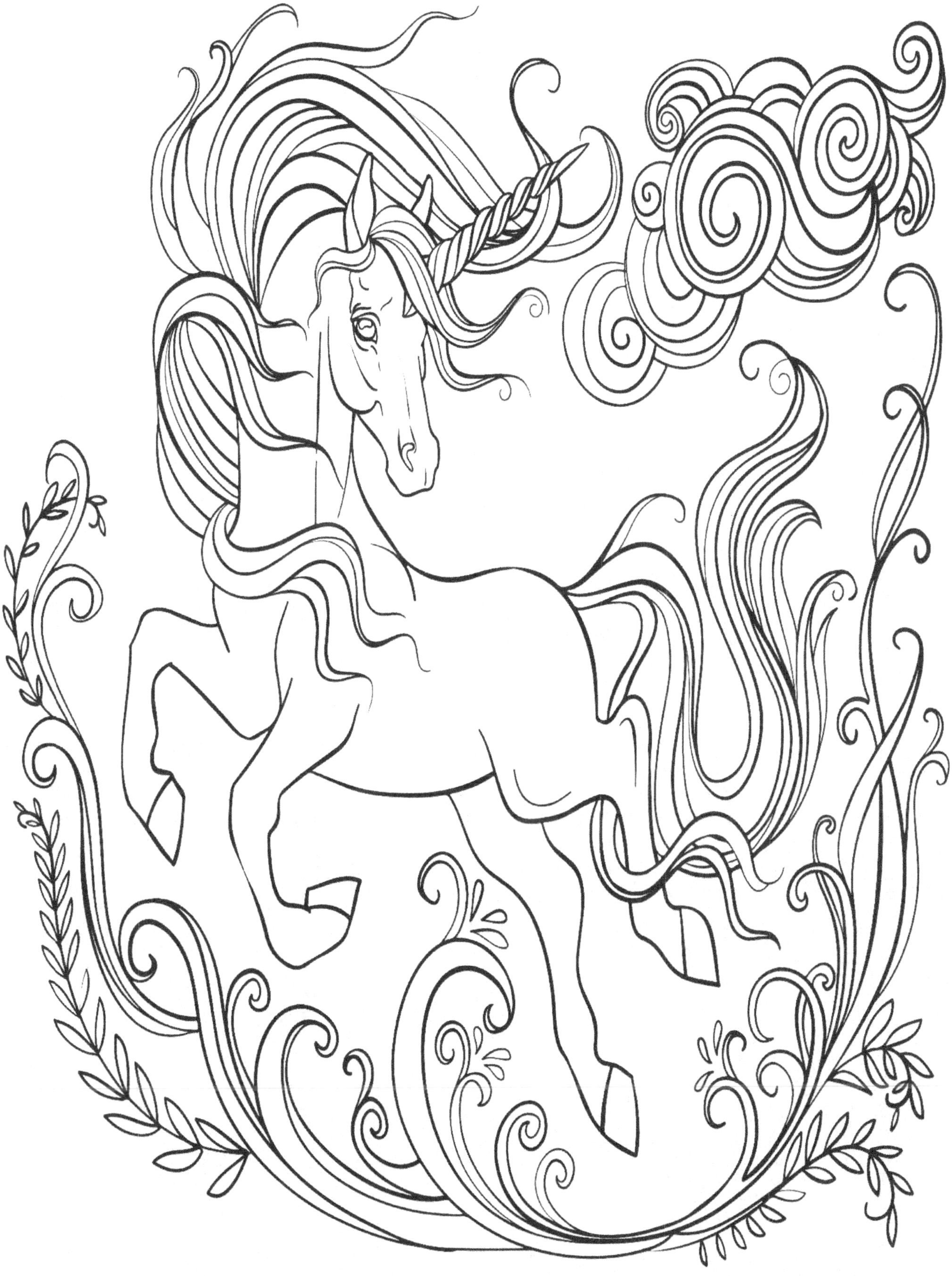

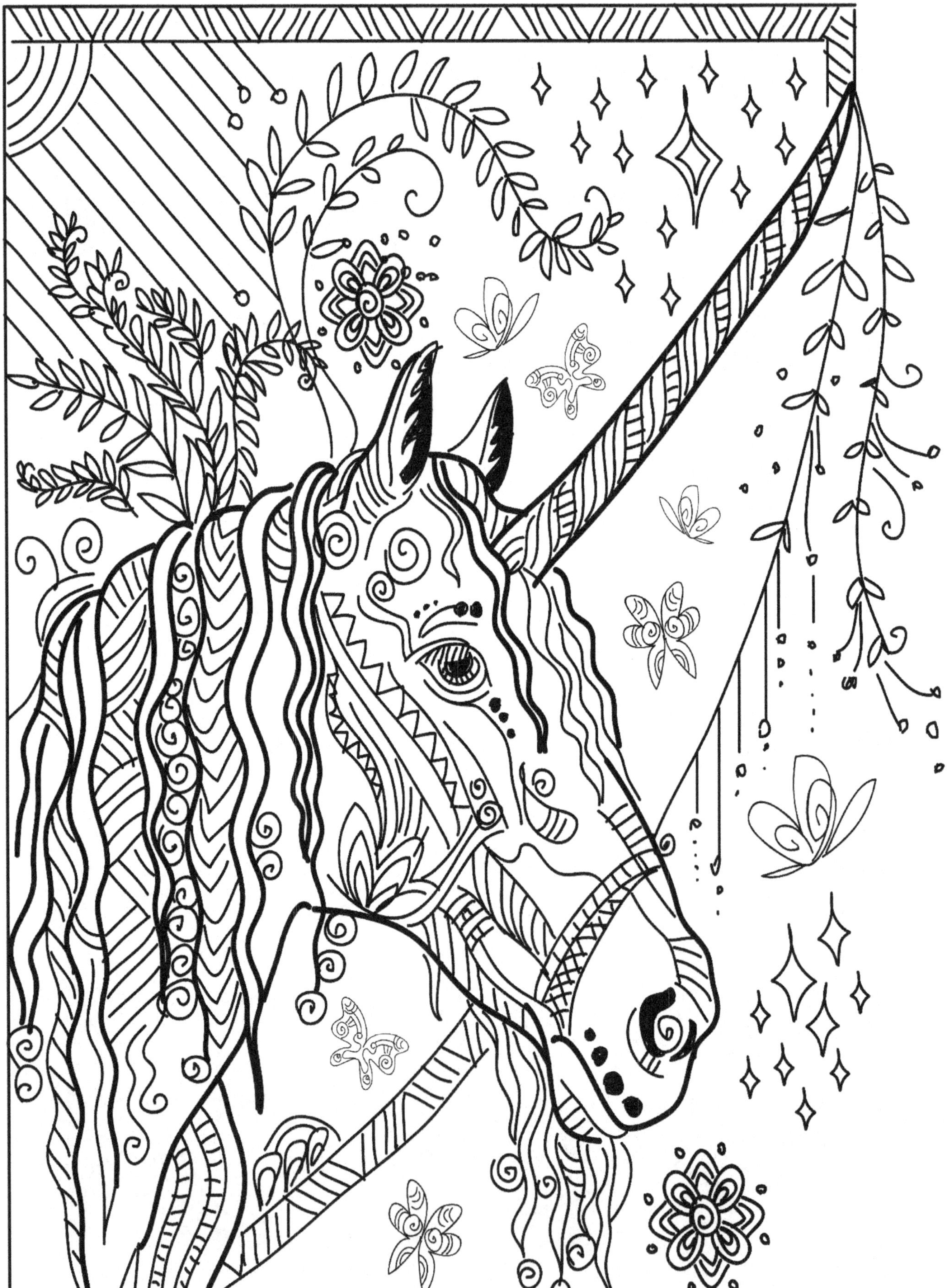

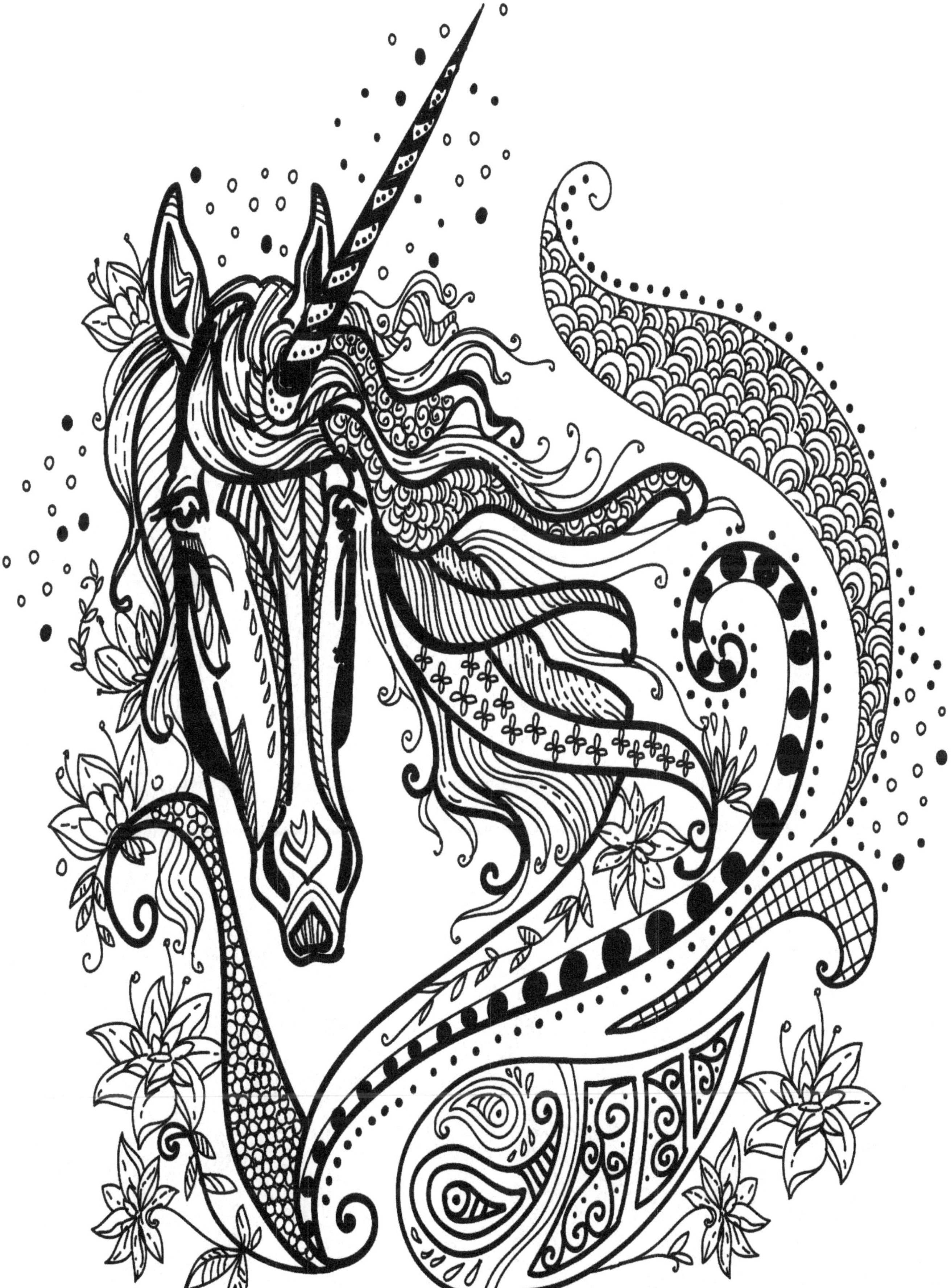

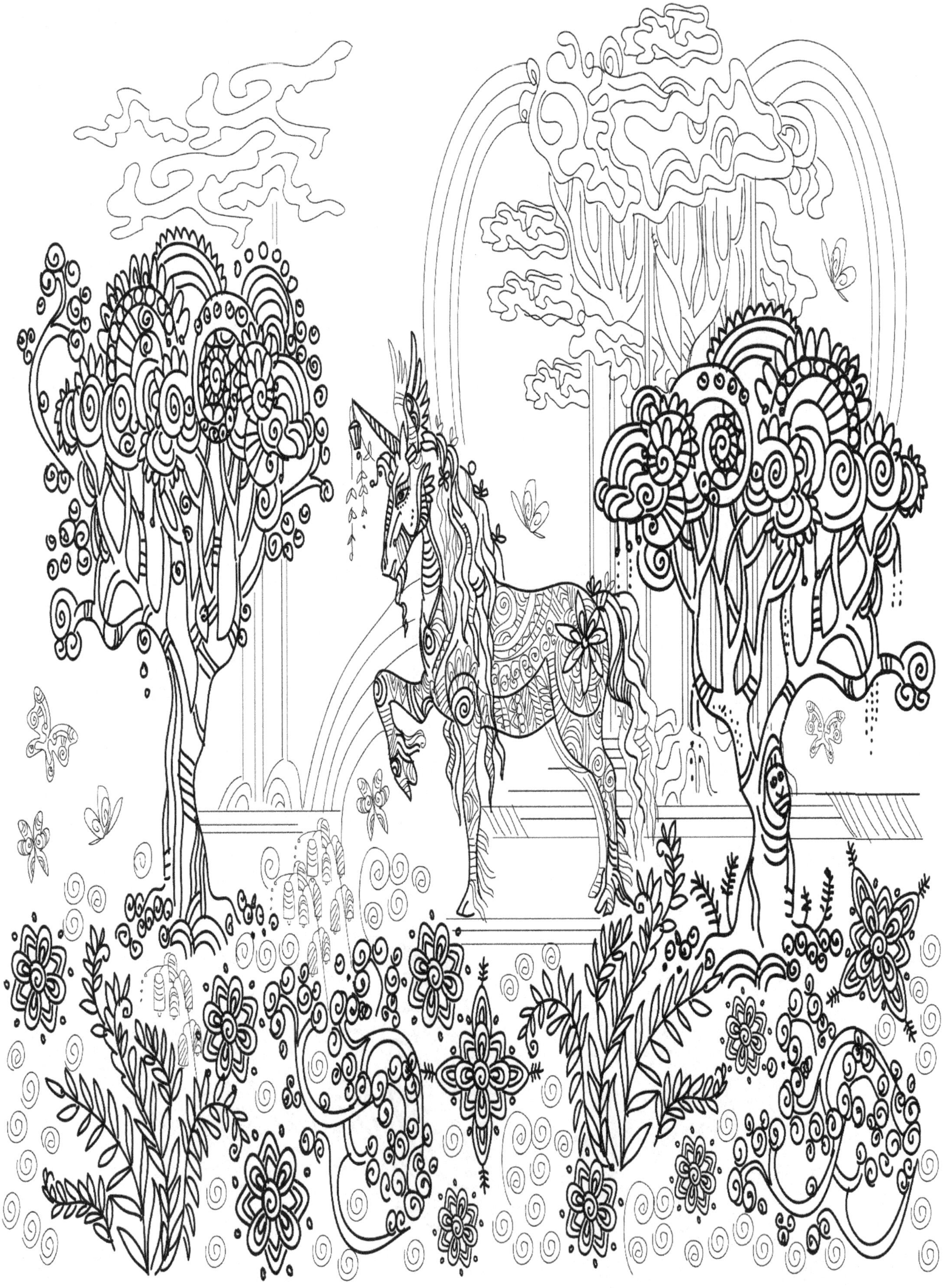

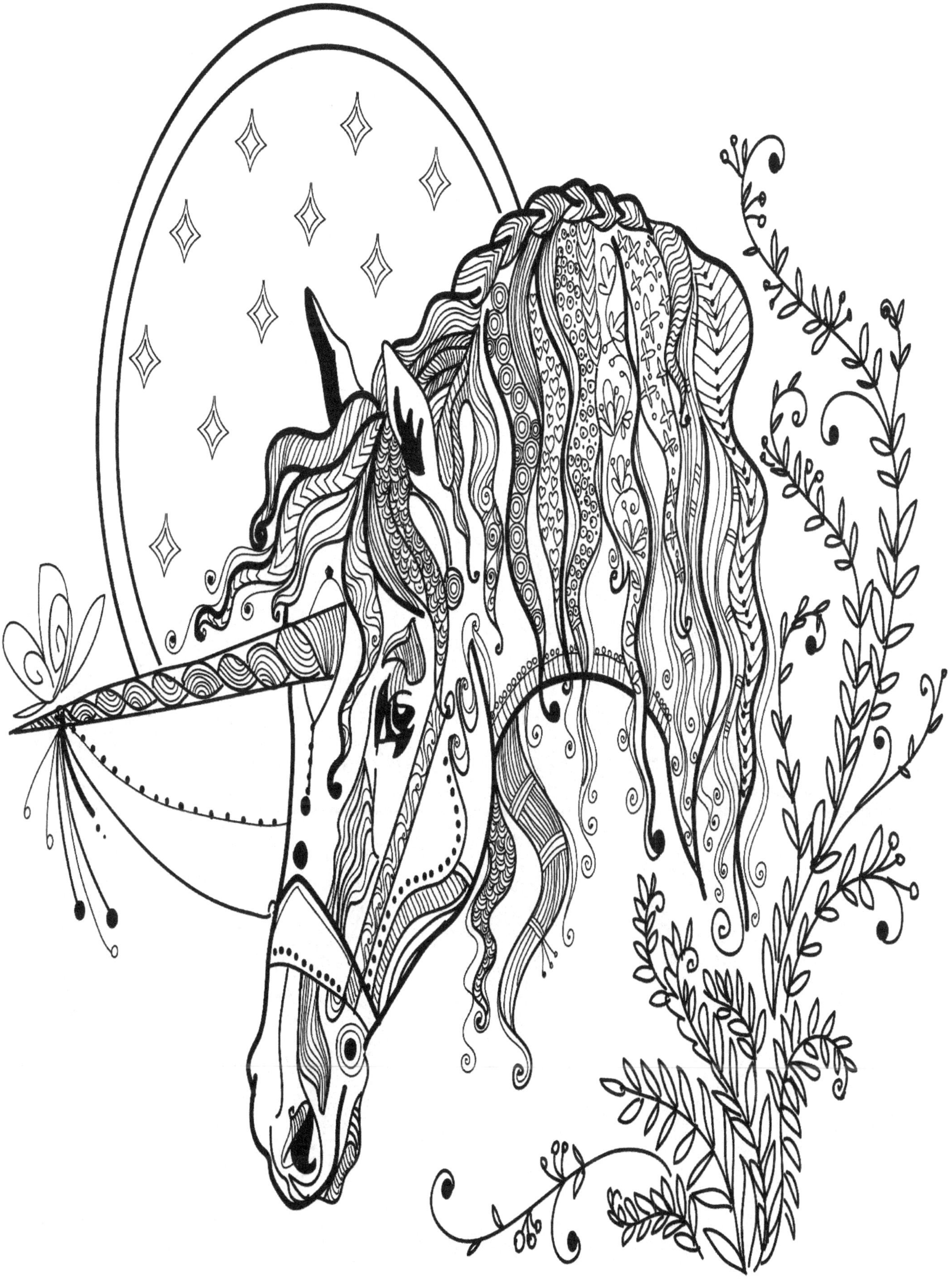

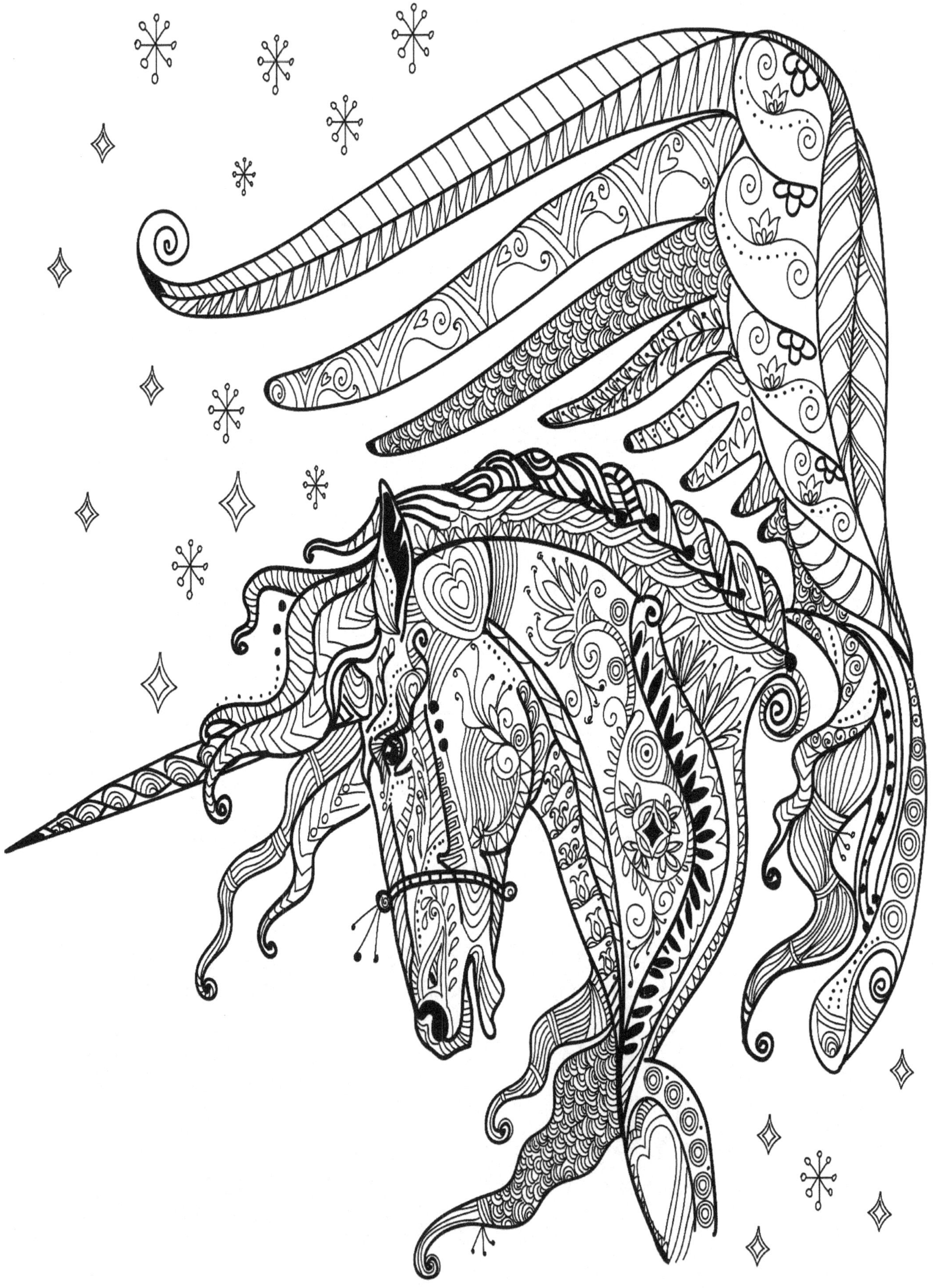

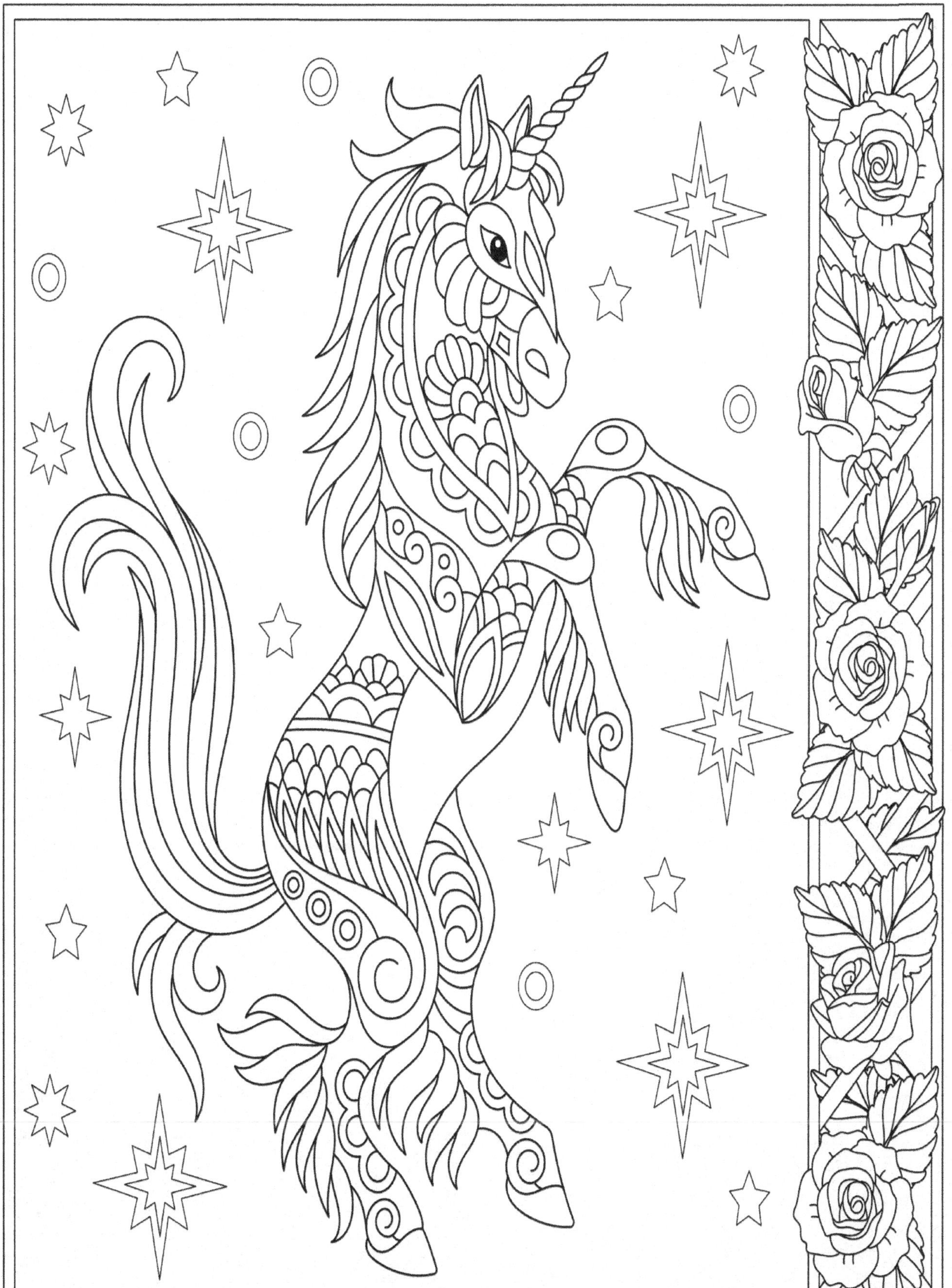

Magic

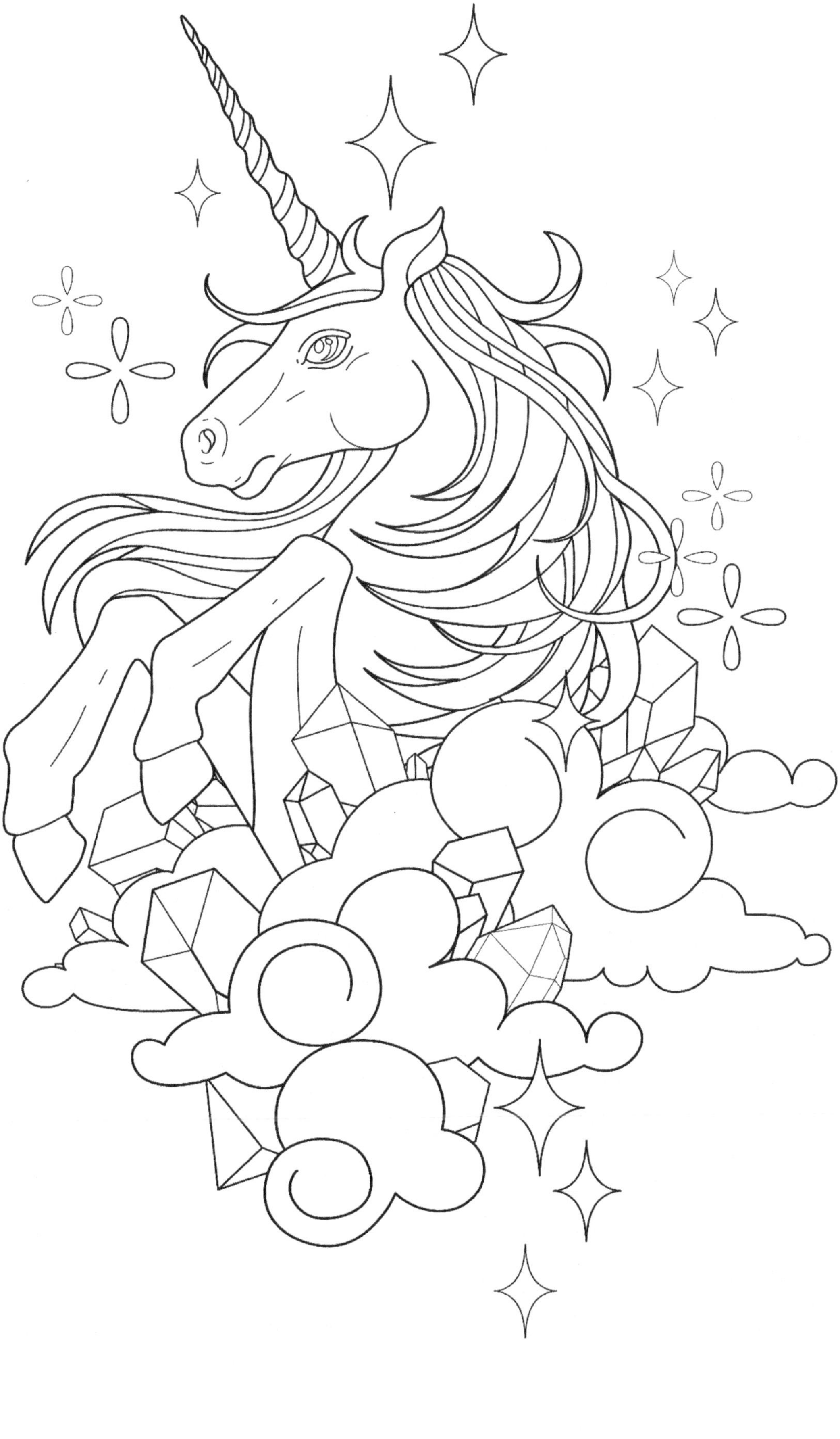

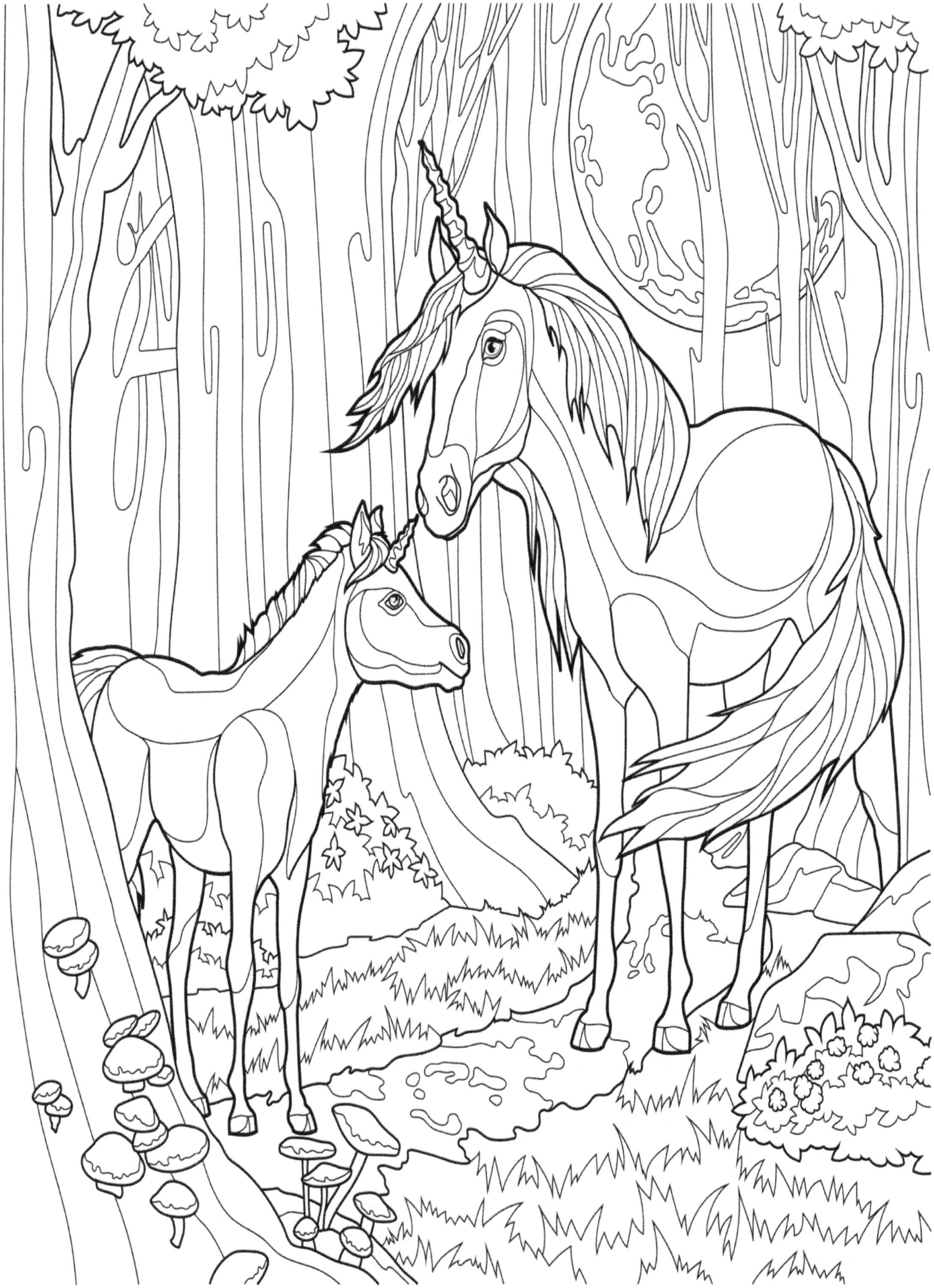

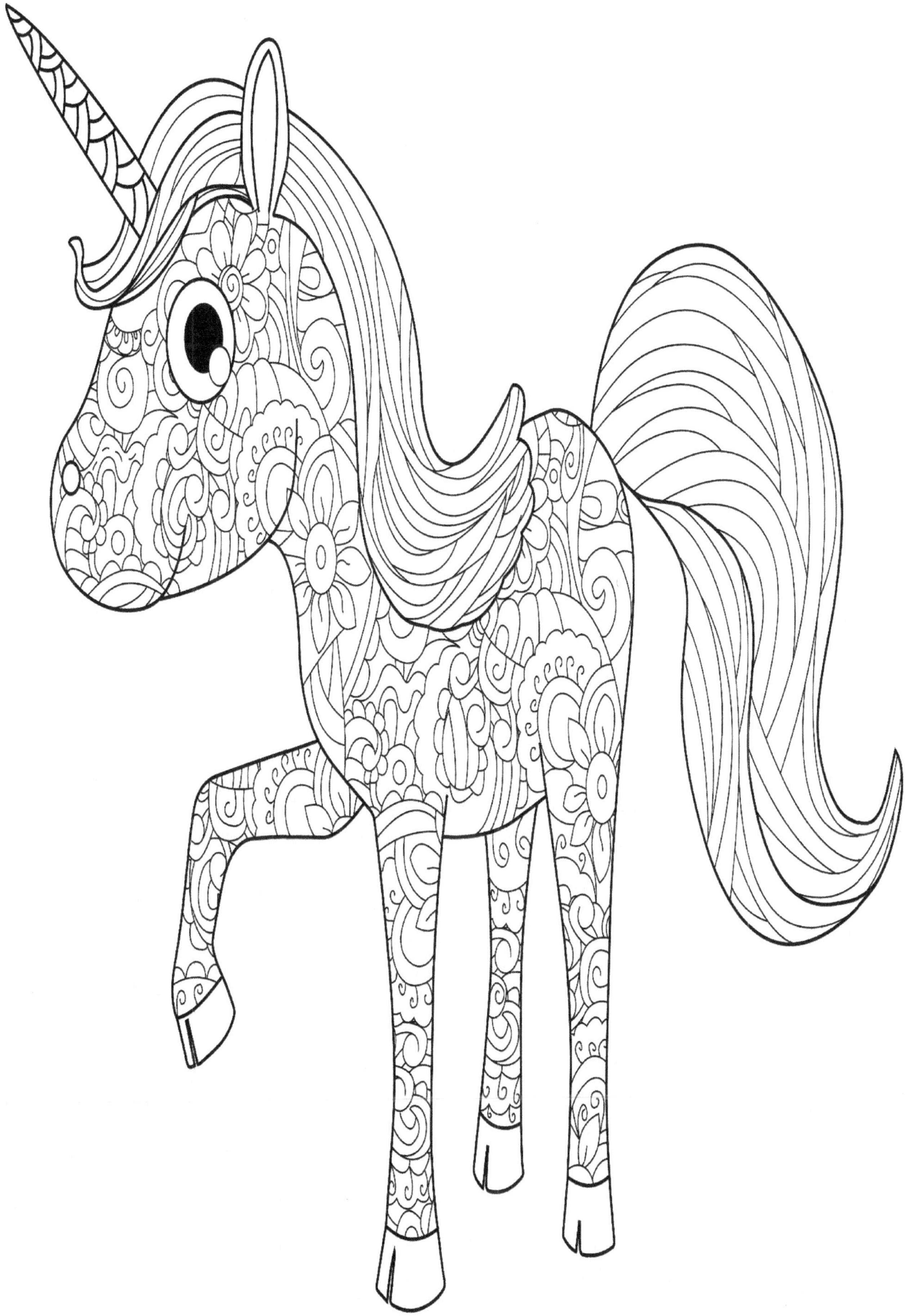

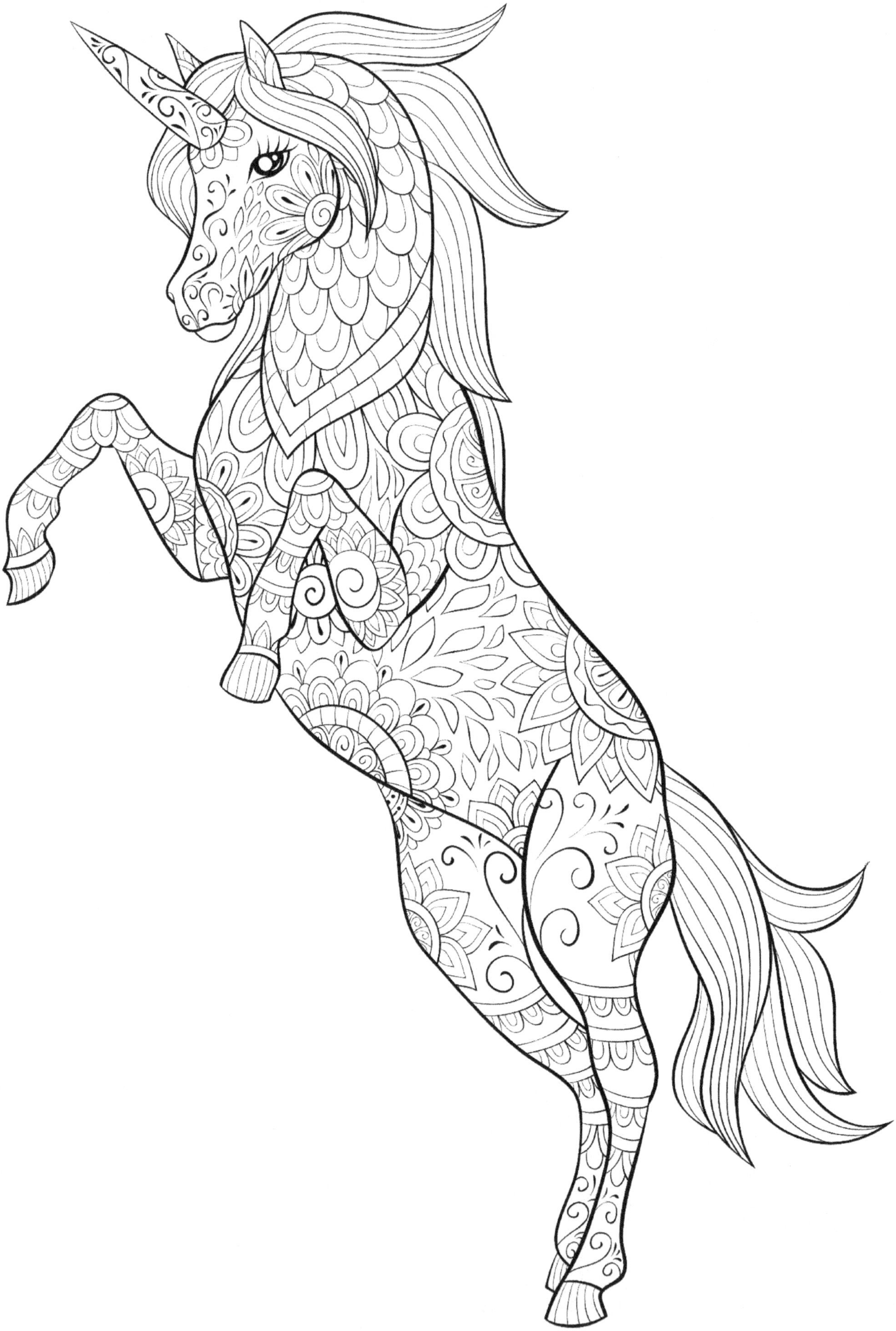

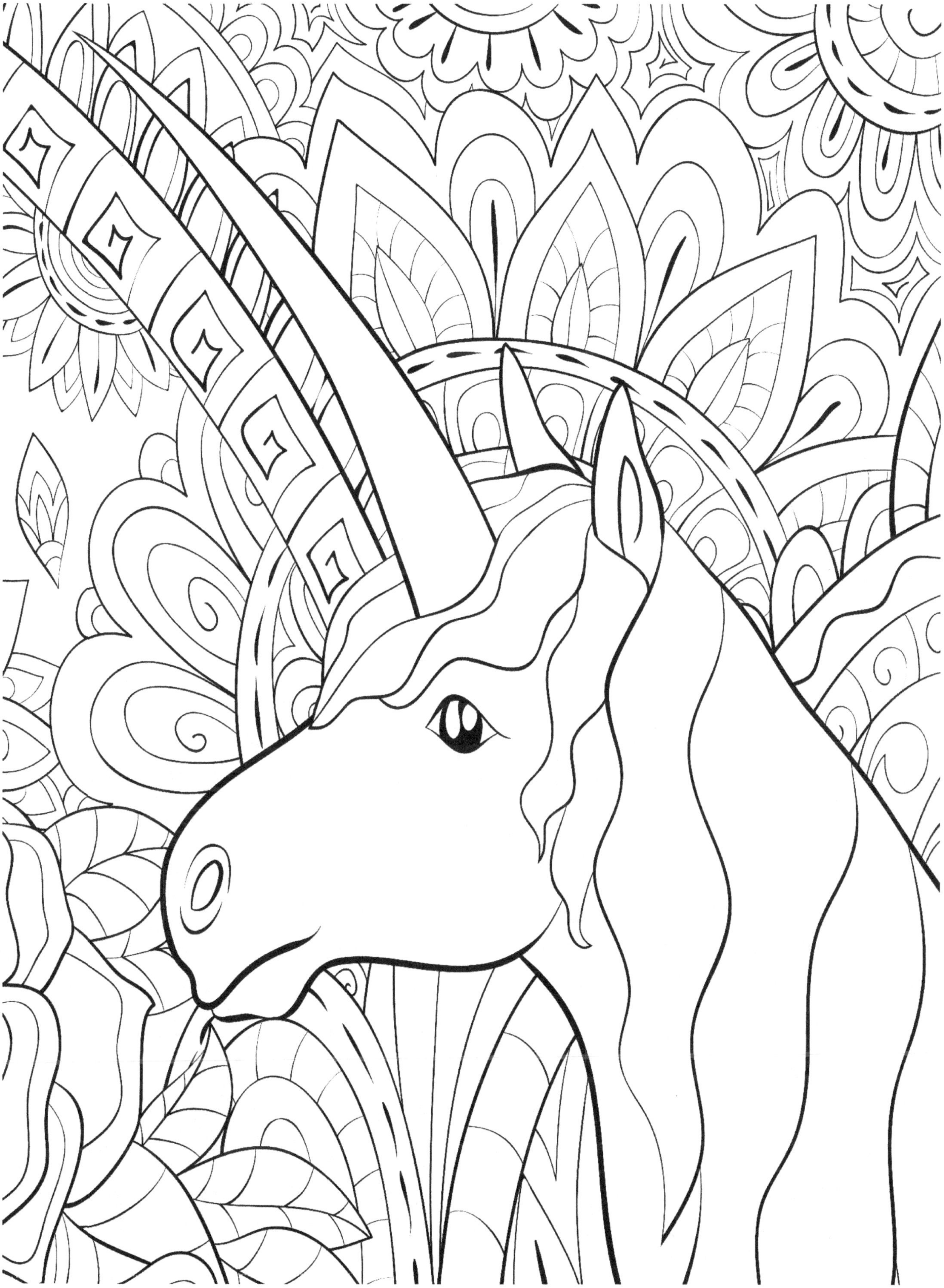

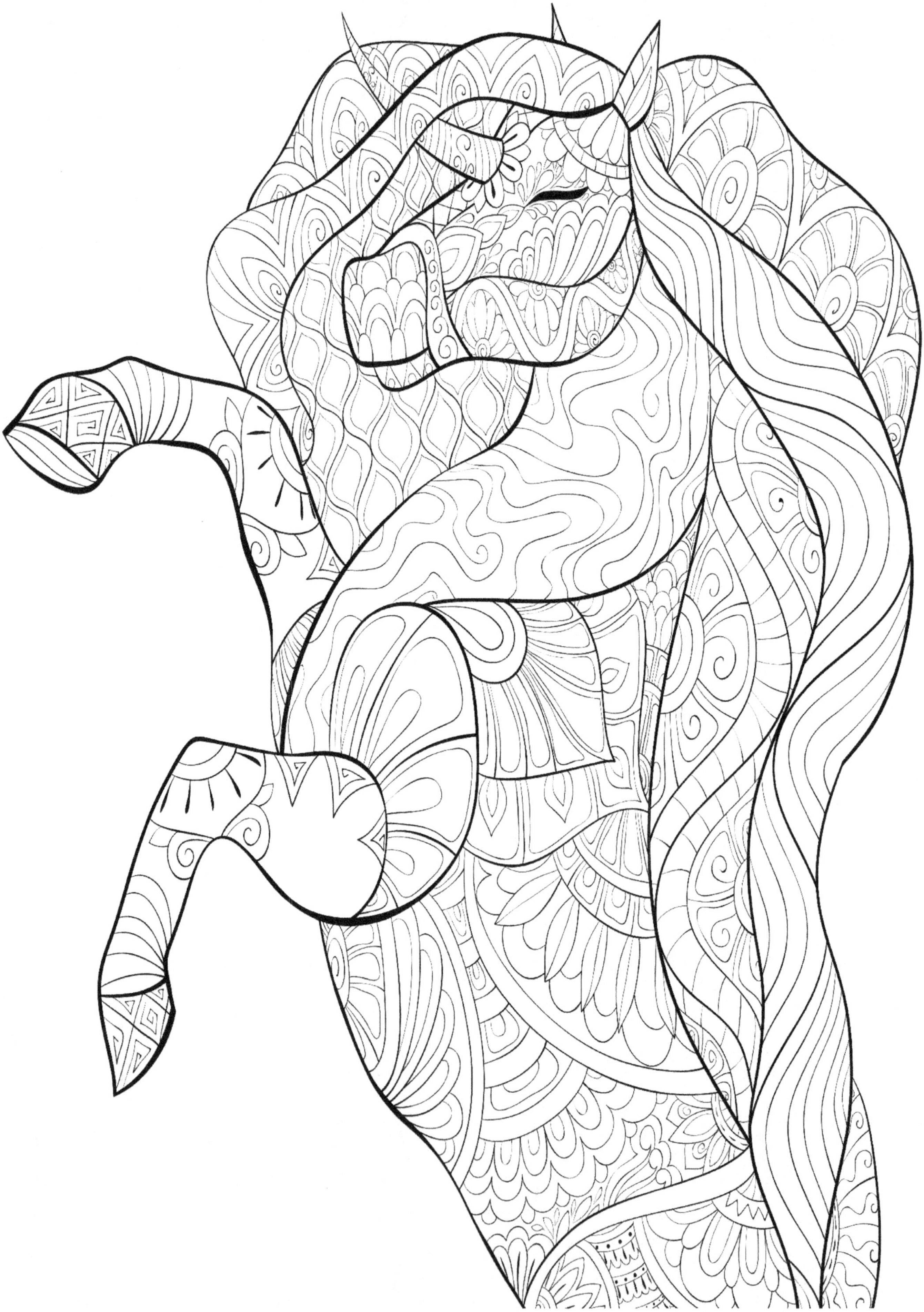

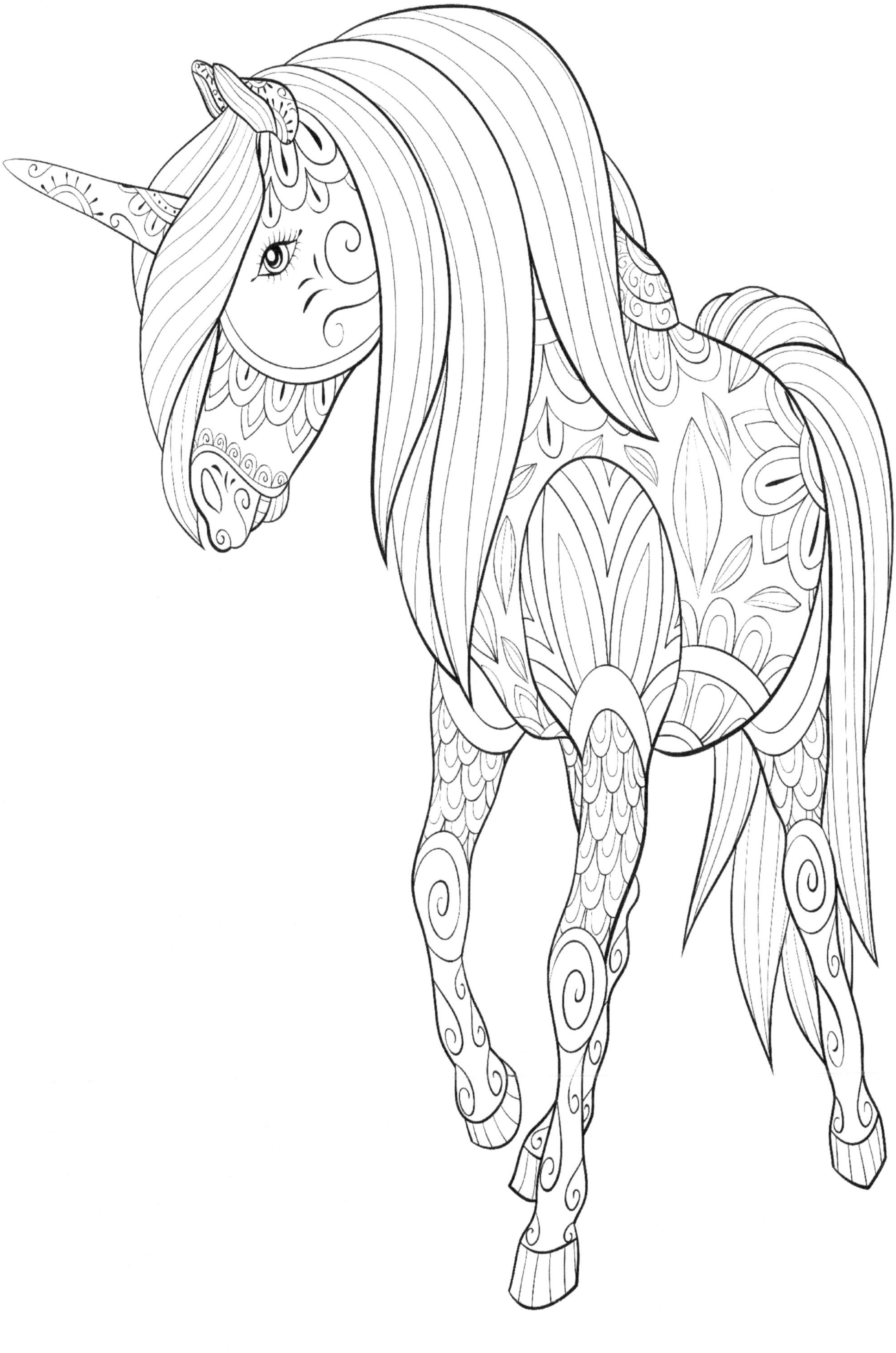

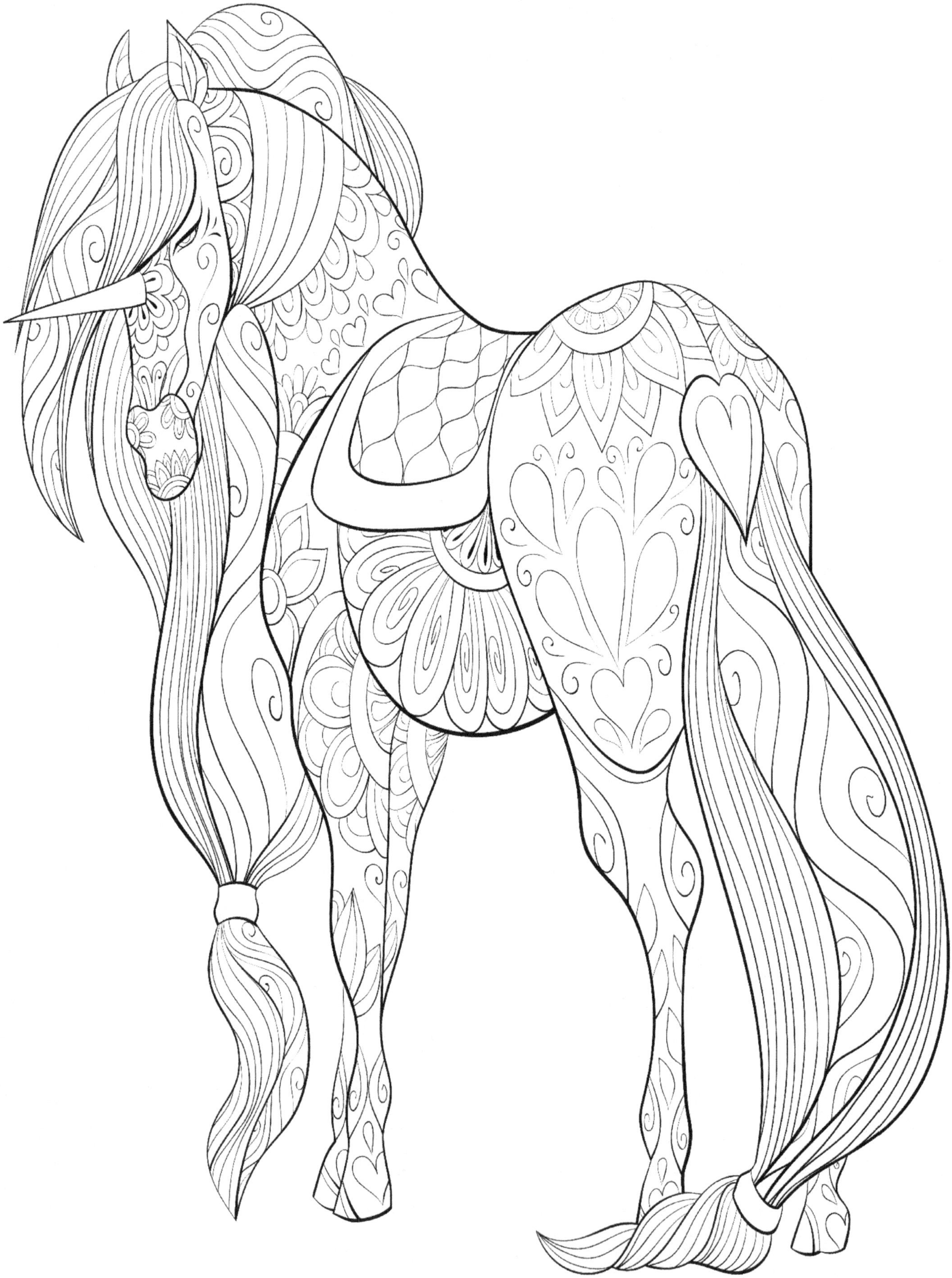

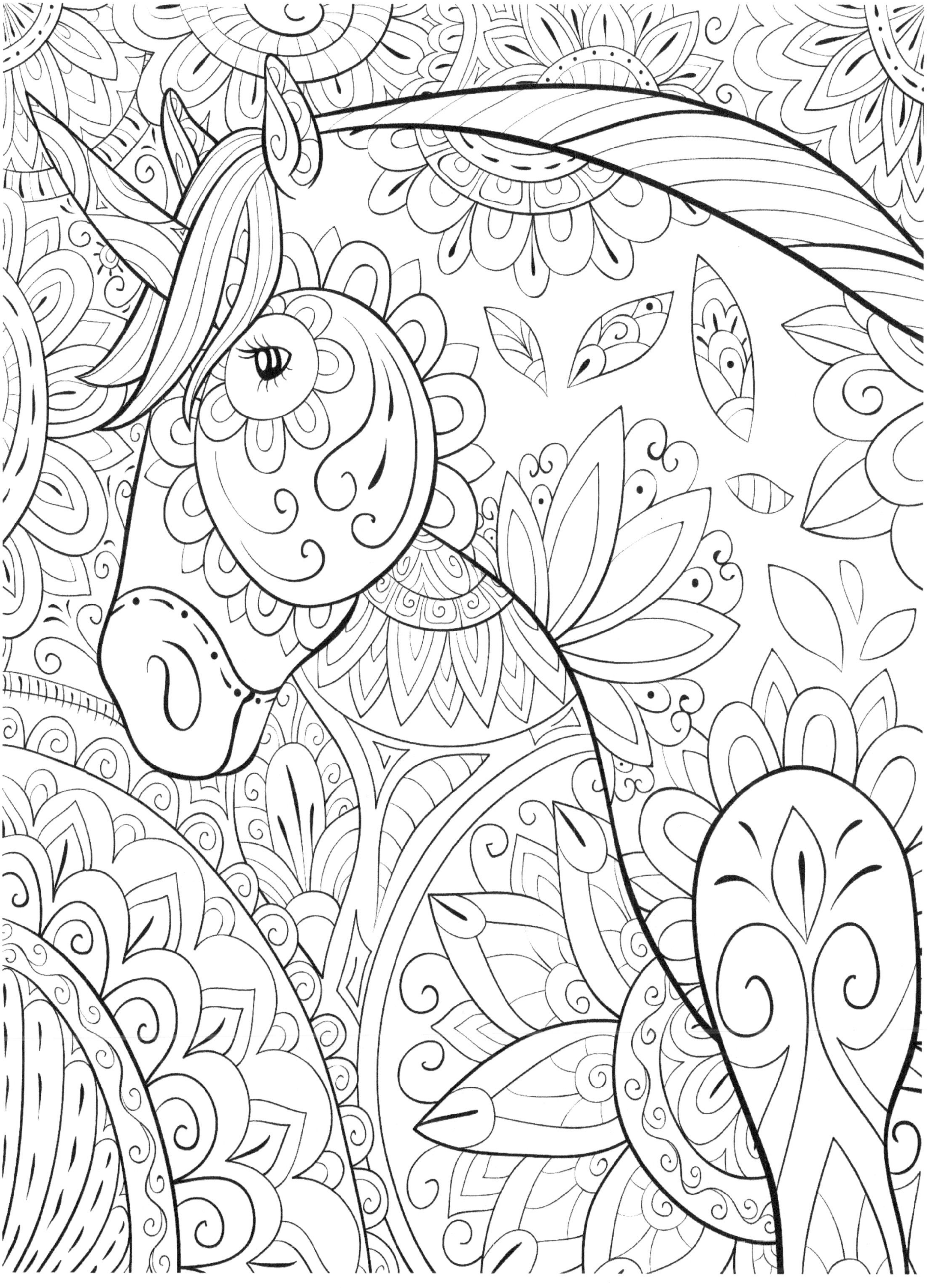

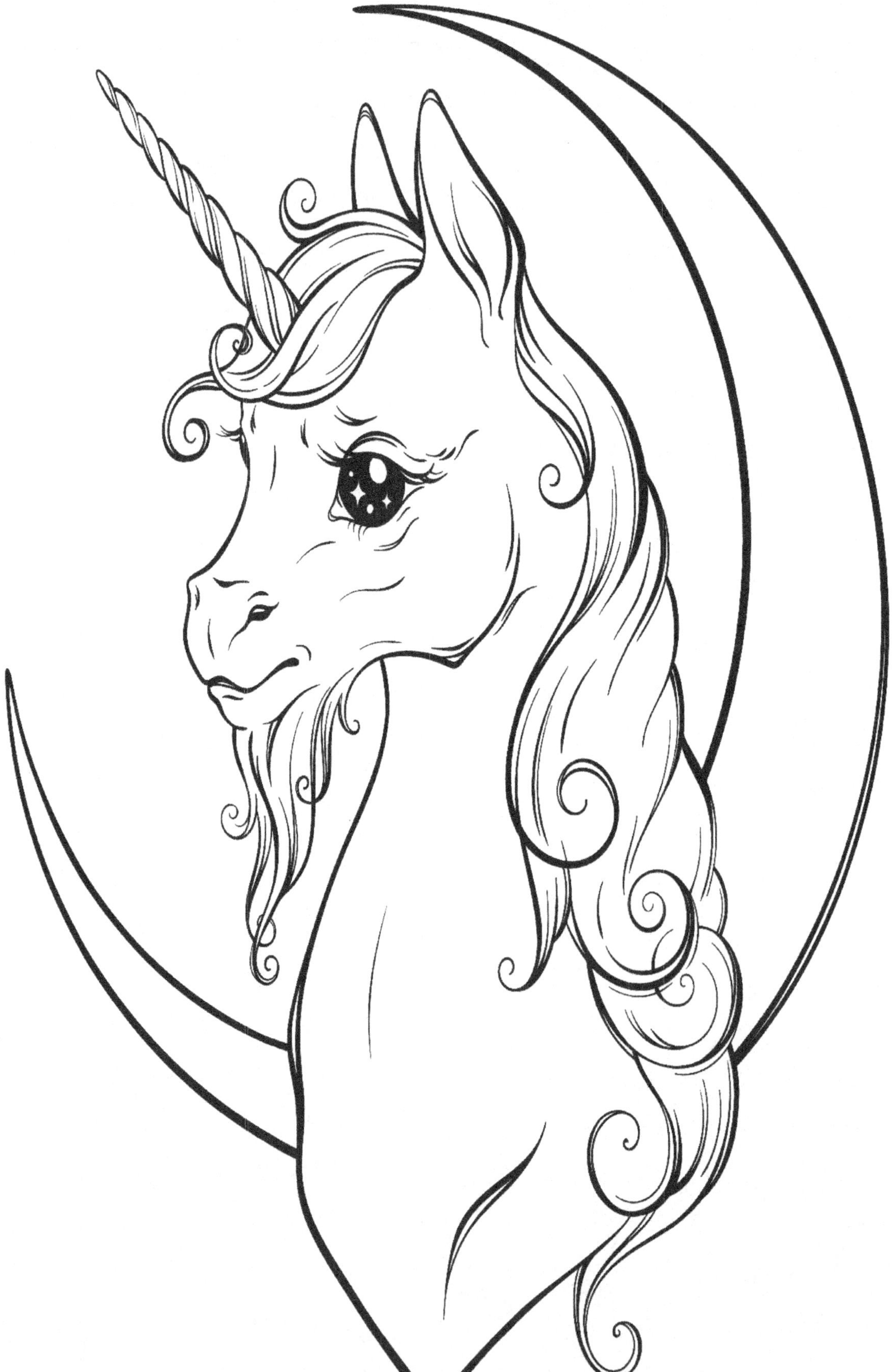

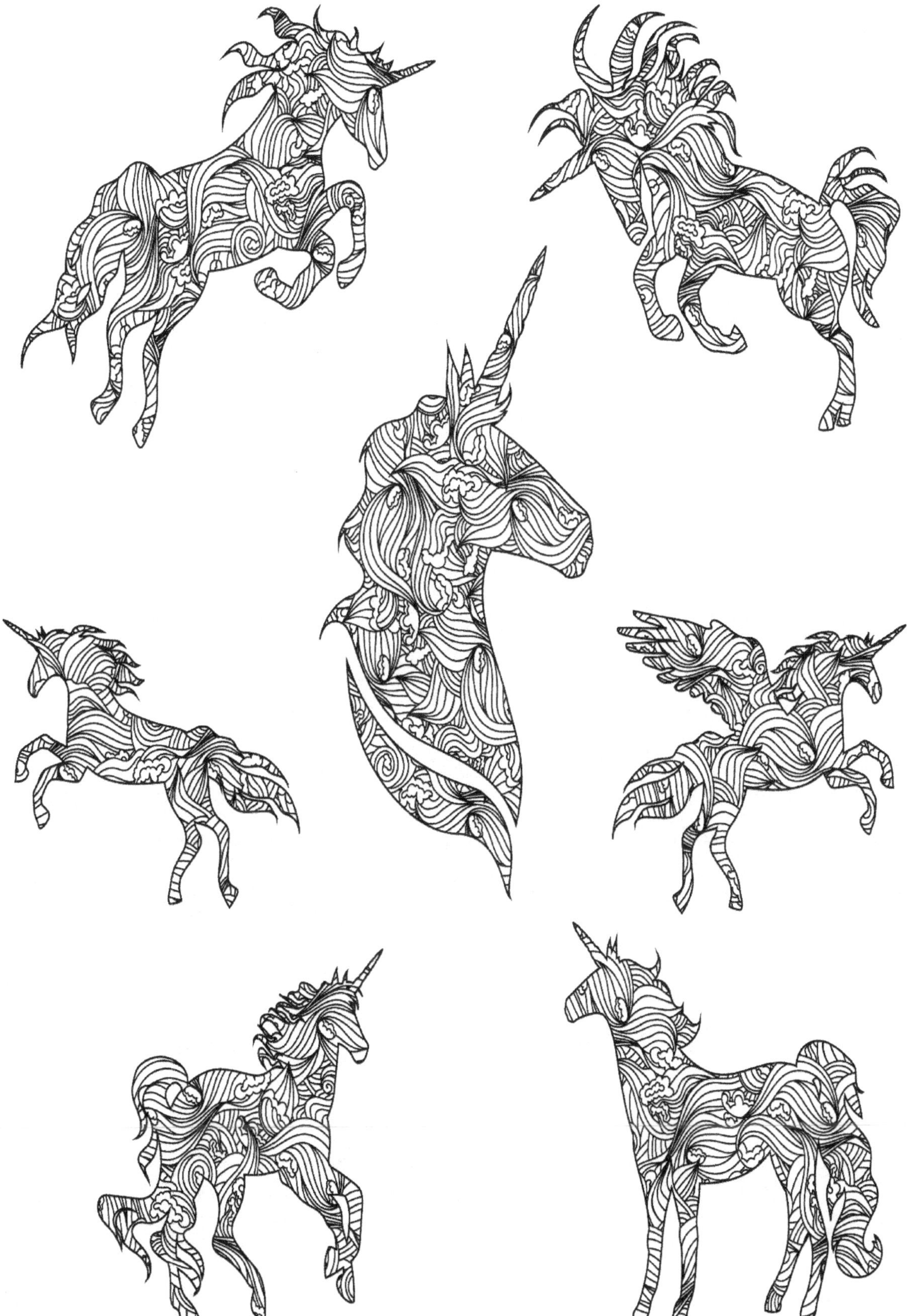

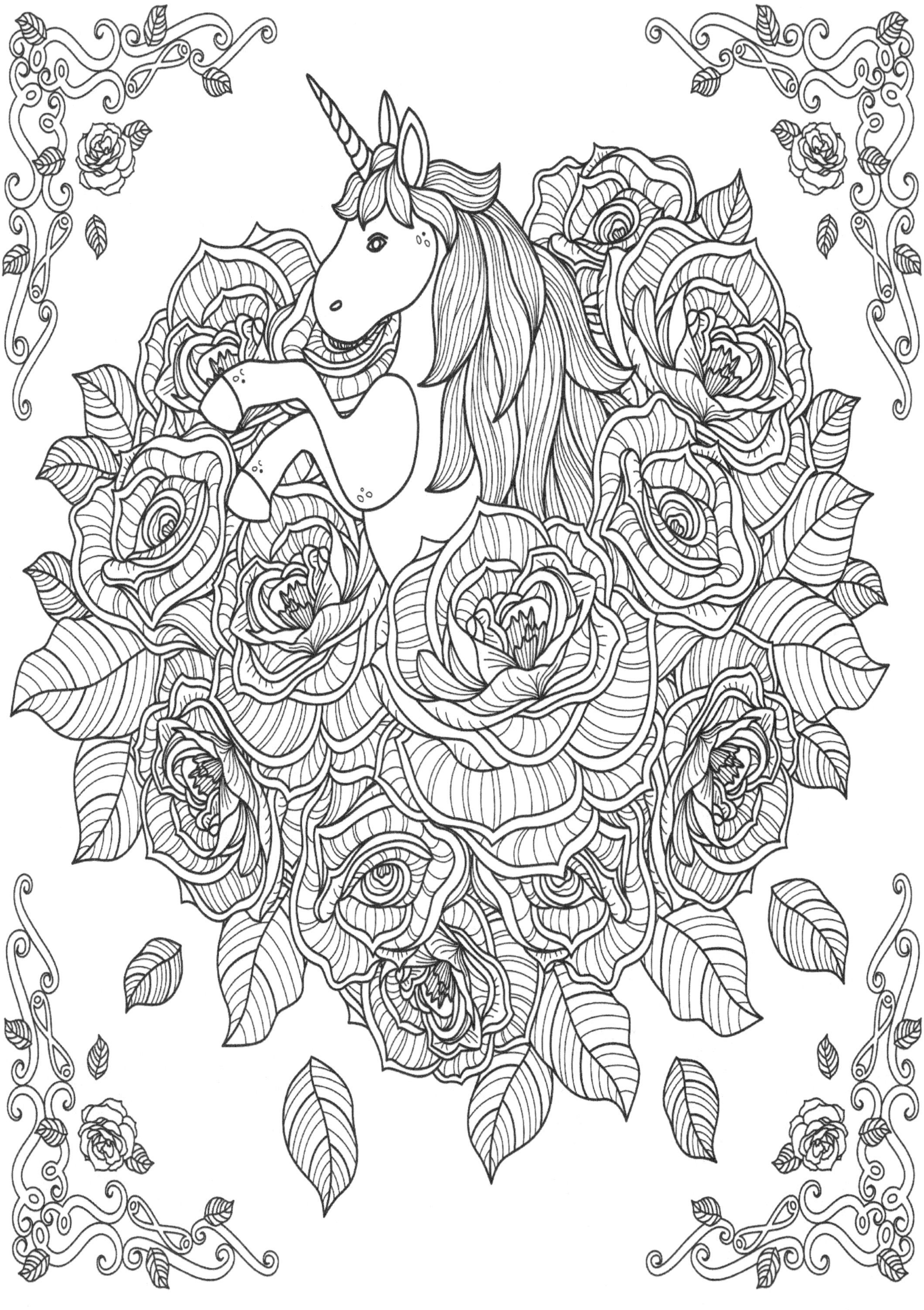

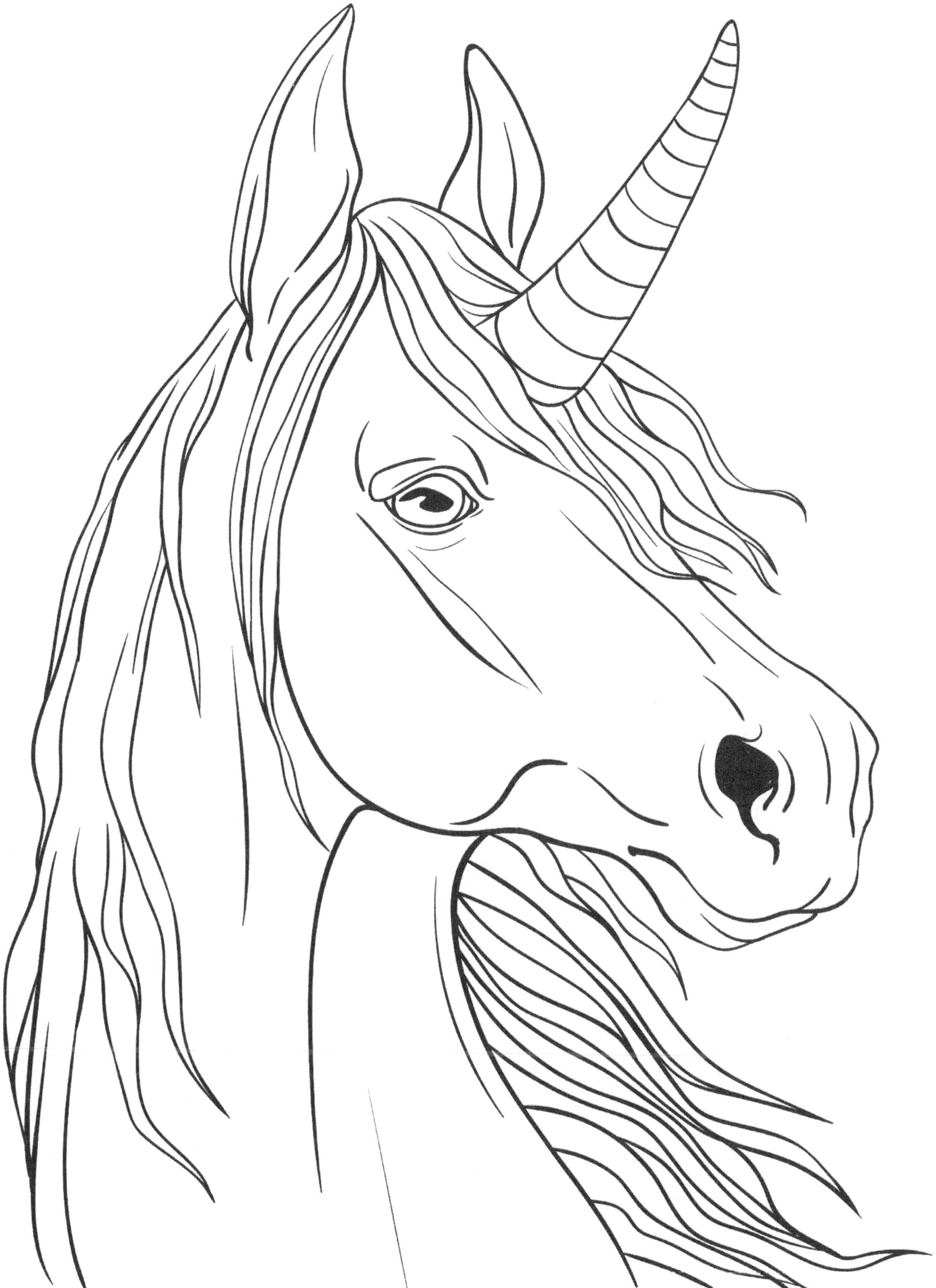

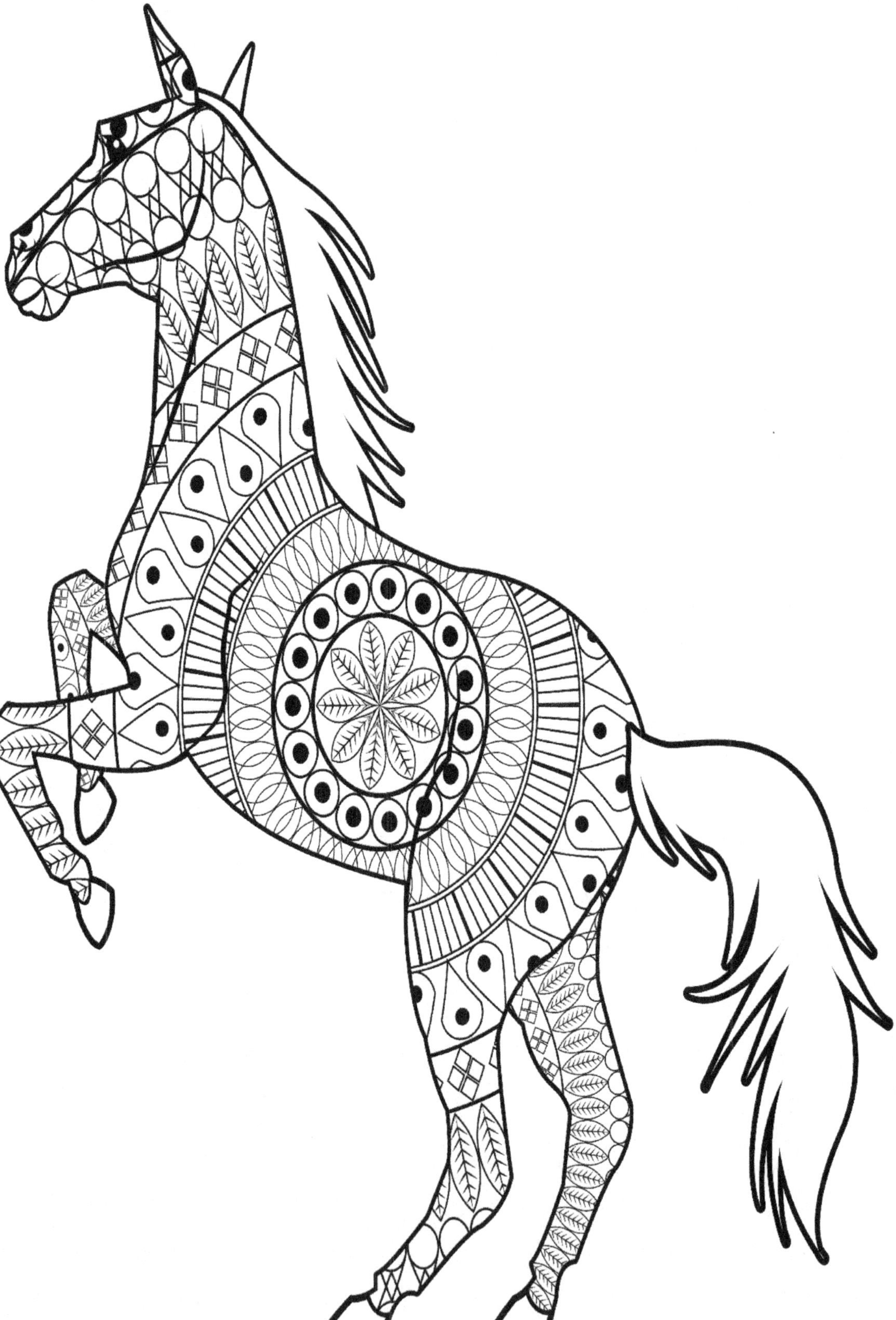

If you enjoyed this book, please leave me a review online.

ABOUT THE AUTHOR

Dr. Wheeler is a physician by day and a writer by night. He enjoys travel, beekeeping, scuba diving, gardening, family time and of course, writing. He is published through Novel Star with his two novels, The Witch of Endor: Vampires and Hammer of the Gods: The Nine Realms Book 1. Collect his entire coloring book series. Mandalas and More, Color Me Butterfly, Fantastic Animals, Fantastic Designs, Fantastic Cats, Fantastic Dogs, Fantastic Horses, Fantastic Sea Life, Fantastic Flowers, Fantastic Skulls, Fantastic Foods, Fantastic Christmas, Fantastic Dinosaurs, Fabulous Designs and Fantastic Unicorns.

For younger children look for: The Adventures of Bumble the Bee in both full color and coloring book formats as well as Fairy Tales and 3 book series. Many of Dr. Wheeler's books are available in e-book, paperback and audiobook formats. His novels are also available in hard cover. For lovers of prose, check out Mystical Musings: A Collection of Poetry.

Dr. Wheeler continues to produce more coloring books each month and is nearing completion of his Vampire sequel: Vampires: Love and Blood which he hopes to publish in 2023.

BUMBLE
CHICKEN TALES

Coloring Book

RK WHEELER

FAIRY FUN

RK WHEELER

BUMBLE

The Bee Who Couldn't Fly

BY

RK WHEELER

The Adventures of Bumble the Bee: Book 1

THE WITCH OF ENDOR

VAMPIRES

R.K. Wheeler

RKWheeler.com

BUMBLE
Beetle Invasion
COLORING BOOK

RK WHEELER

FANTASTIC ANIMALS

STRESS RELIEF

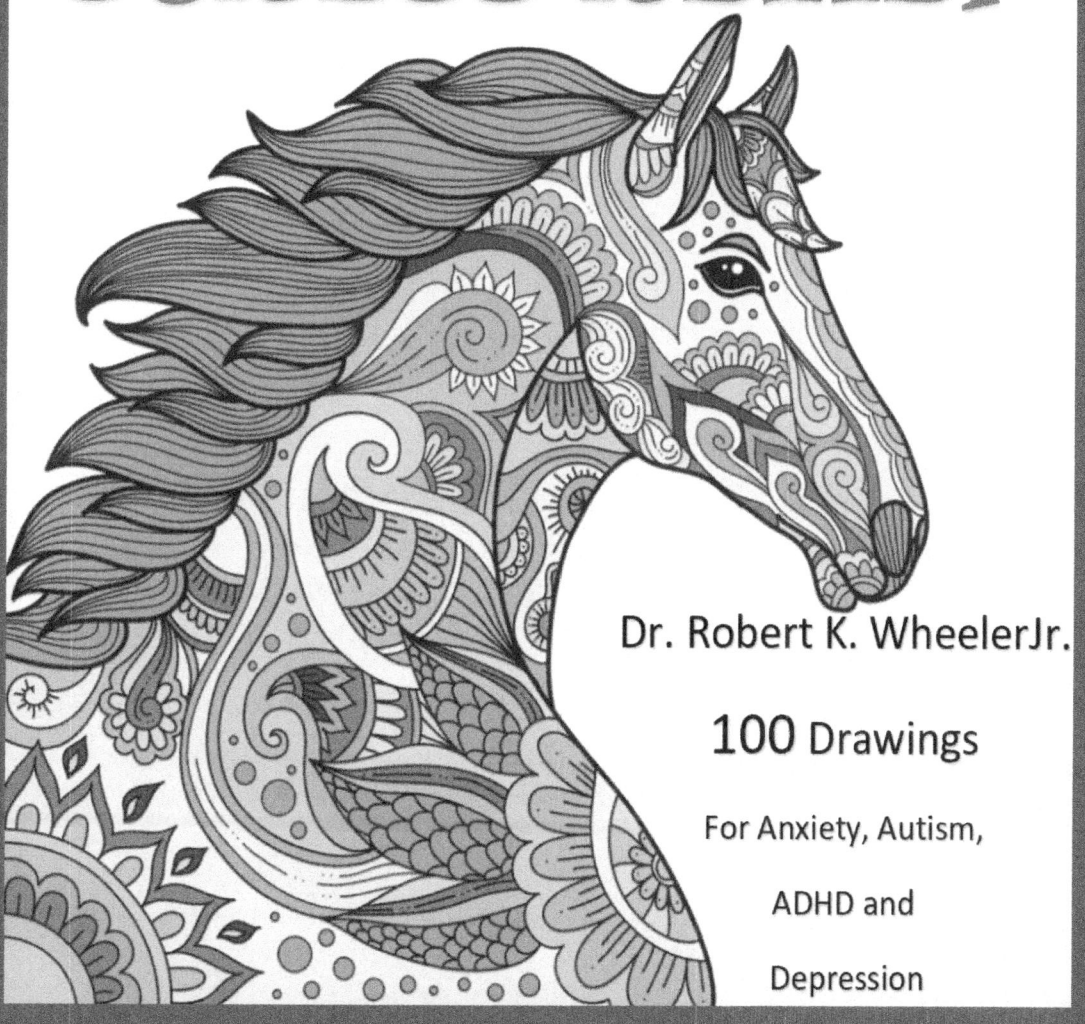

Dr. Robert K. WheelerJr.

100 Drawings

For Anxiety, Autism, ADHD and Depression

ADULT COLORING

BOOK

Made in the USA
Columbia, SC
22 January 2023